# What People Should Know

# To Have a Safe And Successful

# RETIREMENT

By

Mark Kovach

# ACKNOWLEDGEMENT
# AND
# DEDICATION

I would like to acknowledge and dedicate this book to Joan, my wife and the most wonderful lady, friend, companion, and soul mate a man could ever ask for in this world. Joan has been my inspiration over the years, and without her constant nagging at me, in a very nice way, I would never have finished this book or the other books I started years ago that you can view at the end of this book. Joan has been there by my side encouraging and motivating me and she has been my editor and companion throughout the years I have been writing these books. Also, I would like to extend a very special thank you to the two most wonderful children a man could ask for: my son, Lance, and my daughter, Sherrell. Both of my kids are grown now, but nevertheless, they have been great contributors to all of my books, even though they did not realize it because I learned so much from them as they were growing up with Joan and me. I just want to thank Joan, Lance, and Sherrell for all their contributions and the patience they have shown over the years, and to let all of you know I love all of you and how proud I am to have you as my family.

# CONTENTS

# INTRODUCTION

This book, entitled *"What People Should Know To Have a Safe and Successful Retirement"* has been written based on our retirement experiences over the years and to the many requests we received because people wanted more retirement information as opposed to reading personal autobiography that the first half of our original retirement book was based on. Therefore, this book has been revised and rewritten and is focused on particular items that are and should be important to anyone thinking about their retirement years in advance, close to retirement, or those who have reached retirement age at 62 or beyond that allowed them to completely retire and may not be sure of what to do in retirement or for the rest of their retirement years without ever having the fear of running out of money in thirty or forty years of being retired. Today, people everywhere are trying to tell other people how to retire, yet they are nowhere near retirement age themselves, which is like going to a divorce counselor who is divorced to get some advice on divorce—good luck. Nevertheless, the contents of this book is aimed at teaching the multitudes of people who think that they will never be able to retire how to become well-off and well-to-do by teaching them to live within their means, as related through our own personal retirement experiences. However, when we asked different people how they go about living within their means, we were usually given generalities as opposed to specific information. Nonetheless, we decided to give everyone specific information on how to reduce their costs in several different categories, including on how to enter retirement as debt free as possible. Therefore, without having to be rich or wealthy, people can still enjoy the freedom of retirement, regardless of when they retire, and without having to worry about going back to work in order to survive.

As you read through this book, you will notice that my wife and I are in the business of helping people to better themselves financially. Having spent eighteen years as a loan consultant serving the Southern California coastal regions, I managed to retire at the ripe old age of forty-two. Then we decided to write a training manual for the mortgage banking industry. Two years later my wife and I opened the "Professional Loan Officer Training Center," which was located in Lake Forest, California. This school became an immediate success, with standing-room only for the next three years in our classroom. Next, we decided to publish a book entitled *Home Buying and Financing 101*, which one can buy from *amazon.com* as it is in its Second Edition. It is highly recommended for anyone who is thinking about becoming a loan officer or for anyone thinking about buying, financing, or refinancing a home, as we relate insider home buying techniques as well as the most thorough financing information one can possibly get their hands on.

Currently, I am retired and have a master's degree in Business Administration with a major in Business Finance. Likewise, we are the foremost leading authority and expert in-and outside of the United States concerning the financing aspects and interworking of the "Negative Adjustable Home Loan" that, unfortunately, has been removed from the home loan market place at this time. Furthermore, what has qualified us to help the people get back up on their financial footing is what we accomplished this during the worst financial recession that America has ever encountered since 1929. Due to the fact that my wife and I have lived through this learning process to become well-off and well-to-do by living within our means during this recession so that we could retire for the rest of our lives and not have to worry about money or having to go back to work in our retirement years, has now allowed us to assist other people by showing others how they can do the same.

Before going any further, let's clarify the difference between *"RICH and WEALTHY"* and *"WELL-OFF AND WELL-TO-DO."* People who are rich or wealthy have either inherited their riches or wealth as they became rich and wealthy through the operation of businesses, have won the lottery, or are in politics where they usually steal from the masses. On the other hand, people who are well-off and well-to-do have developed a plan of action that eventually resulted in them being able to, basically, do anything they want, anytime they want, and without becoming rich or wealthy. Now, you might be asking yourself *"HOW CAN THIS BE POSSIBLE?"* Well, you're reading the book, so you are about to find out for yourself, as this book is all about how we became *"WELL-OFF AND WELL-TO-DO"* without becoming *"RICH OR WEALTHY"* through the process of "PLANNING," the same as you are about to learn, only without having to go through years of failures as we did in order to learn the successful ways that led us to a wonderful retirement, so that we could bring this knowledge to you. Likewise, it is also true that one can become well-off and well-to-do without starting a business, and without becoming rich or wealthy, and yet, be able to do whatever one desires providing they do what the successful businesses do to stay in business, and that is to establish a *"PLAN OF ACTION,"* which also includes a "BUDGETING PLAN" in the event that something goes wrong or an economic down turn or recession occurs again.

Today, my wife and I live a carefree lifestyle in Texas and do anything we want, when we want to do it. Furthermore, we now have access to as much money as we need and spend it when and how we want and could care less what Big Government thinks or does. We are unaffected by its actions or inactions, the same way you will be independent in your retirement years, and that might also include another pandemic should another one occur in your lifetimes, so let's get started.

# ONE

# CONGRATULATIONS

## Have you Planned Your Retirement And Are About to Retire, Or Have Reached Your Selected Retirement Age?

## Now What?

Great question, and our suggestion is to take 1 to 6 months off or longer when you first retire and just relax and think about what it is that you would like to do or accomplish in your retirement years if you have not already done so. If you are married, then both of you can decide what you would like to do together or separately depending on your desires. To give people an example: My wife and I have our own separate desires where I write books and study the medical industry on the internet and she writes a Women's Bible Study Blog under the name of Joan's Women's Bible Study (com). However, we are both avid treasure hunters and we travel all over the United States after having spent a considerable amount of time researching the type of treasures we are interested in. This activity in and of itself keeps us in excellent shape and now that both of us are in our seventies we will continue to treasure hunt as long as we can, along with our other activities. In the mean time, we also suggest that you start designing and making out a retirement plan if you haven't already done so, but realize that your plan has not been tested and therefore it will need a lot of tweaking as time goes by. Furthermore, we suggest people make out a spread sheet and start keeping tract of all of your monthly and annual expenses for a period of two to three years. The reason for doing this is to make sure that you have an accurate track record recorded of your expenses so that you will be able to make an accurate forecast of your retirement costs that will allow you to forecast what you can expect to spend for the rest of your retirement years. Yes, we are aware of all of the so-called retirement experts (who are not retired) trying to tell people how they should do certain things without having any first hand experience other than what they have heard or read. Unfortunately, people cannot rely on hearsay, assumptions, or speculation coming from non-retired individuals that do not maintain any actual retirement experience. Nonetheless, we will be covering more on this situation when we discuss budgeting and finances in another chapter.

One thing that should be noted is that a lot of this information will be determined depending at what age you elect to retire because your spending habits will decline the older you become. You may not go out as much, or you may not need two or three vehicles any more thereby eliminating maintenance, fuel, and general upkeep fees, or clothing fees because you find no need for them any more. There are a lot of different cost factors that will be eliminated as time goes by and these monies can be added back into your retirement accounts or emergency-fund savings accounts or medical savings accounts. However, for those of you who elect to retire earlier at age 62 and before age 66 you will normally need and require more monthly income because you will more than likely want to do more things that you have been looking forward to doing once you retire. Likewise, you will be younger, more energetic, and capable of still leading an adventurous life style and your financial obligations may not decrease for several more years. However, just remember that you may not have any monies coming in once you retire so you will need to be more astute at controlling your finances.

People who elect to retire at 62 or younger should realize the importance of making sure that they have some sort of a written retirement plan regardless of when they retire. Even though such a plan may not be very accurate it will nonetheless suffice until you have spent some time being retired that will give you a basic understanding of what you will require financially, so as to keep yourselves going until you can start claiming additional income in the way of monthly social security checks. It is also important to remember that all social security monies today are deposited directly into one's checking account or other bank accounts. Therefore, be sure to record the amount you will be receiving every month so that you can record this amount every month into your elected checking or other bank accounts.

Possibly, the number-one reason that most people never manage to get ahead in life is that they are too busy trying to live up with the "JONES SYNDROME," which simply means that there are people who just have to keep up with the "JONESES." In other words, the JONESES buy a new car, so you buy a new car. The JONESES buy a boat and you buy a boat, the JONESES put in a swimming pool and you put in a swimming pool; all of which you cannot afford even though the JONESES can. So you must show the JONESES that you can live up to their standards even though you cannot afford to do so. The sad part about this syndrome is that it is almost impossible to get out of until it is too late—when people either walk away from their obligations, which in turn may lead to divorce, and/or end up in bankruptcy or out in the street. Having lived most of our adult life in Southern California, we have witnessed the effect of the "JONES SYNDROME" that has had on the people on several occasions over the years where they lost everything they owned, especially, when money became tight, as in the recession of 1982, when the bottom fell out of the housing market—just as it was doing again in 2008 when we began writing the first version of this book.

In any case, if you and/or your loved ones happen to be caught up in the JONES SYNDROME, you need to put the brakes on as soon as possible and get out of it if you want to have any sort of chance of becoming "well-off and well-to-do" in the coming years and be able to "live within one's means" in retirement. Let's put this in its proper perspective: should you be unable to get out of the JONES SYNDROME, then more than likely you will end up broke, lose your home, lose your cars, file for bankruptcy, or worse yet, end up out in the streets begging for food and shelter, as the JONES SYNDROME is a no-win situation. When and if you manage to sit down and figure out that you do not need the newest and most costly vehicles to go to the supermarket or drop your kids off at school, and you don't need to spend thousands of dollars remodeling your home every five years, and you don't need the forty, fifty, or sixty-thousand-dollar monthly credit card debt like the Jones, then you may be able to learn how to become well-off and well-to-do. Note, that we said you *may* be able to learn how to become well-off and well-to-do. This is because you will be required to make some additional major adjustments in your living arrangements, but only if you succeed in getting out of the JONES SYNDROME. Remember, recessions come and go, but now the reader should be able to weather the storm with this information, especially, if they are planning for retirement or are about to retire or they are in retirement.

So that every one of the readers will get a complete understanding of each chapter, we are going to relate the exact experiences that took place in our own lives that eventually led us to learn how to become well-off and well-to-do and to get ready for living within our means in retirement.

Back in 1976 at the ripe old age of twenty-seven, I bought my first home in Anaheim, California. In the following year, we sold the house and bought our first business, which was a printing company located in Irvine, California. We were also blessed with a beautiful baby boy, who was turned into a brain-damaged, handicapped child by the doctor. He is still living with me and my current wife today and is just as precious now as when he was born—but that's another book to be written at another time. Nevertheless, one of the reasons that we were successful was because I had a background in printing, a bright business consultant, and a good accountant, along with a great attorney. Even to this day, we believe in surrounding ourselves with "tens"—people who have far more knowledge than us—especially in business, where too many mistakes can cost one their business and livelihood in a blink of an eye.

Business was great in those days, and unfortunately we got caught up in the JONES SYNDROME. We had a new Ford 150 van for the business, and we drove around in a 1972 Cadillac. Then we decided to buy a Mercedes 240 diesel since all of the local business owners were driving Cadillac's, BMWs, Lincolns, or Mercedes. Next, we decided to buy a boat, and we bought a brand-new, twenty-five-foot IMP Day Cruiser so we could take our business clients out fishing and cruise over to Catalina Island on the weekends. Since we were making a lot of money at the time, we also decided to move from our little apartment and rented a beautiful home in Lake Forest, California, where the wealthy upper class lived in those days, and we became one of the would-be, might-be, could-be, pretend wealthy people. We had everything everyone else had in our neighborhood, and we were living very large and barely within our means. After all, as long as business continued to be great and expanding, we saw nothing wrong with living large at the time—sounds like our government.

Business continued to get better and better as time went on, and we kept living larger and larger, buying furs and diamonds for my first wife, great clothes for our son, mingling with the wealthy, and just having a grand old time. However, we were not saving any money for a rainy day, nor did the thought ever cross our minds to even consider saving money. In 1980 we were again blessed with a beautiful baby girl and the spending again continued as business was exceptional, and even though we started to see interest rates increase a little, we did not concern ourselves with anything other than trying to figure out what to buy next.

So we just kept on spending and living large until the beginning of 1982, when our business loan interest rate went to 23.5 percent that year and almost cost us the loss of our business. Only by clamping down on the spending, which was not an easy task, did we manage to survive. Nevertheless, 1982 came and went, and although we managed to weather the interest-rate storm, the following year started to look even better than any of our previous years in business, so we decided to look around and buy a home for the family. Naturally, we wanted the best, so we only looked at the new homes that were being built in the same wealthy area where we had been renting. Since the kids were getting bigger and older, we decided to buy a new home in the Lake Forest area for about $185,000 (which now sells for a minimum of $850,000 to

1 million dollars in today's California's real estate market). We even got an offer from the home owners we were renting from to buy their home for $116,000, but decided against it because we wanted a brand-new home, as we were young, dumb, and lacked a lot of real life experience.

Finally, and after looking at several homes, we decided to purchase a new home in a new development not far from where we had been living. However, we did not know very much about the mortgage business. Even though we were qualified to buy the home financially, we were offered a Graduated Payment Mortgage (GPM) by the lender, and since we didn't understand how the loan worked, we kept refusing to sign the loan documents, thereby making the lender very upset to say the least. So we finally went to the lender's office and sat down with the loan manager and asked him to explain exactly how this GPM loan would function in the event that the interest rates ever went through the roof again. As reluctant as the loan manager was, he finally indicated that there was no life cap on the loan, and in the event the interest rates decided to go back up to who-knows-where, our mortgage payment would also continue to go up along with the interest rates. Therefore, after taking a few minutes to figure out just how high our monthly mortgage payment could go, I decided against buying the home and everyone in the room— including my wife at the time—went ballistic. It wasn't until a year or two later, when I entered the mortgage loan industry, that I learned how the GPM loan really worked.

Basically, we were qualified at a specific interest rate of 8 percent, and our initial payment would have been based on 6 percent for the first year, 7 percent the second year, and back to the original 8 percent interest rate that we were quoted by the lender in year three. However, once the interest rate reached the 8 percent mark, and since there was no life cap on this loan, and in the event that the interest rates decided to start moving up again, our monthly payment would continue to move up along with the interest rates. Now, as long as the interest rates did not increase like they previously had, we would have been all right. However, if the interest rates decided to go through the roof again, we would have a monthly mortgage payment based on an interest that may have gone as high as 23.5 percent, as we had recently experienced. So if you took a loan amount of approximately $184,000 and amortized this amount over the remaining twenty-seven years left on the loan at an interest rate of 23.5 percent, our monthly mortgage payment could have gone from $1,348.47 in principal and interest to as much as $3,540.73 in principal and interest, and there would be nothing that we could have done to get out of the loan other than refinance into another loan or be foreclosed on.

Even though the interest-rate market has never gone through the roof again since 1982, I still did not get a warm fuzzy feeling at the time we were involved in the loan process, as I was wondering what would happen in the event there was another runaway interest-rate market. Nevertheless, the loan manager failed to fully disclose the facts concerning the GPM and failed to explain the effects the GPM loan could have in the long run. Therefore, and in hindsight, I had made the right decision at the time since I knew that I could not afford a monthly mortgage payment of thirty-five hundred dollars or more. Little did I know at the time, but my decision was the beginning of the end for my marriage of eleven years. Unfortunately, after the housing event, our home atmosphere started to take a turn for the worse, and a year later, I filed for a divorce. The point that I am trying to make in this chapter is, don't get yourself in trouble if you don't know what you are doing and don't be afraid to seek out professional advice when needed and know what your financial situation is at all times.

A key factor in retirement planning is to make sure seniors stay busy and have something to do all the time that will keep them fit, their minds sharp and constantly working, and their ability to achieve and completing whatever they set out to do. That is why we recommend taking 1 to 6 months off or more when you first retire to decide what you would like to do. You can find a hobby or maybe you already have a hobby that you can enjoy, or maybe you want to travel or take ship cruises to exotic places, or even get a part time job if need be to stay active. However, you will be the best judge of what would you like to do, so do what you want and stay busy for as long as you can and enjoy your retirement because you have earned it and are entitled to be happy, comfortable, and free from the everyday grind of having to work for a living. Don't forget to plan for the long term too because things will change for you over time, as the older you get the less strenuous the activities you will be able to perform. The goal is to stay fit, alert, active, and not to send yourself to an early demise, allowing yourselves to age gracefully.

We once heard that the more one exercises the longer they will live. Well, we don't know about that or even if it is true, but we do know that the more active one is in retirement, including exercising, the healthier one will be in retirement regardless of how old one gets. As an example; we have seen people in their 90's and 100's that are in wheel chairs and looking at them one cannot tell if they are still alive. We have also seen people in their 90's and 100's still working out and exercising and getting around very well and still driving. The key is to keep moving and never stop until one can no longer function and are called to their final home. As stated earlier, we are in our seventies and when asked how old we are no one believes us because we do not look our age. To learn how we do this will be explained in the next chapter.

To give people a couple of examples, we knew of a guy that was 93 at the tine who was still lifting weights and is still doing so even now at 76 years old. We knew of a gal who was 80 years old who was also still lifting wights and running along with a person who was 112 when he renewed his drivers license. It is amazing what people can do when they put their mind and bodies into staying in shape even thought they are retired. Staying healthy seems to be the key to longevity as long as one stays active in retirement and we are sure that there are many more retirees that fall into these categories.

# TWO
# THE IMPORTANCE OF STAYING HEALTHY IN RETIREMENT

Since we cannot express enough of the importance for seniors to stay healthy in retirement, and because no one else ever talks about this important subject, we will cover a few things that we do that keeps us not only very active, but also very young looking and pain free. Now that both of us are in our seventies, people are always asking us how old we are and we always ask them how old do you think we are? The responses are anywhere from our forties to our fifties at which time we just smile and thank them for their compliments. The key to our youthfulness is our daily exercise workout schedules, and our diets and taking our vitamins along with some other very important nutritional supplements. Likewise, we also contribute our outstanding health to staying away from the medical, pharmaceutical, and food industries along with avoiding the products being sprayed by the chemical industry, but we will get into that in a little more detail later in this chapter.

# My wife's daily 6 day workout schedule

We treat our exercises as a work schedule and every morning we exercise in our bedroom and here is my wife's exercise schedule. For six days a week she starts out with a half horizontal windmill swing with both arms doing 1 set of 10. Next she does a small horizontal circular motion with her arms stretched out making 3 small circles, then 3 medium circles, and 3 large circles and her next exercise is basically the same, but making the circles backwards. Next she puts her arms in front of her and close to her upper chest horizontally and then pulls her arm straight back similar to a breast stroke exercise doing 1 set of 10 and on 11 she stretches her arms completely out 1 time only.

Her next exercise she calls a Tea Pot exercise where she swings one arm over her head to the left with the arm fully extended and bending as far as she can in that direction, and she repeats this movement to the right doing 1 set of 10. Then she does something similar to a toe bending exercise where she bends over and dangles her arms for a count of 10. Next she bends her knees slightly with her hand on her hips and makes a forward bouncing movement with her knees doing 1 set of 10. Next she does a toe swing where you spread your legs apart as far as she can, but comfortable, and then swings side to side bent over touching her toes for 1 set of 10.

Next, laying on the floor, she does leg lifts doing 2 sets of 5 and then does 2 sets of 10 of what I would term as a dying cockroach position kicking her legs out and up wards with each leg going in the opposite directions. As she is still in this position she then bends her knees up just a little and grabs her inner thighs and pulls them back thereby tightening the thighs doing 3 sets of 5. Then still on her back she lifts her legs straight up and does the splits with her legs for 1 set of 10 which also tightens the inner thigh. While still on the floor she turns on her side, right or left to start and then lifts her leg as high as she can doing 1 set of 10 and then turning to the other side and doing the same thing again with her other leg. Next she does a bicycle doing 3 sets of 10. Again in the same position she bends her knee and holds each one with both hands doing 1 set for a count of 20 on each leg independently. Next she does a bicycle crunch with her hands behind her head, knees bent, bringing her elbows forward to her knees for 1 set of 10. Then still on her back with her arms at her side and bending her knees using her feet she lifts her pelvis for 1 set of 10. Then in the same starting position with her legs straight out she again lifts her pelvis for 1 set of 10. Then she sits up and spreads her legs and with both hands together as she stretches forwards trying to touch her toes and rotates from toe to toe doing 2 sets of 10. While still on the floor she gets on her knees, similar to a runners starting position and then arching her back up she moves down and up thereby strengthening her back doing 1 set of 5 only.

After the floor exercises she does these weight exercises on Tu, Th, and Sat only, by sitting in a chair and does weightlifting with a five pound weight doing bicep exercises doing 1 set of 10. Still using the 5 pound weight she does a wrist exercise where she places the wrist on her knee and allows her hand to go down at the wrist and back up again for 1 set of 10 with each hand. Next she does a standing tricep exercise behind her head by lifting the 5 pound weight over and above her head letting the weight drop down and then lifting it back up doing 1 set of 10. This exercise builds the triceps, the upper back, the shoulders and neck muscles.

Now using two 3 pound weights, one in each hand, she does what she calls the weed eater exercise where she simply swings one arm out in front of her from side to side 6 times and then repeating the swinging movement in the other direction with the other arm 6 times doing 1 set of 6 with both arms. Next she puts the two weights together with arms stretched out in front of her and then swings both arms from side to side doing 1 set of 6. Next she uses our hand grips and does 2 sets of 10 and then uses our Grip-master that is designed to strengthen our fingers for playing the piano and guitar doing 1 set of 10 for each finger on both hands and then she does all fingers on both hands doing 1 set for a 10 count. Next she does a chin exercise by placing a foam rubber ball under her chin and forces the ball down with her chin for 1 set of 10 that keeps the chin and neck from sagging and the tendons tight. Then she takes the foam rubber ball again and places it between her legs in the inner thighs and squeezes it with her thighs doing 1 set of 10.

Now for maintaining her balance she does a crossover walk crossing over one leg to the left for 6 steps and then back again with the other leg for 6 steps doing 1 set of 6 for each leg. Next is walking on her toes first forward and then backwards for 6 steps and then walking only on her heals forward and then backwards doing 1 set of 6. Then she does a pelvic thrust by holding on to our dresser and lifting her heels off the ground and thrusting the pelvic forward for 1 set of 10 that is good for the calf muscles and for tightening the buttocks. Then she does another balance exercise by lifting one leg up at a time and holding on to her knee for a count of 20 on each leg and does 2 sets of 10. Note: Depending on your balance you may want to balance yourself by holding on to something with the other hand. Next she holds on to the dresser and moves her legs backwards to a point where she can lift one leg at a time moving the leg up as high as she can for a count of 15 then bending her knee for another count of 15 doing 1 set for each leg. This is the end of her daily exercise routine everyday for 6 days and covers about 20 to 30 minutes or longer depending on what shape women are in. In time all of these exercises can be done in 15 to 20 minutes and you are now ready to start your day.

# My daily 6 day workout schedule

Mine is a little different in that on Monday, Wednesday, and Friday I do a short workout exercise consisting and starting with forward large windmill arm circles for a count of 10 and then making the same large arm circles again going backwards for a count of 10 while spreading my legs apart a little more than shoulder width. Next I spread my legs as far as I can and bent over I swing my arms and touch my left toe and then my right toe and rotate back and forth until I reach a count of 20 thereby touching each toe 10 times. Next, I stand up straight and bend over to again and touch my toes (or the ground) for a count of 10 and then one more time I touch the ground and hold it for another count of 10. The next step is to do 10 jumping jacks and then I walk forward and backwards for a minimum of 10 steps on my toes one time only and then on my heels forwards and backwards 1 time only for a minimum of 10 steps. Next I do a balance exercise lifting one foot off the ground for 30 seconds in a forward position and then the other foot for another 30 seconds. Then I lift each foot again backwards behind my heel of the other foot and again for 30 seconds for each leg. Next, holding on to the dresser I do 2 sets of 10 of the pelvic thrust and afterwards I stretch out as far as I can lifting each leg backwards one at a time for a count of 15 then bending the leg at the knee and again holding each leg up as high as I can for another count of 15. The final exercise is where I turn sideways lifting each leg bent at the knee lifted as high as possible and hold this position for 30 seconds for each leg. This exercise is to strengthen the Sartorial muscles that aids the hip and flexes the knee and helps stabilize balance. Next I do 2 sets of deep knee bends for a count of 10 each with legs spread apart about shoulder width. This ends my exercises for these three days of the week and it should not take longer then 15 or 20 minutes to complete these exercises.

# The next are 3 daily workouts for men

These next exercises are for Tuesday, Thursday, and Saturday and the first part involves lifting weights. However, caution is in order here because lifting too much weight or using the wrong weights for a particular part of the body can cause serious physical damage and harm to anyone for long periods of time. To give the reader an example, I have been lifting weights as a body builder for over 50 years now and never had a problem until I reached the age of 68 a few years back. Even though I had professional body building weight trainers years ago no one told me what could happen to you as you age while still lifting weights. Nevertheless, I was still lifting 55 and 60 pound dumb-bell weights at 68 when one day I started lifting as usual and doing bicep arm lifts on my right with 60 pound single dumb-bell weight and everything was fine until I switched to the left hand and arm and when I started the fourth rep I tore both the upper and lower tendons at the elbow. To say it hurt would be to put it mildly and after dropping the weight naturally I tried doing another set with the right hand and arm and everything went fine, or so I thought. I immediately went to the internet to find out how to cure the torn tendons and after a few articles I started applying cold and hot packs to the damaged areas. The next day my left arm turned completely black and red because of the blood leakage, but after a few weeks of using hot and cold packs everything turned out fine. However, I was not able to lift any more weight with my left arm for about a year even though I kept trying only with lighter weight.

Nevertheless, that was not the bad part of the incident because after lifting with my right hand and arm, the next day I almost fell trying to get out of bed. As it turned out my entire right side of my body went completely numb and I could not even stand let alone walk because nothing seemed to work on my right side. Nonetheless, I decided to wait and see if things would get back to normal and by noontime still nothing seemed to work. Therefore, I had my wife drive me to a medical facility because I thought I may have had a stroke because of the way my system was functioning as I have been studying different medical problems that can occur to the human body, as well as the medical industry for over 43 years, but that subject will be covered in another chapter.

Anyways, after having blood work, blood pressure, and an EKG, and then a brain scan everything turned out okay and I decided to go home even though they tried to get me to stay in the hospital. However, when I pulled out my medical power of Attorney (POA) and the doctors and nurses saw what I had, they basically didn't bother me any more and I walked out of their facility after they had given me all their BS about dying or dropping dead and had me sign their release papers. I then told them that I had extensive knowledge concerning the medical industry and was well aware of what they do to people if one allows them to, and left. The next day I went to see a Sports Chiropractor who told me that I had extreme muscle wasting on my right side that has caused the numbing effect and that it would take some time to get back to normal. That was back in December of 2017 and as of now in June of 2020 I am finally getting back to normal even though I took a couple of weeks off before starting to lift weights again in January of 2018.

Basically, the bottom line according to the Sports Chiropractor was that what happened to me should have happened once I was in my mid fifties and he could not believe this didn't happen to me until I was 68 years old. Naturally his advice was to use much lighter weights because as one ages there is muscle wasting that occurs no matter how good of shape one may be in. So now I am down to lifting only a maximum of 35 pounds, 30, 25 and 20 pound weights depending on the exercises I am doing at the time. Therefore, one needs to be very careful when choosing the amount of weight they intend to lift. It is better to start with lighter weights and increase the weight as long as it doesn't bother one.

So here is my weight workout exercises in the mornings for the days mentioned. The first exercise is for the biceps using a 25 pound weight on each arm one at a time doing 2 sets of 10. Then doing the same thing again using a 30 pound weight doing only 1 set of 10 and then the 35 pound weight for 1 set of 6. Next I do a wrist curl with the 30 pounder on the knee letting the weight pulling my hand down and I do 2 sets of 10 and then the 35 pounder for 1 set of 6 on each hand. Lastly I do standing tricep exercise behind my head by lifting the 30 pound weight over and above my head letting the weight drop down behind my head and then lifting it back up doing 2 sets of 10 and again with the 35 pounder for 1 set of 6. This exercise builds the triceps, the upper back, the shoulders and neck muscles. Next I use two 20 pound weights and swing both arms out horizontally, as far as I can to support the weights, to the sides doing 2 sets of 10. However, at the end of the second lift after the count of 10, I extend both arms out one more time again holding the weights horizontally for 30 seconds. Remember, if you are going to do this at the end of the last set be sure to start with only 5 to 10 seconds holding the weights straight out horizontally and eventually work up to whatever will be comfortable for you. After doing 2 sets of 10 with the 200 lb. HEAVY GRIPS, I do 2 sets of deep knee bends to a count of 10. The last exercise I do in the morning is to pull a lawn mower cord doing two sets of 10 only on the right arm so as to correct a dislocation problem that I have in my shoulder according to the Chiropractor. Remember, be very careful with lifting weights and always start with light weights and work up to heavier weights as time goes by, if one wants to.

# The second half of my exercises on these days

Basically, I originally started out with doing 5 sets of 10 push ups and built up to 5 sets of 20 over time and the same applies to these other exercises except for the next one. Next I lay on the floor in a push up ready position and extending just my arms pushing the upper body up as far as I can bending the back up and extending the neck as high as possible doing 2 sets of 10. This exercise was taught to me by another Chiropractor in order to keep the Sciatica nerve in place and she has been right for several years now that I have been doing this exercise. I used to do 5 sets of 20 on both of these next exercises and 5 sets of 20 leg raises. For dizziness exercises I stay in the sit-up position with my legs pulled up and knees bent lying flat on the floor on my back and very rapidly raise only my upper body and head, kinda of like a sit-up crunch for 2 sets for a count of 15. Next, I roll over to on my right side cocking one leg and raise my upper body sideways as fast as I can all the while swinging my head towards a fixed object and then again doing 1 set of 10 on both sides. Next I take our little foam rubber ball and place it under my chin while standing and holding it firmly in place I force my chin down for a count of 8 only. This exercise will strengthen the tendons in the neck while firming the neck skin below the chin eliminating any possibility of having sagging skin.

After putting everything away like rubber mats, towels, foam rubber ball, I again do 2 sets of 10 of the deep knee bend squats. The last exercise again is pulling the lawnmower cord with the right hand and arm only that keeps working my shoulder until it goes back into place, if it ever does. Needless to say, the shoulder doesn't bother me very much, but as time goes on one never knows and that is why it is very important to be careful when lifting weights. When one starts lifting, start out with 5 or 10 pounds for the senior men and 2 to 3 pounds for the senior women. Over time both men and women can increase their weight lifting weight depending on what you are comfortable lifting, but the key to staying in shape and healthy is consistency with each of your workout schedules. Likewise, it is advisable to start out doing less then trying to do more. Start with 1 or 2 sets doing only 2 to 5 repartitions instead of 1 or 2 sets of 10 repartitions and gradually build up to 10 repetitions. The easiest way for both men and women to do this is to increase by one extra rep once a week or two until you reach 10 reps. It's really not necessary to do more than 10 reps as the goal is to build stamina, strength, and staying in good physical condition instead of building large muscles groups; and by all means don't hurt yourselves by over doing anything elaborate or unusual, just be consistent.

Two more great exercises that everyone can do at pretty much at any age is walking and pool exercising. Walking can be done anywhere and that includes wherever you go shopping or window shopping and any other places one may have to walk. These can be very short walks, medium walks, and long walks depending on one's physical capabilities. The same will apply to pool exercises providing one is available for you to use, but exercising in water can be a little strenuous depending on what one is doing. However, there are exercise pool instructors available or one may be provided by your community so just check around on one's computer. People can also find pools at most gyms today and they can also find various exercises on the internet that they can learn to utilize in swimming pools.

Furthermore, there is no reason for seniors to do nothing after they retire and to stay healthy and remain active as one needs to exercise whether it is at your homes, the gym, or wherever you may be or whatever you may be doing, try to stay as active as you can for as long as you can and enjoy your retirement. Remember, don't procrastinate or make excuses to stay in shape as you will be rewarded by your efforts whether they are small or large sessions on your behalf as only you will be rewarded in the short and long terms of your healthy retirement. The key to staying healthy is to keep moving regardless of how old one may be or get to be, but remember not to over do any exercises.

# THREE

# KEEPING YOUR MIND ACTIVE AND YOURSELF BUSY

One of the biggest downfalls of retirement is that a lot of seniors think it is time to not only retire, but to stop doing everything and lying around doing nothing. Those of you who decide to resort to this do nothing attitude will be the first to pass away because you simply have nothing to look forward to. Don't fall into this thought process as this is the time of your life that you have been working for all of your life so take advantage of it. You may think of turning your hobby into a business, or you may want to work part-time doing something you enjoy, or you maybe an avid hunter, fishing people, hiking people, traveling people or a myriad of other activities that you have considered doing. You may want to donate your time to some cause that you believe is worthy based on your working background or through your life experiences. Helping the children is always a worthy cause, especially, to the less fortunate and handicapped. Trust us, as you can always find something to do that will help you stay busy.

Be on the constant lookout for senior discounts and don't be afraid to ask for senior discounts everywhere you may decide to go or places you visit. Always think of paying yourselves first after all your bills are paid and paying off as much debt as possible before retiring will make life in retirement a lot nicer for you now and in the long run. If possible, paying off your mortgage is a major plus factor because you can start with establishing an emergency fund (if you haven't already done so) that should be able to cover all your monthly expenditures for a period of six months or more. Be sure to keep these monies in a very safe place where you will have immediate access to them should you ever need these emergency funds. As an example: Our people may have total monthly expenses around $2500.00 per month times 6 equals a little over 15, 000.00 that they would have immediate access to in the event of any emergencies that may arise at any time in the future. This example should give everyone an idea of what they will need to put away in the form of an emergency fund. Granted it may take several years to save these emergency funds, but in the long run it will be well worth it.

People should decide on a retirement age factor and remember that your age will determine your Social Security (SS) benefits. We elected to retire early at 42 and had to wait until 62 for one of us to start collecting SS and the other one waited until 66 at the time. However, it took one of us almost 5 years just to catch up with the other's income that they had been receiving from SS although the income of the one who retired at 66 is now a lot further ahead of the one of us who started collecting at 62. Nevertheless, it doesn't make much difference to us now as it did when we were younger. The reason for collecting early was to travel and treasure hunt across the US, so we bought a 35 foot motorhome and went from place to place and had lots of fun for a change. Like everything else, the older we became the more trouble the motorhome became with the upkeep until we finally sold the motorhome. Now we travel in our custom built off road Suburban that does just fine on and off road and stay in hotels and again that has been just fine for us. However, we also take a black light and a GPS signal detector that will detect AI, any magnetic field signals, a camera laser detecter, an RF wireless signal detector, and a GPS tracking device all in one neat little compact unit. Our unit is called a GPS Signal Detector K 68 that we purchased on Amazon and so far no complaints. We use it at every hotel or places we stay at and if we detect any hidden cameras or anything else in the rooms we simply call the local police. When they arrive we register our complaint and off to jail the perpetrators go after clearing the room as these spy devices are against the law when trying to capture pictures of people taking their clothes off or taking showers or doing both in these hotel rooms. Well worth the money if one is elects to travel.

The point being made here is to stay busy doing something and keeping your brain sharp and active and staying physically healthy that will keep one away from the Medical and pharmaceutical industries as long as possible. Find something to do that will keep you active and busy and under no circumstances just laying around watching TV or whatever, doing nothing, as this inactivity will do nothing more than put one into a hospital causing all kinds of diseases such as diabetes, cardiovascular and others making one's next stop into the morgue. Stay active, stay busy and stay alive for as long as you can.

# THREE

# SECTION II

# THE DIET

Our last recommendation and suggestion is to pay close attention to your diets. Again we cannot stress the importance of maintaining your over all health as a senior. Just look around and one will notice that obesity is on a rampage not only in the United States, but also all around the world. It has been reported that there are currently over 1 billion obese people around the world with approximately two-thirds of the American population that are obese. As of this writing it is projected that over 80 percent of Americans will be obese by the year 2050 causing a medical crisis which is now in the making and on a rampage in America. What is causing this obesity phenomena around the world can only be contributed to the different food chemicals that are being used on our food supplies and the lack of physical activities. Furthermore, other countries are either importing theses food products or they are being grown in poor soils.

A lot of America's foods have been outlawed in several countries due to the chemicals that are being used on our agricultural foods products. Also foods that are classified as having GMO in them are forbidden in several countries along with our meat and fish farm products. These foods are poisoning our people and causing major problems in America and around the world. In America, chemical companies are using a chemical called glyphosate (gly-pho-sate) that can't even be washed off our food products no matter how many times you wash products sprayed by this chemical. The worst food products that anyone can buy and consume in the US now is corn, potatoes, and apples that have been sprayed with glyphosate and all this information is available on the internet. To counter act glyphosate one can use chicory root and therapeutic probiotics that are in blister packs AKA as TCP. Any other probiotics are pretty much worthless and there are an unbelievable amount of probiotics on the market. However, some of the worst are sold in bottles and even though TCP's may cost a little more, stay with these probiotics that come in sealed blister packs.

It is important for retired people to try and adjust their diets to suit their needs and at the same time be healthy. I will use myself as an example: I don't go to doctors because I don't trust any of them and most of them are mountebanks anyways. Nevertheless, a couple of years ago I developed a cataract in my left eye and went to a cataract specialist to get my eye checked out. What it came down to was that I was to see a doctor to determine if I was physically fit to have cataract surgery. Anyways, this mountebank decided to do a glucose test and got a reading of 241 and immediately told me I had diabetes and I busted out laughing. Needless to say, I started to question this doctor as to how he could possibly make that assumption when he didn't even know me? This mountebank didn't even ask me any questions concerning my eating habits or anything else for that matter, but simply stated that he could not recommend any cataract surgery for me at that time.

Next, I returned to the surgeon who informed me that he had spoken to this mountebank and stated he would not be able to do the surgery unless I had more eye tests. In other words, they were just starting to crank the medical money machine on me or so they thought. Unfortunately for them, I had been investigating the medical industry for over 43 years now and what they didn't know that I knew wouldn't hurt them unless I was to speak out. The main point that I learned very early on is that doctors will lie, cheat, and steal anyway they can to get one's money by way of "recommending" further medical tests that are basically, a waste of time in the majority of cases. Nevertheless, I went along with another eye test that proved that I did not have diabetes and all of these doctors had to erase this information from my records or be sued. They complied and I didn't have to sue them, however I am not one to sit around and feel sorry for myself so I decided to investigate this cataract eye condition.

What I found out was very interesting in that once a person is diagnosed with a cataract the medical industry immediately tries to rush a person into surgery the same way they do with just about everything else, especially, with cancer clients, when in fact, there are always alternatives available. First I found a product called "Can See" that is used to eliminate cataracts so I bought some. However, after a year of using this product I saw no results, so back to more investigation. Next, I located another company in Israel that sold a product called "Cataract Terminator" and tried their solution for about 8 months. Only this time I started to see very large objects, but not clearly in my left eye so back to the drawing board. This time I found a product called "Cataract Clear" in the United Kingdom and since having been using this product I am now beginning to see out of my left eye that I had been told that because of the density of the cataract, surgery would be the only solution to regain my eye sight.

Not only am I seeing more and more out of my left eye using this product, but I expect my left eye will eventually return to normal in time because I have been using this product now going on 6 months. This just confirmed my investigation facts concerning the medical industry in that they couldn't care less about alternative solutions to anything that would interfere with their income. Nevertheless, I changed my diet completely around by constructing my own diet eating a combination of certain vegetables and eggs every meal. Nevertheless, having spent a couple of years trying to eliminate these cataracts, I ended up getting cataract surgery because none of this stuff mentioned above managed to work well enough. Even though I wasted a lot of time and money trying these products, none of them were capable of eliminating any of my cataracts.

Yes, we know that there are a myriad of diets that are being pushed in the market to entice people to spend their money on, but we have found that designing one's own diet is far better providing one knows what they like and don't like in the way of healthy foods. We have found that by designing one's own diet that one can be content eating the same thing over and over again without getting bored with the repetitiveness. Simply by changing the little bits of meat we eat and add a little spaghetti noodles and refried beans as a side dish and we stay extremely trim and healthy all the time. One day a week I eat nothing but a large salad and really pig out, but hey, salad will not add any weight that we have noticed and we stay at our weight consistently. Remember, this is our custom designed diet for us and since everyone is different people can custom design their own diets and be sure to keep it healthy. In the beginning it may be a little difficult to adjust to, but in the long run it will be well worth it. Likewise, don't be afraid to enjoy the things you know you shouldn't eat to treat yourself once in a while.

Understand that everyone has a different conception of what a diet is and means to them. Others will try different diets in an effort to find the right one suited to them and that is okay. The key is to find a diet that one can live with and stay healthy with that will allow them to stay fit and healthy. Likewise, there is no problem switching from one diet program to another diet program providing one is achieving their goals, whatever they may be. This whole chapter and there sections have been related to everyone so that they will be able to live a healthy, vibrant, and exciting retirement with as little medical intervention as possible. In fact, the seniors who are over a hundred years old all have the same common denominator in that when asked what contributed to their longevity they all replied "Staying away from Doctors." Now, we don't know about anyone else, but that sounded like very sound advice to us.

# FOUR

# IRA's, ROTH IRA's, AND 401K's

Everyone will have their own opinion concerning IRA's or Roth IRA's accounts and whether or not they are viable accounts to have for future savings for retirement. Our answer is maybe or maybe not depending on what one's own personal thoughts are concerning these financial tools. Before deciding on an IRA account lets look at the reason for establishing one of these accounts and who set them up and for what reasons.

In our opinion, IRA accounts were established by the government to be a sort of a forced savings account for people all across the US that would also allow the government to borrow funds against these funds for their purposes the same as banks do with people's money because these accounts would collectively accumulate tremendous amounts of monies over time. However, if any person happened to need the money in their IRA account before they were entitled to withdraw their monies, they would be fined and penalized to the maximum allowable by law. The IRA accounts, in our opinion, are one of the best deceptions ever developed by our wonderful government, except for the thirty-year, fixed-interest-rate mortgage loan program—which happens to be the worst loan programs ever developed by the government and banking institutions in the United States. This information is all explained in our other book entitled "Home Buying and Financing 101 Second Edition."

Before moving on, let's view the IRA from a different angle. The idea behind the IRA initially was to convince people to be allowed to place a certain amount of their earned income into an account that would not be subject to taxation until they were ready to retire and withdraw the IRA funds, but only up to a certain amount each year (note: people are being told what to do with their own money). Upon reaching retirement, the government would then tax people based on a lower income bracket and at a lower tax rate than they would have had if people had not placed their monies into an IRA account. Moreover, the IRA accounts were targeted at younger people who were about to enter the working world, and they were promoted initially as retirement accounts, which became college accounts, grandchildren accounts, backup insurance accounts, etc. I am completely surprised and amazed that the government overlooked the opportunity to market IRA accounts as backup Social Security do-it-yourself account, since they keep telling us that we are running out of Social Security money—which is not true even though the government keeps taking our Social Security monies to use for other purposes.

So the initial concept of the IRA account was to allow people to put money away until they reached retirement age and be taxed at a lower rate on these monies. But the government knew what the people did not know, which was that sooner or later something would happen where the people would need to withdraw their IRA monies to help them out of a particular situation. Since the government is well aware of the saving habits of the people in this country, they knew that people would not be able to leave their IRA accounts alone for fifteen, twenty, twenty-five years or longer. Therefore, when people made an early withdrawal from their IRA account, they are fined, penalized, and assessed for taxes at a higher rate—just for using one's own hard-earned money. Over the years we have seen people get slammed with these kinds of fines and penalties because they needed to respond to some situation they could not have foreseen years before when they opened their IRA account. Again it is my recommendation to put one's money in a stockbroker's money market account rather then in an IRA account any day of the week where people would have immediate access to any funds they need at anytime. One last thing concerning both IRA and Roth IRA accounts, the government has relaxed certain rules concerning withdrawal requirements from these IRA accounts, but only as a means to pacify all of the account holders as they are still telling people what they can and cannot do with their own monies in these accounts.

Again in our opinion the 401k program is viable, but only if one can participate where the employer has matching fund contributions. However, people need to know that the employer will have direct control over these accounts even though they are controlled with guidelines by the government. In other words, people will be entitled to their funds including the employer's matching funds even though these funds can be invested in the Stock Market. This means that if the Stock Market crashes, so does the money in your 401k. We have seen and read about people losing over half of their 401k accounts over the years because of the Stock Market and trust us when we say recovery can take a long time. Another very important factor to consider is in the event a person decides to leave their company, be sure to get as much paperwork as one can on their 401k account and the company it is with so that people will be able to claim their monies in these accounts when they turn 65 or older. People would be amazed to know how many people forget about claiming their 401k accounts and lose these monies because they did not take these precautions simply because they forgot.

It is our opinion that a person interested in investing in an IRA, Roth IRA or a 401k program take their monies and put them into a mutual fund account like Vanguard fund, Fidelity fund, Schwab fund, T. Rowe fund, or others where one can have immediate access to their monies if needed. Also consider putting your monies into a Brokerage Money Market account because they usually guarantee up to fifty-million dollars as opposed to two hundred and fifty-thousand dollars in a bank account.

# FOUR

# SECTION II

# MAKING A RETIREMENT PLAN

When we say make a retirement plan, we mean for people to write down what they expect to accomplish in retirement whether it be a retirement goal that you always wanted to achieve or looked forward to, or paying down or paying off debt before and after retiring, or reducing your possible tax bills. All this and a whole lot more will be necessary in order to have a comfortable retirement and it will require intelligent people to make out their written plans in order to be successful at being able to retire living comfortable in their retirement years. This also means being able to live within their means in retirement. However, it is important that people realize that the plans they make can and should be variable as everything will change as people grow older and their requirements and priorities will change as time goes on because seldom does anything remain the same for very long.

Starting with looking at what people want to achieve or accomplish in retirement and since everyone's ideas will be different, we will use our situation to get our point across. We, being my wife and myself wanted to continue to treasure hunt and travel wherever we wanted whenever we wanted and since we already had a small 22 foot motorhome we decided to trade up to a new 35 foot motorhome that we would use to accomplish our goals. After outfitting this unit we started traveling all over the US. hunting buried treasures and visiting various places as we traveled. Because we were still young at 59 and 66 we were able to treasure hunt using our motorhome for seven years before selling it as we were now 66 and 73 and tired of traveling with the motorhome as it was big, long, cumbersome, and costly to maintain, but it was fun during the time we used it. Now that we are in our seventies we still treasure hunt, but now we travel to and from our destination in our custom made Suburban that we beefed up when we treasure hunt off road and usually stay in hotels or motels along the way, and actually it is less expensive. However, we don't have the energy that we use to have as we did in our sixties, but we still do all right as we stay in excellent shape.

Likewise, our spending habits changed quite a bit now that the motorhome is gone and we elected to add this extra money towards our retirement accounts. This by the way is something people ignore because they just like to spend money. Nevertheless, any extra monies we accumulate always gets put into one of our retirement accounts that may or may not be eventually used in our latter years. If these funds are required by us, then they will be there, otherwise they will be transferred to our estate according to our wills that will then be distributed to all of our kids upon our demise.

Which brings us to another subject that should be discussed and eventually marked off your retirement plan once completed and that is having an Estate plan or Will drawn up and filed away to be used when needed. Why people overlook this process is beyond us unless they are planning on donating assets to charities because they don't have any children or anyone else to leave their money and assets to. When both of us retired we had our attorney draw up our Wills that can be changed or added to or subtracted from as our situations change the older we become. We elected to do a Will for each of us that will transfer everything we accumulate in our estate that is to be transferred and divided up by the executor of our estate to each member on both sides of our families according to our Wills. Nevertheless, and because we are not attorneys and we don't know much about other state's requirements, but in Texas, estate plans are not necessary as a Will, will take care of everything as if one had an estate plan. This process is a lot less complicated and easier to do and the cost factors are a lot less in Texas even though a Will will go through probate court. Therefore, this is definitely something you need to discuss and get taken care of in the beginning of your retirement or before retirement or sooner whether it be a Will or a Trust because everyone will have different circumstances.

# FOUR

# SECTION III

# PAYING DOWN OR

# PAYING OFF DEBT

This option in our opinion is a rather important subject because it can have a major impact on people's retirement planning and the goals they would like to achieve in their retirement years. Again we will be using our situation as an example so people can get a better idea of what they can expect when their time comes to retire.

When we retired, no one told us anything about retirement and how our personal debt would effect us going into retirement and therefore we never paid off any of our debts before retiring. Not that was a big mistake for us at the time, but had we known sooner we would have definitely made an effort to eliminate as much debt as possible before retiring. Furthermore, the internet was just starting back then and there were no articles that had anything to do with retirement planning like there are today, so we had to learn the hard way. Believe us when we suggest that people planning to retire, a few years away from retirement, or have reached their retirement age that they decided to retire at, will be a whole lot simpler in retirement without having any debt. Unfortunately, we were not that lucky along with the rest of the retirees that had to learn the hard way. Carrying as little debt as possible into retirement will give people a lot of breathing room and not force them into thinking like they will never make it in retirement or be able to retire. That is also why writing out a retirement plan can make all the difference in the world to those that plan ahead.

Fortunately for us, I had been in the military and a Loan Officer for several years and the one thing I was good at was thinking very fast on my feet, so I started writing a retirement plan for us even though we were now retired. The first thing we did was to design an income budget sheet that you can see in chapter 9 that would give us an immediate view of what was coming in and what we needed to pay out thereby giving us a direct analysis of our current real income situation at any given time. Here we are 11 years later in our retirement still utilizing this same income budget sheet. In the meantime my wife went to her computer and started making out a spread sheet that we could use daily to record our transactions on and then be able to compare it with our monthly income budget sheet to determine if we were all right in our spending. If these two sheets did not match up, we would find out where the problem was and make our corrections. We did this for 3 years before we were able to assess exactly where we were financially every month and year in our retirement and we still do it every year as it has become a habit for us.

The advantage to this was showing us what debts we were paying down and how much more we had in order to pay off our remaining debt all the while maintaining our sanity. By doing this and sticking to this regime we were able to become debt free in three years except for our mortgage that took us another 2 years to completely pay off our home thereby eliminating our 30-year mortgage payment in 5 years, even though we could have paid it off in three years, but why get stressed out? People, we cannot even begin to tell you how relieved it is to be debt free except for our home taxes and insurance for our three cars and home that we now pay once a year. As the monies keep rolling in each and every month we are now spending less and less every month and year because we no longer have the commitments and we require a lot less as we get older.

Naturally, everyone will have their idea of how they will deal with their debt in retirement, but for those who can manage to pay down or pay off as much debt as they can before retiring will be a big plus for them when they enter retirement. Furthermore, paying off one's mortgage is probably the biggest factor facing the majority of people about to retire. Therefore, our suggestion is to pay off all the debt one can before retiring including their mortgage if they can. If people can't pay off their mortgage, try to pay as much as you can afford and deal with the rest once retired. The biggest key to paying off debt is having a plan and always knowing what your financial situation is at all times and even though it may require paperwork it will be well worth it when anyone decides to, has to, or is forced to enter retirement.

# FIVE

# THE DOWN SIZING
# CONTROVERSY

Let's analyze from both the good and bad perspectives in one's retirement situations instead of what people are being told to do in the internet articles. However, understand that downsizing is strictly a personal decision as no one is required to downsize no matter what other people may think or say. Furthermore, the decision to downsize or not will be based on several factors of which you will be the only one who knows what these factors are and no one else.

This is strictly our opinion, but since our home is paid for except for the annual taxes and insurance, we see no reason to downsize regardless of how old we become in the years ahead. As long as we both maintain our health and stay busy our 2,500 square foot home suits us just fine along with our one acre back yard. As long as we can take care of the place everything will be fine and if we get to the point where we can't take of our place by ourselves, then we will just hire the people who can do the work for as long as we can. Therefore, our home is our home and we have no intentions of downsizing just because someone thinks we should as it is none of their business what we do with our property.

Let's give people another example: We knew of a guy and his wife who lived up in the mountains in Arizona who had a beautiful 7,500 square foot ranch home on 25 acres of land and they both loved the peace and tranquility of their place in which they retired. Needless to say, they stayed busy all of the time taking care of this place. After about ten or so years of owning this beautiful ranch his wife was diagnosed with a cancer and she managed to survive for another year and a half before she passed away. However, the guy decided to keep on living in his 7,500 square foot ranch home because he enjoyed the open spaces the ranch afforded him. However, after a few years living alone in such a large home he decided to downsize and moved down to Phoenix in Arizona where he was having a small home built that was only 5,000 square feet in size because he didn't want to think he was being cramped up. Nevertheless, this guy past away a few weeks later and everything he had was left to a charity.

The point of this story is that here was a guy who decided to downsize because of loneliness and yet believed that he needed ample space in which to downsize. In other words, this was a personal decision for this guy even though it may sound excessive to the reader, but to this guy moving from a 7,500 square foot ranch home to a 5,000 square foot home was a considerable downgrade for him. As people can now understand, downsizing to a smaller facility is nothing to be taken lightly as everyone will have different ideas of what downsizing will mean to them. Likewise, by downsizing, people will also need to get rid of a lot of their household items, and at the same time people need to realize that the majority of their items will be sold at a loss that will also depend on the size of their new facility. Depending on how much one has to get rid of, we would suggest bringing in an auctioneer in order to minimize excessive losses on your items, unless of course you have more money than you know what to do with. Again, in our opinion, downsizing is not for everyone, especially, if you own your own home. With all the technology we have today and that is being developed for the future, makes living in your home a long time while being retired in this day and age a very viable solution. People can have in home medical care, a lot less expensive and more personal than what they would receive at any hospital. There are several companies that make mobile electric chairs and other devices that will allow seniors not only to remain mobile, but to allow them to continue to do the things they need or want to do around and in their homes.

Therefore, there is no requirement or need to downsize in today's home living environment. One of us is pushing towards 80 in a few years and the other one is seven years behind, but we both remain in top physical health and condition. Likewise, we contribute our health by staying away from doctors at all costs because the leading cause of death in the United States is medical care according to the American Medical Association right behind cancer and heart disease. We do not take any drugs of any kind and we are both health nuts that take a steady regime of vitamins daily and nightly, but again that will be in our next book that will be directed towards seniors to assist them in staying healthy and busy while they continue to age in their retirement years.

Moving on to seniors and people who want to downsize or need to downsize. These will be seniors who are tired of all the upkeep they've been doing around their homes as well as those who can no longer handle these tasks. This will also include the people who are no longer capable of living in their homes for various reasons. If a sickness overcomes certain seniors and it is not just a mild sickness, these seniors will have a need to downsize to a facility that they feel comfortable in even though it may not be what they had expected. Going from a 2, 3, 4000 sq. ft. or larger home into a 800 to 900 sq. ft. home or even a 1000 or 1500 sq. ft. home, condo, or trailer park will be a major change that will take time to adjust to if the need or desire arises.

Nevertheless, unless there is a reason to downsize we would recommend against it as there will be a lot of things to consider regardless of what people may be told from sources one may not even know. Again, our advice to everyone including retirees or future retirees is to always seek out some sort of professional advice from people you do not know and who do not know you. The reason for this is to avoid any conflict of interest from the people you know or associate with on a regular basis and, especially, family members as they may have ulterior motives that may benefit them and not you. Seniors need to consider that any and all transactions that they become involved in whether they intend to downsize their home, invest their monies, and/ or address medical concerns, be sure you discuss your matters with the most qualified professional you can find in any particular field.

When it comes to addressing medical concerns stay away from doctors, but make sure you consult with someone who is knowledgable in the medical field or who are familiar with your particular situation. It is also important that seniors take advantage of bank services and brokerage services as these people are constantly dealing with all kinds of financial situations. We have found these personnel to be of great service with a lot of knowledge, but be sure you maintain an account with these banks or brokerages if one is going get the information they desire.

To give people another example, we have been with our broker for over 30 years and have stayed with him during 2 different moves from other brokerages. Not only does this brokerage give us superior service, but we can ask any questions that we may have concerning finances, savings, and recently advice concerning our Wills. All of his information has turned out to be substantiated and superior in its quality over the years we have been doing business together. The other nice thing about a stock brokerage is that they guarantee one's monies anywhere from 25 to 50 million, whereas banks only protect people's accounts to 250 thousand, so naturally, our choice is the brokerage.

One more thing we want to mention before moving on is for those seniors who do plan to downsize they should consider hiring and using an auctioneer when selling their home items thereby making sure they are getting a fair price and not just giving their items away. This would include cars and anything else one considers to be valuable including collectables. Make sure they are appraised before the auction so you have proof and evidence of the items values.

# FIVE

# SECTION II

# FINANCIAL PLANNERS

We were going to include financial advisors in the title, but since financial planners and financial advisors are, basically, the same we will deal with just the one title that will include the advisors. People have to be very careful when dealing with any of these people as any one can hang their shingle or sign, as one may prefer, indicating that they are a financial planner or advisor even though they have no experience. In time we believe this will change, but as of this writing anyone can hang their shingle advertising that they are a financial planner or advisor as they prefer. These people may have all sorts of fake degrees and certifications hanging on their walls in their offices in an attempt to gain their future client(s) being you, and gain their trust to make them feel comfortable. However, don't and we mean don't take these displays seriously as they may not be accurate at all. Our recommendation to all seniors is to make out a list of questions that you want answers to concerning your situation and not anyone else's. Be careful because these people like to talk as that is how they make their living trying to convince anyone that they know what they are doing. The reality is that none of these people may know what they are doing and we will tell you why we know this is true.

What started us questioning these people was because we never had any reason to require one of these financial planners or advisors while we were growing up and going through life, having kids, and basically, surviving like the rest of the population. So why would anyone need a financial advisor just because we are retired? Great question and we decided to learn what these financial planners and advisors were all about. Naturally, we started going around and dropping in several of these offices over the years to see what they were all about. We never made an appointment and we never got turned away as curiosity got the better of these people. So, just like these financial planners and advisors do, we would make up different scenarios as we went along to test the general knowledge of these planners or advisors in order to determine if they knew what they were talking about.

According to our records over 80% of these planners and advisors did not pass our test and no where were they any smarter than the average bear. However, they were excellent at their presentations and had mastered what little they did know. At the end of our investigation with all of these financial planners and advisors we decided that we would be much better off on our own. Likewise, what we did not expect was that the banks and stock brokerages started using the terms of financial planners and advisors thereby grouping themselves with the street financial planners and advisors as if it was a sort of competition. Furthermore, it was now becoming more difficult to determine who was more than qualified to be the real financial planners and advisors. Therefore, we decided to stick with our stockbroker who we knew was a great financial planner and advisor concerning any complicated financial issues along with our banking personnel where all the advice was free of charge.

Seldom have we ever lost any money in the stock market with our broker's advice who has the title of financial advisor and never have we ever lost any monies with our banks. Therefore, why would people need a financial planner or advisor? In our situation, never is the answer, however, for a professional such as a doctor, lawyer, big time investors and others who do not have the time to do their own investments then qualified financial planners or advisors would be a good choice for these type of people. Moreover, most of these people will get their references from their colleagues and their referrals will be very legitimate in the way of professional financial planners or advisors.

The bottom line will ultimately be left up to one's own personal decision and their ability depending on their sagacity to assess financial planners or advisors they chose or are referred to should they desire to have someone else control their investments. Nevertheless, if one decides they want to try a financial planner or advisor, it is our recommendation to hire one of these financial planners or advisors after checking them out thoroughly, then only let them handle just a little bit of one's monies. At the same time, they can take an equivalent amount of their monies and invest it the way they like and then compare the results at the end of 1 or 2 years against the financial planner or advisor. In our opinion one is guaranteed to determine who will be the best and wisest person to handle one's own monies be it the financial planners or advisors or yourself. Again in our opinion this is the best way to decide who would be more qualified to handle one's monies and remember, it is all a risk and who knows, you just might get lucky.

# FIVE

# SECTION III

# ANNUITIES

Are annuities good or bad investments strategies for retirees? The answer to this question will naturally be up to the retirees and the amount of monies they want to invest in any given annuity. Since annuities are usually purchased from and backed by insurance companies it would be wise for one to do their research before committing their monies to something they may or may not understand because annuities can be complicated. There are long term annuities where one invest with an insurance company that in turn makes payments for a specific period of time that can also be for one's entire retirement or until they pass and the client will also pay fees to protect their income.

Annuities can provide growth and protection, they can guarantee an income depending on the amount one invests in an annuity. Annuities may offer some tax advantages and protect one who they may pick to receive their annuity when the annuity holder passes. Annuities can be Delayed annuities where one starts to receive income sometime in the future or most annuities are classified as Immediate annuities where people can start receiving their income immediately. There are also Fixed and Variable annuities. These annuities are usually tied to the financial markets and naturally the variable annuities are more risky as an investment because one could lose their monies with this type of annuity as opposed to a fixed annuity. However, should one be interested in participating in the financial markets they will be investing with a managed portfolio via the insurance company. This process will provide an opportunity for income growth, but we would recommend that one takes their time and thoroughly question anyone involved in this process and be sure the insurance company provides one with at least ten years of their past returns that one can have to verify. There are also additions that can come with a variable annuity, but like anything else there will be additional charges associated with any of these incentives or as insurance companies refer to them as additional features.

There are also Fixed Index annuities that can grow one's monies when you pick an index even though one does not and will not be investing in the stock market, but rather makes money on the performance of the different indices. One can also pick a set rate for a specific period of time depending on their situation. It should also be pointed out that all annuities will have additional features that every insurance company will offer to people because these features make them more money off of your monies, so be careful not to get caught up in the offerings of these extra features.

So, are annuities good or bad? For some, annuities may be good if people can't control their monies and need someone else to take care of this aspect of their lives in retirement. On the other hand, to us, these insurance companies don't do any better than we do with our monies, but then again we have been dealing with our monies for a long period of time and we have been in the banking business for a good period of time. When it comes to annuities we think they can be good for some, but for others that have the ability to control their own monies and invest it properly, it is also our opinion that some people will be better off without having to go through the hassle of setting up an annuity. Over the years we have heard horror stories when it comes to people trying to cancel their annuities because these insurance companies want to keep their monies and will do whatever they can, not to return these monies back to their clients without a fight. Because these insurance companies make their incomes off of these annuity accounts people may now understand why these insurance companies are so reluctant to part with your monies that you have invested in your annuities.

To us annuities are not good or bad because they are just another financial device from our perspective that people can utilize before or when they are in retirement. What it comes down to is what people think is better for themselves. However, we do have some suggestions when it comes to annuities and they are to make sure you have an attorney who understands annuities and take copies of your annuity contracts for your attorney to review and offer you advice if needed before signing any annuity contract. Don't be afraid to question these insurance companies as to how hard will it be to cancel one's annuity and be sure to write their names down and what their status is with the insurance company. The last important thing to remember is that the people investing one's money at an insurance company is nothing more than a financial planner or advisor hired by these insurance companies. Therefore, it would also be advisable to know what their investment backgrounds are and how long they have been in the financial business. These financial planners or advisors should have at least 5 to 10 years of experience in their fields and ask what they specialize in or are they just general financial planners or advisors? The more one knows of who they are working with or who is handling their money and their educational backgrounds in these insurance companies the less likely they will encounter any problems may be.

# SIX

# LET's TALK RETIREMENT FINANCES

People are constantly being bombarded by others that think they know how everyone should figure out how much income they will need in retirement and yet none of these people are retired. In other words, they are just regurgitating something they have read or heard as their advice is not based on any real life experiences. Then they have various calculators that are supposed to assist people in figuring how much money they should spend or how much money they should be able to withdraw every month or how much money they should have to retire on.

People, all they are doing is selling calculators that no one needs because all of this information can be calculated with any ordinary calculator. The problem with all of this is that there is no way to make any accurate calculations until one has been retired for at least one, two, or three years in retirement is better. All the rest is just an exercise in futility because people entering retirement have absolutely nothing to base their retirement spending on to be able to determine how much they will or will not need. Once a person's income is cut off when they enter retirement the best thing that one can do is to cut back on their spending as much as they can for the first two or three years in order to determine what they might need to support themselves in retirement.

What we did was to make out a spread sheet of all of our fixed monthly payments along with as much of our variable monthly payments and recorded these figures every month for the next two years. At the end of the second year and after tabulating all of these figures from both years we were able to realize what we were required to spend and what we could spend if we wanted to. By going through this process we now knew what we were required to spend vs. what we could spend allowing us to maintain our living standards.

People are always telling people on the internet that they can retire on eighty percent of their working income having no idea of what people were making. Our question is, how does one think they can make such an assumption having no knowledge of what people spend or do not spend? Unless people have these figures there is no way anyone can determine what they cannot spend or what they can spend after retiring and actually have any idea of how much of their working income savings they will be able to spend based on a fantasy percentage figure.

Granted some people may be able to live on eighty percent of their working income once they are retired whereas others may find out that they will have to cut back and live on 70%, 60%, 50%, or even as low as 30% of their working income. Nevertheless, no one will really know their real figures until they construct a means to track their spending requirements over a given period of time. People can forecast all they want, but until they have their real figures recorded over a couple of years they will just be guessing, which in our opinion puts them on the path of retirement uncertainty and destruction.

No one will have the same set of circumstances regardless of their situations, but in order to survive in retirement and not have to go back to work depending on when one retires, the more financial information they are able to accumulate the better off they will be in their retirement years. The good news to this situation is that as time goes on in one's retirement years the less money they will eventually be required to spend thereby giving them more and more income and the relief of knowing that they will be okay in the long run.

One thing that the majority of people forget is to plan for inflation that can have a major impact on people's spending habits as most people do not take inflation into consideration when they retire. Furthermore, since no one knows how much the inflation figures are or will be in the coming years it is always beneficial to base these numbers on the previous year. Even though the inflation numbers may not be totally accurate, if one uses the previous year's inflation numbers and add them to their spending spreadsheet at the end of each year they should be able to make any necessary adjustments to their spending requirements for the following year while they are in retirement.

In our opinion inflation has gotten way out of hand in America based on the median household income in all fifty of our states. Basically, we are talking about the middle class all across America and as of this writing Alaska's median take home income was reported as being $59,250.00 and Mississippi being the lowest at $33,403 annual take home income after taxes. This in turn meant that the average household median income all across America is roughly $46,326.50 and then everyone wonders why people cannot save enough for retirement? The only thing that we can come up with concerning inflation is GREED that is eventually going to destroy our economy simply because people will not be able to buy the products or items they need in order to survive.

When people have to spend ridiculous amounts of their money that all these greedy businesses want for their products, it will be just a matter of time before a major disaster takes place in America. Just look at new automobiles that cost 40 to over 100 thousand dollars just to go from point A to point B and back again to point A, and they wonder why there is such a huge used car market. How about the ridiculous interest rates that are drowning our citizens in debt with their greed or just look at our housing market where they are financing for 40 years and soon to be 60 years just so people can have a roof over their heads that they can call home. What about your average cell phone that is already over a thousand dollars that is no where worth anywhere near that amount of money. Furthermore, if people think that is bad, just wait until 5G hits the market because all the current cell phones will have to be discarded and new ones bought if people want to utilize the 5G networks at a predicted dollar amount of 1 thousand 5 hundred dollars per phone.

In our opinion this is just pure insanity because there is no reason to be ripping people off just because businesses think they can get away with ripping people off instead of giving them a fair deal. Today is Black Friday and as an example we will use this day's prices that are being presented at just about every major retail outlets all across America. People these prices are the real prices that all people should be paying for any product they are buying. However, the day after Black Friday these retail outlets will again increase their prices to rip people off once again when they could have sold all these items on a regular daily basis that they are selling to people on Black Friday attempting to make people think they are getting a deal when in fact, that item should be selling at these Black Friday prices on a regular basis.

Okay, so much for our ranting and time to get back to retirement finances. Another thing that people can forget about is the so called 4 percent rule that they are always talking about on the internet indicating how much people should be able to withdraw and live on in retirement. People there are no set rules because this is all based on someone's assumptions and, frankly, we consider this to be feckless information. Depending on the age one retires whether it is at 62 or 66 or later makes no difference because everyone's situation will be completely different. As long as retirees have a complete understanding of their finances using a spreadsheet to monitor their necessary and variable monthly and annual expenses they will be able to really discern what available percentage of income they can or cannot live on from year to year.

Basically, the bottom line is that there is no way for anyone to determine if they managed to save enough for retirement. Likewise, no one will be able to tell people how much they should have saved for retirement because they do not know anyone's particular situation. In reality everything will be determined on one's working career and how much money they were able to accumulate in IRA's, 401K's, Health Savings Accounts, pensions and any other sources of income they may have accumulated over the years before they retire.

# SIX

# SECTION II

# LET's TALK RETIREMENT

# FINANCES

Another thing people talk about when retiring is taking or getting a part time job. If people enjoy working or just want to work after they retire there is nothing wrong with that providing they are in good health and in full control of their faculties. Also the extra income they make can be beneficial, but one should be careful of the tax consequences they could be exposed to while continuing to work. Likewise, retirees should check with their accountants or even the Social Security Administration to determine just how much more money they are entitled to make so that they don't have to pay any additional taxes or have their Social Security taxed. In addition to the financial rewards these retirees will remain in good health as all retirees need to keep themselves busy in order to stay in good physical and mental shape.

Another thing we have heard about on the internet is suggesting that retirees automate as many financial services as they can, but we are in disagreement with this idea and we will tell people why. We acknowledge that technology is great, but it is not perfect and, therefore, we do not trust much in the way of financial technology. The more sophisticated technology becomes the more sophisticated the hackers become and until someone can come up with a plan to stop hackers no one will ever be safe. That is why we never put any financial information on our computers, phones, or anything else that is electronic because it can be hacked. Paranoid? No, just cautious when it comes to our financial well being, especially, as we get older because it is much easier to forget little things as one ages.

When companies like Yahoo, Equifax, the Medical industry, AOL, AT & T, Facebook, Apple, and several banks, just to mention a few that have been hacked along with other companies there is no telling whose information has been compromised. Everyone's information can be stolen by hackers and used for various reasons and there is very little people can do about it until it is too late. Usually, when people find out their credit has been ruined and it will take a considerable period of time to correct the damage that has been done, this is the reason why we never record any financial information on our electronic devices. Nevertheless, we do not recommend retirees use automated services unless it is absolutely necessary. Another little tidbit people should know about is that 80% of all stolen identity theft occurs from the information given to doctor offices, clinics, and hospitals. Never give these people one's driver license number or social security number under any circumstances as it is not required by law. If these companies want a photo have them take one for their records, but even that is not necessary.

Investing is another area in the world of finances that can include a lot of different investments from stocks and bonds to investing in all different kinds of real estate as long as one knows what they are doing because all investments are risky no matter what they are. However, there are exceptions such as bank certificates of deposit (AKA CD's) that can be for short periods of time to long term CD's. Nevertheless, one can check with their banks for information on various information concerning different investments their banks offer and there is no charge for asking questions. When it comes to other investments like stock and bonds, we recommend that one find a stock broker who has been around for at least 10 years that they can ask for advice. Most of these people are being referred to as financial advisors to handle this sort of business for the banks. Also check out the independent stock brokers at reputable brokerages and again ask all the questions you want because the information will be free of charge if one is inclined to invest. The other nice thing about stock brokerages is that they will protect your monies as high as fifty-million dollars as opposed to only two hundred and fifty-thousand dollars at any bank.

For those of you that may be relying strictly on their Social Security (SS) monthly payment while in retirement, our recommendation would be to wait as long as possible before applying for your SS payments in order to get as much as possible. For those of you who do not want to wait or can't wait for one reason or another for their SS payments, you need to understand that it will be more difficult to survive on such payments. Although there are ways to stretch one's SS payments that we will be discussing in a later chapter.

Another way to increase one's finances is to learn to live within one's means before or after retirement. People are always telling or suggesting that people should live below or within their means, but none of them ever take the time to explain exactly what they mean or how to go about living below or within one's means. Be that as it may, we have devoted an entire chapter that will assist all people to understand what those words really mean financially, and how anyone rich or poor can benefit by living below or within their means that we will be discussing in detail in another chapter. In the meantime, let's look at some other financial situations people should know.

One of our big no no's is that there are technically no reason for anyone to go back to college once they retire unless they have the finances required to give away to the school systems for no reason. On the other hand if a local college is offering free classes on a subject that one might be interested in, then by all means enroll in the course and be sure it is free. Once retired, all people should keep their minds functioning as this will keep them alert and sharp for a longer period of time, especially, as they continue to age. We have conversed with 90 and 100 year old people who were extremely alert and sharp as ever and when we asked them what contributed to their alertness, all of them basically stated that they were always studying or learning something new. With that said, it seems beneficial for retirees to keep their minds functioning the best they can regardless of their situations. In our next book for retirees we will be giving them advice on how we go about accomplishing this feat and what we take to maintain our health and longevity.

Before leaving this chapter we would like to mention another source of income that may be available to a lot of retirees in the event they really need extra income in their retirement years and that is the Reverse Mortgages. This is another program that we are not interested in because of all the downfalls that can come with these types of loans. Like anything else, the reverse mortgages have different issues that one should be aware of before applying for this kind of loan and one should make sure that this is the type of loan that people are looking for before making a final decision. As we have mentioned before, if people are not quite sure of what they may be getting into with a reverse mortgage, seek out as much professional help as one can and don't be afraid to talk with the FHA or lenders that offer reverse mortgages before accepting and committing to accept this type of loan. Furthermore, be sure to have an attorney that is familiar with reverse mortgage loans before signing for a reverse mortgage.

# SIX

# SECTION III

# LET's TALK ABOUT

# REVERSE MORTGAGE

# FINANCES

Since we have already written on this subject extensively in our HOME BUYING & FINANCING 101 SECOND EDITION book, and because of all of the requests we had been receiving from our first edition, we will include some of the important information here in this section in addition to a little more that people may not be aware of concerning reverse mortgages. The only reason that we are going to elucidate on this subject is because people are always asking us and wanting to know about the advantages and disadvantages of the " Reverse Mortgage." Likewise, the reverse mortgage is another way to gain valuable additional finances in one's retirement should they need it and providing they own a home and have sufficient equity that can be used for getting this type of loan.

Like most everything else, there are both good and bad aspects of the reverse mortgage. Since 1988 there has been continued updated advancements, in addition to increases in FHA loan limits that were set at $625,500 as of this writing that have now been increased and one should check with the FHA or other lenders for any other new limits. Nevertheless, one has to be 62 years old or older, and interested in financing home improvements, or supplemental retirement income, or pay for healthcare expenses, or paying off their current mortgage. The nation's consumer protection agency is the "Federal Trade Commission" (FTC), and the FHA is responsible for funding approximately 90 percent of all reverse mortgages under the heading of the "Home Equity Conversion Mortgage" (HECM) in today's marketplace. However, other lenders have entered into this market place and offer different loan structures, so be sure to check around as one could receive more money according to their loan limits. Nevertheless, people should be very careful to read their contracts or have an attorney do so before signing any contracts, especially, if these lenders offer more money than what the current guidelines of the FHA are concerning reverse mortgages. Should there be any differences in any structures of the contract, a qualified attorney should be able to point them out to you.

Currently, there are three kinds of reverse mortgages available in today's marketplace as follows: 1) The *single-purpose* reverse mortgages, offered by some local state governments and nonprofit organizations that are the least expensive, and can only be used for purposes specified by the government or the nonprofit lenders. Homeowners with low or limited income can usually qualify for this type of loan. For details concerning this loan consult your lender. 2) The *"Home Equity Conversion Mortgage"* (HECM) is backed by the U.S. Department of Housing and Urban Development (HUD). However, the HECM and proprietary reverse mortgages can be more expensive than regular home financing including the upfront costs and even though this reverse mortgage is readily available, it has no income or medical requirements, and can be used for any reason. However, before applying for the HECM there is also a requirement for the people to meet with a counselor, and you can request the counselor to assist you by comparing the cost of the different reverse mortgages. As of the year 2000, detailed limits concerning origination fees charged by lenders are allowable and were approved by Congress from a minimum of $2,500.00 to a maximum of $6,000.00, which is now the law. However, be sure to check as limits are always changing in today's environment. 3) The *proprietary* reverse mortgages are usually backed by companies that develop them, and issue private loans. Again, we recommend that people who elect to apply for these types of reverse mortgages take copies of their contract to an attorney to be reviewed. For what little expense it will cost people to hire an attorney it could save them a lot of headaches down the road.

Nevertheless, for those who are interested in these reverse mortgage loans, there is a myriad of information available on the internet, as well as, the FHA, HUD and other organizations. Moreover, homeowners can choose different payment options such as: Fixed monthly cash advances for a specified periods of time called a "Term Option." There is also fixed monthly cash withdraws as long as you live in your home called a "Tenure Option." There is a line of credit that allows you to withdraw the loan monies at any time, and in any amounts you want until the line of credit proceeds have been used up. Likewise, you can have a line of credit along with monthly payments, and the homeowner can change their payment options any time they want for a fee that will be plus or minus $20.00 or so to make the change.

As a rule these loans have to be paid back when people sell their homes, or when the surviving borrower dies, or when one no longer uses their home as their principal resident. An owner can also live in a nursing home or medical facility for a year before they have to repay the loan. Furthermore, people with reverse mortgages must continue to pay their property taxes and insurance, as well as, the up keep on their properties even though there is no tax charged for the use of the reverse mortgage monies. The people should also know that the loan interest on a reverse mortgage will continue to accrue on the loan balance every year, thereby increasing the loan balance should the people elect not to pay down the reverse mortgage balance. Likewise, for those of you who decide to get an HECM reverse mortgage, you will be required to pay a 1.25 percent insurance premium each year, as of this writing on the remaining loan balance because the loan is being insured by the FHA. Nevertheless there are a few things people need to remember when it comes to reverse mortgages in addition to the aforementioned. Basically, the money people receive on a reverse mortgage is not considered taxable income, but it would be wise to check with the appropriate government agencies or your FHA advisor before signing any documents. As long as the homeowner meets their obligations of the loan they will not be forced out of their homes, but failure to meet the loan agreements could result in a foreclosure. The reason for this is because banks are not in the business of owning homes, but they do want their money back. Why and for what reason we could never figure out, (just joking) but they do want their money back and they will add a lien to the title assuring the bank that they will get their monies back sometime in the future.

In addition, there are considerable up front closing fees, but these fees can be financed into the reverse mortgage loan. Reverse mortgage loans function like home equity loans in that any homeowner can apply for a home equity loan whereas one has to be at least 62 in order to apply for a reverse mortgage loan as stated earlier. Both home equity loans and reverse mortgage loans will have closing fees, but the home equity loan may have higher interest rates as opposed to the reverse mortgage loan where the closing fees are paid up front thereby keeping the interest rate lower, in theory anyways. Also, home equity loans can be financed for far shorter years than reverse mortgage loans where they are not paid back until the owner passes or has left their home for 12 consecutive months as mentioned earlier. Both loans can have their closing fees financed into their loans, but be sure to mention this when applying for a home equity loan.

Granted the heirs will be entitled to inherit the home through the estate of the deceased, but there will be a lien on the title that will include the amount of the reverse mortgage owed along with any and all accrued interest including any and all mortgage insurance monies owed. However, because the reverse mortgage is a non-recourse loan, meaning that the borrower or their estate can never owe more than the loan balance or the total value of the property the mortgage solution will be limited to foreclosure and the borrower will never be liable for any deficiencies that may occur because of the foreclosure. One last item that people should realize about reverse mortgages is that their medicare could be effected, however, be sure to check with the FHA personnel or call medicare and ask how a reverse mortgage could affect some of these government benefits. Again the majority of this information can be explained in greater detail on the internet by going to the FHA reverse mortgage site where one can verify everything we have stated here concerning the reverse mortgage programs available.

Furthermore, there is another caveat that no one tells people about the reverse mortgages. However, we will not go into the calculations concerning these owed monies as they can become very complicated. However, we have done this in detail using different examples in our Home Buying & Financing 101 Second Edition book. Therefore, if anyone is interested in knowing the real facts about reverse mortgage loans and what they can really cost the heirs to pay back these loans or lose these homes because they cannot afford to pay them back, this book would be worth reading. This is where the problem with reverse mortgages can come into play because no one told the heirs what a reverse mortgage could cost them to buy the home back.

As for the bad aspects of the reverse mortgage, and in our opinion, and even though this loan was originally designed to assist elderly persons who are having trouble, and struggling to make ends meet in their retirement years, the reverse mortgage today, like the reverse mortgages in the years gone by, are designed to let the investors take your home along with the rest of your home equity. Question: Why does our government always start advertising, and promoting the reverse mortgage when interest rates are at their lowest point? Answer: Because this is when the government, and private investors can make the most money when they take your home back in order to pay back the reverse mortgage loan, and then they take the rest of the equity that is left in the home.

In the event that a homeowner does not have anyone to leave their home to in the way of family, relatives, friends, or in the way of a donation, then a reverse mortgage may be a good way to go to live out the rest of their lives with extra monies. However, if one wants to leave their property to their loved ones and at the same time they get a reverse mortgage, the chances are, they will lose their home to the federal or state government, or a private reverse mortgage lender. Why? Simple! All of these lenders are aware of the national statistics concerning household incomes, and the savings habits of the people, and they know that the odds are in their favor.

This book reveals several saving techniques relating to cash monies, social security monies, downsizing, reinvesting and saving monies every month, and how to put these monies back into one's retirement accounts, just to mention a few topics, as this book is filled with many savings techniques. This retirement book will also show people how to live within their means and how to go about accomplishing this endeavor. At the same time, we will show everyone how they can become well-off and well-to-do before they reach retirement or if they are already in retirement, and never having to worry about going back to work again in order to survive in their retirement years. In our opinion, and as mentioned early on, unless one does not want to leave their home to family members, relatives, friends, or in the way of a donation, then a reverse mortgage may be a good way to go to live out the rest of one's life having extra monies, and having no more home mortgage loan payments. On the other hand, should people considering a reverse mortgage, and have family, relatives, friends, or they intend to make a donation of their home, then people should, at all costs, stay away from a reverse mortgage unless the people know that their family, relatives, or friends, have the financial capability to pay back the reverse mortgage loan including any and all accrued interest.

# SIX

# SECTION IV

# LET's TALK ABOUT EMERGENCY FUNDS

We are always hearing about having an emergency fund in case of any emergencies that may arise at anytime in the future. Having said that, it is easier said than done. As always the media and financial writers make comments without assisting or instructing people on how to go about to do such a simple thing as establishing an emergency fund. Don't worry because we are here to assist anyone and everyone on how to go about establishing their emergency fund, but first we need everyone who has gone through the epidemic coronavirus in 2020 should now understand the value of having an emergency fund.

So far we have gone from January to December having people restricted and ordered to lock themselves down to keep this virus from spreading. These restriction orders were implemented by each State's Mayors or Governors who then decide to determine when the people could be released from their confinements. By doing this these Mayors and Governors have exceeded their authority according to the Constitution of the United States of America. By doing this caused massive layoffs and massive unemployment filings that broke the system along with harming the Social Security and Medicare systems. In addition, there were people that hoarded thousand of different items such as food items, paper items including toilet paper, hand sanitizers, and other items that caused shortages of the items for other people and yet these Mayors and Governors did nothing about this situation. In other words, the United States and the rest of the world was not prepared for such an event and many people not only died because of this virus, millions of people had to go without the aforementioned supplies all because the United States

Government along with the State Mayors and Governors did not have any policies in place to stop this hoarding from taking place.

Had America had hoarding policies in place then everyone would have been able to obtain these items without any problems, but instead, people were just thinking about themselves and no one else. Then we also had the profiteers who bought up everything they could get their hands on and then they demanded huge prices for items that should have cost people the regular prices they were originally sold for. Next, America had the medical crisis because America did not have the necessary supplies in the quantities necessary that were needed to aid in assisting the people who were in dire need of such supplies. Again, America was at a loss because of the greed of the Corporations and Companies that moved over seas in order to have their products manufactured cheaper than they could be made in America.

All of this activity ended up costing America billions and billions of dollars simply because America was not prepared. Granted the President at that time had nothing to do with the epidemic and yet his response was excellent after realizing just how big the virus problem was and he took the necessary response to try and correct the problem. Nevertheless, the President was being given false medical information by his advisors (who had been advisors in the White House serving several Presidents over the years) because they did not know what they were doing at the time. Furthermore, people in our Congress were ignoring the warning signs and actually inviting people to come out of their dwellings because they thought this was all a hoax being propagated by the President. Unfortunately, it did not turnout that way and then panic and fear set in because of the fear mongering by the media outlets, medical personnel, and our own Congress along with these long time advisors to the Presidents who had no idea of what they were talking about concerning the pandemic.

Nonetheless, and getting back to the emergency funds, we now believe that the people will understand why they should have an emergency fund. When it comes to retirees, they can establish an emergency fund simply by taking 10 to 15 percent of their monthly social security (SS) monies and establish an emergency fund. As an example, say you retire at 62 and receive the minimum monthly payment around $700 or $800 dollars. At 10% one would save $70.00 and at 15% one would save $105.00 per month every month. If these numbers are too much one can cut these figures down to where they feel comfortable. Likewise, all seniors can determine just exactly what they would like to save for their emergency funds. The goal is to try and save the equivalent of six months income in one's emergency fund. Granted it may take several years to do, but you will be glad you did if another epidemic ever arises or some other crisis occurs in the future.

Now for the working people, and yes we know that they think it is impossible to accomplish because of all of their other living expenses, but a few dollars here or there will and can make a big difference in a situation like this epidemic or any other crisis that may occur in the future. Again, all it takes is consistency for anyone to build an emergency fund for themselves. In this next example we will use our situation to explain how it worked for us. During our first marriages neither one of us managed to save for an emergency fund and actually we never even heard of such a thing in those days.

We both met while we were in the real estate business with one of us working for a real estate company and the other one working as an independent real estate loan officer. Needless to say, we hit it if off and we became a team where one sold homes and the other did the financing. After a month or so we were getting along so well that I asked her what she was going to be doing for the rest of her life? When she asked me if I was asking her to marry me, I told her that we had nothing better to do and we decided to get married having knowing her for about a month. That was 31 years ago when we tied the knot and it has been the greatest marriage one could ever ask for except for our up's and downs, and that is my opinion anyways as I have never asked her, her opinion, but nevertheless, we are still together.

Anyways, we were going through some tough times having had a couple of serious earthquakes in California. Then came the year 2000 and what little money we had we spent on supplies that would carry us for about 2 to 3 months if need be even though nothing happened, but we had enough to support us for the next few months without having to spend any more money except for our vehicle gas requirements. Fortunately, we had downgraded our living standard by selling her condo that was in Laguna Niguel and located a couple miles from the Ritz Carlton in Dana Point, California and bought a mobile home in San Juan Capistrano that was a mile from a very popular beach. Our expenses went from $2200.00 a month to $575.00 per month that included the land lease. By down grading we managed to save $1,625.00 per month and living in a newly rebuilt mobile home that we completely rebuilt in order to save money.

Having explained to my new wife that by down grading we would be able to eventually get out of debt by paying off all of our bills, getting rid of our credit cards and using only debt cards from now on. She wasn't sure, but she agreed and in a couple of years we no longer had any debt, so we decided to open our own Real Estate Processing Center, a Real Estate Office, and a Real Estate Loan Center in Irvine., California. As it turned out, this was an excellent choice for the both of us as the money just kept pouring in, and if one of our companies slowed down the other two would keep us going for as long as we wanted.

Being in California, most of our business revolved around $650,000 to 2.5 million dollar properties and it wasn't long for us to start getting ahead even though we were in our late forties and mid fifties. It is amazing how fast time and life goes by because in just a few years we would reach retirement age even though one of us retired at 42. So now the race was on again to put enough money away to be able to retire once we reached 62 and the other at 65. We figured that we had 8 years before one of us would reach age 62 and a couple of more years for the other to reach 65 in ordered to be eligible to file for social security benefits. Therefore, we needed enough money to be able to buy a place to live and enough money to support us for a least 8 years.

We both looked around at several states to move to because we knew we could not afford to live in California with the inflation going on in the housing market and decided to investigate Arizona, New Mexico, Nevada, Utah, Colorado and Texas. To make a long story short we settled on Texas as it was the only state at the time where one could get their monies worth buying a home and having some property to go with it. So, we packed up our motor home and headed for Texas and after a month looking at over 10 houses seven days a week during that time until we finally found a home to buy. After making the deal we headed back to California and sold our mobile home for an unbelievable price and moved to Texas.

At the time it seemed like the logical thing to do even though we were approaching retirement age and buying a new home going into retirement. However, we figured that we could pay off the home in 3 years so we decided to take the risk even though we wanted to be debt free in retirement. Five years later everything was paid off in 2009 when we read an article in the financial section on the internet stating that people should have an emergency fund in the event that something should break on one's car or in one's home. After thinking about it for a while we decided to start an emergency fund and started with $100.00 per month. At that time we were spending around $36,000.00 a year and according to the articles we were reading we figured we needed 6 months of capital for any given emergency that may materialize in the future. So our goal was to save at least $3600.00 for how ever long it took to raise at least $21,000.00 or $22,000 that would cover us for a six-month period of time if need be in an emergency situation.

Having been in the real estate financial business one thing we learned is that people always under estimated what they think they need regardless of whether it is a crisis or an every day event. Therefore, we figured another 10 to 20 percent would just about do it so we set our goal at an emergency fund at $22,000.00 dollars. To understand what we are discussing here is that we managed to save only $13,000 dollars when this virus epidemic hit in January and now in May we still have enough emergency funds to carry us another several months if need be concerning this virus lockdown.

When the lockdown is over we will start replenishing our emergency funds again until we reach our goal as mentioned above. But now, maybe people will learn and understand the value of establishing an emergency fund for themselves because no one ever knows what the future may bring. Being prepared no matter how little one can put towards their emergency fund it will always benefit them in the long run. We originally started with $5.00 dollars a week to build our emergency fund and now it is $500.00 per month or nothing more than what we spend for lunches every month for 3 people. Plus we have enough money to feed or help someone that may be in need at any given time while we are out and about.

Regardless of what people decide to do, make sure that you always have access to your emergency funds. Even if the financial institutions along with the banking system decide to lockdown and shutdown, one needs to maintain access to their emergency funds in the event that things get out of hand as no one can predict what the future may bring in the way of disasters or any other problems that may develop in the future.

As of this writing, we have no idea of what some of these State Mayors or Governors will do when it comes to allowing their people to discontinue being locked down. Some of these Mayors and Governors are indicating that their lockdown orders could last through the summer months and some State Governors have not indicated when they will rescind their lockdown orders when all they had to do was make the suggestion that all people should wear masks.

# SEVEN

# HEALTH CARE COST

# AND

# MEDICARE

We know the majority of people have heard all the hype about health care cost in retirement that we totally disagree with, but then again we are health nuts and seldom if ever do we ever have any health problems. On the other hand there are people who have several health problems and most of them had these medical problems before they retired. However, there are retirees who will develop some sort of medical problems while they are in retirement or before they retire for one reason or another that they will have to deal with whenever they occur and the only question will be, how they will be able to deal with their medical situations financially.

Like most people we have read where it can take anywhere from $250,000.00 to over $300,000.00 to handle routine medical problems in retirement. Therefore, the question is, where do they come up with these figures? Likewise, and to the best of our abilities and since we do not go to doctors, we guesstimated people will spend approximately $11, 000.00 dollars per year while they are in retirement. Based on this number, which we just pulled out of the air, would indicate if one was retired for twenty years their medical cost would be approximately $220,000.00 in medical bills. If people managed to live for 10 more years that would indicate that they will need approximately $330,000.00 to waste or rather spend on medical care. Be that as it may, retirees can now make the necessary adjustments based on these figures as of this writing because we all know that medical cost increase at ridiculous rates annually and, eventually, the government will need to step in and stop these runaway increases because there are no reasons for them other than greed.

When we mentioned adjustments based on these figures above, we meant that retirees can start deducting from these medical cost while they don't use them. Example: If one expects to live for another 30 years when they retire and depending on the age they retire, they can expect to pay a lot less while they are retired. Let's say one retiree at 62 and expects to live until 92 and assuming they stay away from all medical services by the time they are 72 they can readjust the aforementioned medical cost figures down by $110,000.00 because they no longer require these monies for a 30 year period. In other words the longer one lives without requiring medical services the less money they will need to save to carry them forward while they are retired.

Let's look at another example, a person is 80 years old and stands a good chance of reaching 100 years of age who retired at 66. They no longer need $330,000.00 to cover them for medical expenses and since they never used these monies they no longer need them and can deduct $110,000.00 thereby leaving $220,000.00 to cover them for medical expenses for another 20 years. This scenario will continue to repeat itself over and over again regardless of when one retirees so we would not put too much emphasis or become stressed out trying to save this amount of money just to cover medical expenses. People can also purchase insurance plans that are designed for these types of situations in the event they don't already have insurance coverage.

The upside to this situation is that when a person reaches 62, they can apply for Social Security and sign up for Medicare that will take care of the majority of these medical expenses. However, be careful as medicare may raise the retirement age pretty soon as that has also been discussed in the government and media for some time now. Nevertheless, people will be made aware of any changes to the age requirement in the event medicare makes such a major move in its policies. Medicare is a major benefit and health care program for seniors, so be sure to read or get informed as to what your particular situation may or may not be required when signing up for medicare. Like all other medical programs medicare offers several alternatives that any senior can take advantage of and like other medical plans there will be additional cost involved with these programs.

Currently, as of 2020 people can apply for Original Medicare or Medicare Advantage Programs. The original medicare program covers Hospital insurance known as Part "A" and Medical insurance referred to as Part "B" program. However, people will be responsible for paying a 20% fee in out of pocket cost, but you can use any doctor or hospital one wants throughout the US providing they accept medicare. The Medicare Advantage Program (also known as part C) is referred to as an all in one alternative to the original medicare program in that it bundles Part "A," Part "B," and includes Part "D" programs. However, like original medicare people they will pay a premium for Part "B" should they select the medicare advantage program, but medicare advantage program offers the prescription drug coverage. Furthermore, unlike original medicare people cannot buy separate supplemental coverage with a medicare advantage plan. Also, people need to know that they will be required to use a doctor who is in the network and people will also have to get a referral in order to see a specialist if required.

In our opinion, unless someone is using drugs, the original medicare program is just fine and we see no reason for the additional cost for the medicare advantage programs. People should also know that they will be receiving an annual update Medicare booklet every year, which in our opinion is a waste of money that could be returned to the medicare recipients by not increasing the charges for medical care every year instead of wasting it on printing cost for these booklets. Everyone is aware that medical costs are always going up and the medical industry is gouging the American people, but Medicare could send out flyers indicating what changes, if any, have taken place in the medicare programs instead of printing these booklets every year, especially, in the event of minor changes.

# SEVEN

# SECTION II

# MEDIGAP SUPPLEMENT POLICIES

# AND

# DRUGS AKA MEDICATIONS

All Medigap policies are standardized, meaning that they have to follow State and Federal guidelines that are designed to protect the people and they must be identified as Medical Supplement Insurance. It should also be noted that insurance companies can only sell people a standardized policy and all of these policies, basically, maintain the same benefits. It should also be noted that medigap plans do offer additional benefits so people can choose the one that meets their needs. That said, there are some major changes that will go into effect starting in January 2020, but anyone can get this information via one's State Health Insurance Assistant Program, your State Insurance Department offering these programs, or the Social Security Administration. People should also know that it is illegal for anyone to sell you a medigap program if one has a medicare advantage program. Because there are a lot of facts to be considered before one selects one of these programs, we recommend that one takes their time and do their due diligence and research these programs before one makes a final decision. In our opinion, these programs are feckless as people are just giving free money away to the insurance companies, especially, if they are healthy going into retirement.

We are not big fans of supplemental insurance programs as the original medicare program will serve people just fine. Likewise, if one thinks about it, the chances of one spending more than four days in a hospital is going to be slim to none, so why waste one's money on something they may never use? If people are interested they can go to the internet and look up thetruthaboutmedicare.com and locate a video on U-Tube. The video is sponsored by a doctor who gives people the real facts about these supplemental insurance plans that are constantly being offered in the market place to people giving millions of free money to these insurance companies.

Let's deal with medications AKA drugs. We believe it is about time for the medical industry and the pharmaceutical companies to stop drugging the American people, especially, the seniors. According to the reports that we have read and the seniors we have spoken with it seems that the average person over 60 is taking anywhere from 10 to 16 drugs per day and then they wonder why they are dying off. People, it is reported that 80% of doctors are on pharmaceutical payrolls and as long as they are on these payrolls the more drugs they are going to prescribe simply because that is more money that goes into their pockets. When doctors are being offered incentives like this and being rewarded by the pharmaceutical companies, people stand little chance of being cured or being normal again.

America only accounts for 5% of the world's population and yet the American people consume over 90% of the world's drugs and our question is why? In our opinion this is strictly medical and pharmaceutical abuse based on monetary compensation thereby totally ignoring the people's rights to be treated fairly and properly. Just look at the death toll and immediate problems that has been occurring because of the prescriptions for opioids that were being handed out like candy.

The last we heard was that almost a half of million people had died and millions more were addicted all because of the desire for more and more money by the medical industry. Think about this for a moment, is this really about money and greed or is it about population control? We imagine that one could debate this situation until they turn blue and end up with the same results being absolutely nothing but talk without any resolutions. People, if you want to remain healthy, stay away from any medications AKA drugs that doctors want to prescribe for you, and if they do prescribe drugs have them justify their reasons and protect yourselves.

Recently there has been a product called DSUVIA, which validates a key role in modernizing the treatment of acute pain within the Department of Defense that includes all of the military branches. This product is replacing the use of all opioids that means a substantial decrease in the time a client is required to be in the post anesthesia care unit, or PACU; and second, a dramatic decrease in IV opioid requirements in the PACU. In other words, DSUVIA was tested in 4 clients undergoing abdominal surgery. The nurses in the PACU as well as the anesthesiologists were hesitant to believe a single dose of DSUVIA would be all a client would need for opioid analgesia. To say the results have been quite shocking to some is not an overstatement. Minimum to no other IV opioids are required during the operative process. Normally, they would have been delivering multiple doses of fentanyl during and immediately after the process. The second area of interest for DSUVIA is for the use in senior clients that we will discuss later on in Chapter Fourteen.

Eventually, people will understand that doctors are not your friends and they expect people to be subservient and refer to them as patients, which is a subservient derogatory term instead of referring to people as clients. Think about this for a minute or so, who is the boss, you or the doctor? You are, as doctors don't pay you, but you pay them to provide you with a service and therefore, they work for you. It is time to put these medical personnel in their places as they have assumed they are in charge for years when in fact they are being paid to perform a service for you their client.

Before leaving this section we will leave the reader with this thought and our favorite quote. First the thought by Ivan Illich who warned of the risk of medicalization by dehumanizing and the damaging effects of the so called professional intervention: "The medical establishment has become a major threat to health." Now our favorite quote: "Doctors are people who prescribe medicines of which they know little, to cure diseases of which they know less, in human beings whom they know nothing." By: Voltaire 1692-1788. So true in today's society.

Seniors need to realize that the major problem is that they are being experimented on by the medical industry. This may be hard to swallow, but unless one is born with a disease all diseases are caused by the Medical, Pharmaceutical, Chemical, and Food industries that leads to Physical, Chemical, and Emotional Stressors that we will be talking about in another chapter. In other words, all diseases are nothing more than an adaptive physical response to the chemicals being put into one's body. These can be in the form of drugs, AKA medications, vaccines, that contain dangerous chemicals that will destroy one's body and brain, unhealthy foods that are being produced in all sorts of industries including the medical and pharmaceutical industries. The chemical industries alone is destroying the natural foods we once consumed each and every day years ago, with their deadly chemicals, but more on this later in another chapter.

People need to realize that there are natural remedies for every known disease and every psychological problem that they can encounter today. Nothing, and we mean nothing a person can contract ever needs to be treated immediately because every disease or psychological problem takes time to develop. This includes all Cancers, Dementia, Alzheimer's, Nerve Pain, Depression, just to mention a few and anything else one can think of or be diagnosed as having. Therefore, finding remedies to resolve any of these diseases or psychically problems only requires the time to locate a qualified doctor through "The American College for Advancement in Medicine" that maintains a physicians locator service one can view by going to www.acam.org. and viewing the resource headings. All one has to do is name the decease or psychological condition they have or have been diagnosed as having and locate a natural doctor that will treat said problems with natural methods that have been tested over and over again for ages. Just think, no more drugs, no more slicing and dicing, no exploratory surgery, no more assumptions or speculations, no more might be's, may be's, or could be's, and no more just guessing, but rather real facts concerning one's situation. In addition, the cures are all natural and the cost is extremely low compared to our modern day medical and pharmaceutical industries. Time to consider the natural solutions as opposed to the dangerous medical and pharmaceutical solutions.

# EIGHT

# FINANCIAL AND MEDICAL
# POA'S AND POD'S
# WILLS AND FAMILY TRUSTS

These are areas that we consider to be vital for every person soon to be retired and those people already retired. Since these areas require the intervention of an attorney, it is our suggestion that one interviews several attorneys until they find one with whom they are comfortable, as people will be relating some very personal information to them. The attorney we picked we had known for over 11 years and we were very comfortable, not only with him, but also his entire staff. We originally picked this attorney after interviewing 5 other estate attorneys. As it turned out the attorney we picked had no problem assisting us with our requirements with both POA's, POD'S, and our Will's as there is no need for Family Trust in Texas, but a trust will avoid probate court. However, every state has different requirements so be sure to check around and interview several attorneys that specialize in these areas of the law and check their prices.

Starting with the Financial Power of Attorney (POA) that we had drawn up for both of us plus an additional financial POA for our special needs son in the event that something happened to us or him and we were to pass away or if he unexpectedly passed away for some reason, he would be taken care of for the rest of his life. Basically, a POA is a legal document that gives a person the legal right to make all financial decisions for another person. This may include: Real property and tangible personal property transactions, stock, bonds, commodities, and options transactions. Banking and other financial instruction transactions, Business operating transactions, Insurance and annuity transactions, Estate, trust, and other transactions, Claims and litigations, Personal and maintenance obligations, Benefits from social security, medicare, medicaid, including civil or military service, Retirement transactions and/or any Tax matters. In addition, there may be other stipulations depending on one's situation.

Nevertheless, when a person accepts the authority granted under a power of attorney, they are establishing a fiduciary relationship with the principal. That means one develops a relationship between a trustee and a beneficiary similar to a company that would have a fiduciary duty to its shareholders. A power of attorney is a special legal relationship that imposes on a person legal duties and responsibilities until they resign or the POA is terminated or revoked by the principal or by operation of the law. The fiduciary duties would include: Acting in good faith, Doing nothing beyond the authority granted in the POA, Acting loyally for the benefit of the principal, Avoiding any conflicts that may impair one's ability to act in the principal's best interest; and disclosing one's identity as an agent or attorney-in-fact when acting for the principal by writing or printing the principal's name and signing your own name as agent or attorney-in-fact.

In addition, a durable power of attorney requires an agent to: Maintain records of each transaction or decision made on behalf of the principal or discharged by the court: and if requested by the principal, provide an accounting to the principal that, unless directed by the principal or otherwise provided in the special instructions, must include: property belonging to the principal that has come to your knowledge or into your possession. Each action or decision made by you the agent. A complete account of any and all receipts, disbursements, and other actions of the agent. A listing of all property to include a viable description of each asset and its current value. Cash balances on hand and the name and location of all depositories. Each known liability and include any and all information known for a complete understanding of the property belonging to the principal, and all documentation concerning the principal's property and all information known for a complete understanding of the property belonging to the principal, and all documentation concerning the principal's property.

Any acting power of attorney agent's authority can be stopped if the agent stops acting on behalf of the principal or an event occurs that terminates the power of attorney or the agent's authority to act under the power of attorney. These may include, but is not limited to include: The principal's death. The principal's or agents revocation of said power of attorney. An occurrence of termination stated in the power of attorney. If one is married to the principal and there is a divorce or annulment decree issued by a court of law. The appointment of a guardian of the principal's estate or if ordered by a court. The suspension of the power of attorney based on the appointment of a temporary guardian until the date of the temporary guardianship expires.

It should be noted that the authority granted to a person in a power of attorney will be specified in the Durable Power of Attorney Act. Therefore, if one violates the durable power of attorney act or acts beyond the authority granted, they may be liable for any damages caused by the violation or subjected to prosecution for any misapplications of property by a fiduciary. Anyone considering to become a fiduciary for a power of attorney needs to understand that this is a responsibility that could cause them serious problems in the event they do not understand the consequences they could face if they do not follow the guidelines set forth in the power of attorney. That is why we recommend people have a complete understanding of what a power of attorney means should one take on the responsibility of becoming an agent for another person. Understanding the full ramification of a power of attorney will keep people out of trouble and possibly out of jail or prison. Furthermore, we wish you and your principal a bright future should one need a power of attorney for whatever reason.

# EIGHT

# SECTION II

# THE MEDICAL POA'S

This kind of power of attorney is designed to protect your love one's from any attempts by the medical personnel who may have decided to do something just because they think it is appropriate to do without informing anyone. We carry copies of our medical POA'S with us wherever we go and we made three copies for each of us and carry one in each of our three vehicles. One may never know when they will need a medical power of attorney and we will explain a little later on why they come in handy even if they are not needed to protect one's self from the medical industry personnel.

Basically, a medical power of attorney will have Directives to Physicians that will indicate what they can and cannot be allowed to do in the event that one ends up in a hospital for whatever reason conscious or unconscious. The power of attorney addresses all Medical Conditions and any Terminal Conditions where in the event a doctor indicates that person only has six months to live, providing they receive life-sustaining treatment they have the right to reject or accept treatment, which they have been chosen to do according to their power of attorney. Then there should be Irreversible Conditions that will have the same selection processes available. Next would be Additional Request where one may list particular treatment that one wants or does not want. This can be things like being force fed with artificial nutrition and other fluids or be given intravenous antibiotics or drugs or completely refused by one agent in their power of attorney. As in the financial POA and the medical POA can have any number of backup agents listed in the event that the original agent resigns or is removed from the power of attorney. In ours we have two people listed and in another one we had three people listed who would be capable of protecting our rights according to our POA's in the event our first agent is unable to perform.

Next, they have what they call a HIPPA Release Authority that stands for Health Insurance Potability and Accounting Act of 1996 of which we totally disagreed with. Basically, this added HIPPA section authorizes the release of one's entire medical record information and authorizes any doctor, physician, medical specialist, psychiatrist, chiropractor, health-care professional, dentist, optometrist, health plan, hospital, hospice, clinic, laboratory, pharmacy or pharmacy manager, medical facility, pathologist, or other providers of medical or mental health care, as well as insurance and insurance companies and the Medical Information Bureau Inc. or other health care clearing houses that has paid for or is seeking payment from one for services to give, disclose and release to my agent who is named herein without restriction, all of my individually identifiable health information and medical records regrading past, present or future medical or mental health conditions, including all information relating to the diagnosis and treatment of HIV/AIDS, sexually transmitted diseases, mental illness, and drug abuse.

Maybe now people will understand why we are against this HIPPA Release Authority. In our opinion, all of these people mentioned above have no right to this kind of information unless they can provide the necessary evidence and produce a valid reason they require anyones personal information such as this and the reason why they need this type of information. Unfortunately, we were informed by our attorney that this HIPPA Release Authority was required in all medical power of attorneys, but he was unable to give us a reason why. Nevertheless, we will still be researching the need for disseminating and releasing this sort of personal and private information to determine what course of action we can take to refuse the release of this sort of information without reasonable cause and justification.

Next, one should come to Restrictions which is the fun part because this is where one can list the procedures they do NOT authorize or that are undertaken by any medical personnel. Here we will give people an example of the things that we will not allow the medical personnel do to us based on our 43 year study so far of the medical industry. The medical people cannot conduct an Angiogram, they cannot give medications (drugs) unless authorized by our agent. They cannot do any brain surgery, conduct any Amputations, or perform Sigmoid or a colonoscopy. They cannot conduct Arterial blood gas test, Liver punctures, or Bone marrow test, Spinal taps or Lumbar punctures. They are not authorized to do a Tracheotomy, or Intubation, or use any ventilators, or any kind of Exploratory surgery. They cannot do any MRI's, Cat Scans , or X-rays unless authorized by our agent. They cannot use any Feeding Tubes, Endoscopic test of any kind, no Carotid artery test, and no Heroics and nor are they ever allowed to give us Flu Shots ever. This will give people an idea of what they can demand in their medical POA's.

In addition to the above we have an additional request sheet with more of our requirements that the medical personnel are not authorized to perform on us. Likewise, we included an additional request sheet that we can list things like No Respirators and several more lines that we can continue to add to if needed. It is also important for people to remember that any written demands will take priority over anything that is typed in any legal document. That said, there should be a heading called Definitions that will explain Artificial nutrition and hydration. A section on Irreversible conditions, Life-sustaining treatments, and Terminal conditions. Anyone getting a medical power of attorney needs to read and understand everything written in these areas and if one has any questions be sure to ask questions until one is satisfied with the answers so there will be no mistakes concerning one's obligations concerning the medical POA. Be sure to read and understand the Medical Power of Attorney Disclosure Statement before signing this document as it is a legal document and one's responsibility.

# EIGHT

# SECTION III

# FINANCIAL INSTITUTIONS

# POD'S AND TOD'S

Basically, POD's and TOD's are the same in that these acronyms stand for "Payable on Death" or "Transfer on Death" depending on which kind of financial institutions one uses. In our businesses we use several bank accounts and different banks in order to keep tract of the different areas where we need to spend monies and to be able to analyze these expenditures. However, it also becomes a little more complicated when one is making out one's final decisions to make sure their monies are going to the correct person or persons when one departs from this world. That is when POD's or TOD's come into effect concerning one's last wishes that will be indicated in one's last Will or Testament.

The good news is that these financial institutions will usually have and maintain their own forms concerning POD's whereas stock broker-ages will also maintain their own TOD forms. Dealing with the banks is relatively simple depending on the banking institution one is bank-ing at and all one has to do is spend a few minutes with a manager and express their desires concerning who they want to authorize and name the person that will be allowed to have access to your bank accounts when the time comes. This process is pretty simple as one simply designates the person to whom will have the authorization to close these accounts. In our situation we had to give information on and sign POD's on six different bank accounts including one out of state account and the banks handle all the paperwork that they required to meet our request. Once all the paper work was signed we just continue with our banking processes as everything else is now in order.

The next order of business was to deal with our stock brokerage accounts, but unfortunately, these are a little more complicated because we had to deal with the cash account as well as the various stock accounts. Why the stock brokerages use the term Transfer on Death (TOD) as opposed to Payable on Death (POD) is anyones guess because to us, they are all the same and they all have the same meaning and the same result in the end. Nevertheless, there is more paperwork that has to be signed by all parties involved in these transactions. Be that as it may, everything is pretty much the same as the banks, but one has more paperwork that needs to be looked over that we had to take to our attorney for review.

This process does take a little more time, but the end results will be the same when the process is completed. The only problem we encoun-tered was that our stock brokerage was located in another state and their headquarters was located on the other side of the US. The only reason we mentioned this is due to the fact that some people like to put things off and then forget doing these important little things. Therefore, since these things can sometimes require a lot of time to complete it is better not to put these things off for any length of time.

Another thing to remember is that one is signing legal documents and all banks and stock brokerages will definitely follow the laws of their respective states regarding POD's and TOD's that one signs. Another thing to remember is that because these are all legal documents they can still be changed or canceled by the person or persons who established these POD's or TOD's anytime before they pass away. Likewise, one has the ability to change the recipient or recipients names at anytime prior to passing. However, one has to remember that this process will require even more time to accomplish because all of the paperwork will first have to be recalled by these institutions and then changed and signed again, verified and refiled. So be careful and don't procrastinate and presume that one will have plenty of time to complete these tasks.

# EIGHT

# SECTION IV

# WILLS AND FAMILY TRUSTS

All Wills or Family Trusts can be either very simple or extremely complicated depending on the amount of holdings one has and the number of heirs who stand to benefit from one's estate. No matter what the division may come to, we must warn people that the distribution of assets can cause major problems and divisions in all and any families where the division of assets are not equal or equivalent in values. Yes, we know that people will insist that they will not become upset, disappointed, or enraged when things do not turn out to be the way they expected when a Will or Trust is read. Nevertheless, we have witnessed several situations where the families were completely disrupted, separated, and destroyed simply because a Will or Trust was not divided equally. Notwithstanding, people will learn just how vicious and greedy their siblings will become when it comes to the distribution of assets.

Unfortunately, we have seen this situation occur more often than not and I even had to tell my own wife that this scenario would play out in her own family when their mother passed. Like everyone else she adamantly denied that such a situation would develop within her own family and I just smiled and started laughing to myself knowing how naive people were concerning these matters. That said, we will now give the readers an example of what actually occurs just before my wife's mother ended up passing away, but first, a little background on this family. Granted my wife's family was a very close relationship family that I never knew even existed in this world because my own family was completely the opposite. My wife's family lived in California and my family was raised in Detroit, Michigan and could not be more different than night and day. My wife's other three siblings were very close and loving people as opposed to my family where my other three brothers and myself were always competing against each other and there was absolutely no cohesion between any of us because of the way we had been raised in a very violent family environment.

To make a long story short, just before my wife's mother passed away one of her brothers managed to get their mother to change her Trust giving the majority of assets to him thereby cutting out his sisters and limiting his sisters ability to share in all the proceeds from the sale of their properties. However, one of the sisters had over heard the conversation between their mother and this brother and yet did nothing about it at the time. Nonetheless, the mother passed away and the three siblings ended up splitting a few thousand dollars where the brother that convinced the mother to change her Trust ended up with several hundreds of thousands of dollars. When my wife found out about what her brother had done she could not believe it and was in total shock that anything like this could take place in their family. When I finally approached my wife and explained to her that people will come out of the woodwork when they smell a chance to get free money any way they can, they will do the unthinkable and backstab their own brothers and sisters at the first chance they get.

In my situation and just before our mother passed away she made our old man promise and swear that he would not change their Trust and Wills while she was on her death bed in the hospital and he agreed. However, once our mother had passed the old man flew to Nevada and had his attorney completely cutout his four sons from his Trust and Will and even indicated that he had no sons. Kinda of gives the reader an idea of how close our family was between the parents and their siblings. Again to make a long story short, the three of us brothers got together and sued the old man's estate and Children's Hospital that he left his estate to. Our other brother did not join us as he thought we would take him out because of his paranoia if he showed up at the court house. Nevertheless, this brother did have his attorney fly in and joined the other attorneys that were involved in the law suit against our old man's estate and Children's Hospital because greed never fails when it comes to getting free money. In the end Children's Hospital was instructed to make a rather large settlement with us four boys and yet the hospital made out just fine as the old man's assets were extensive and worth several millions.

Why did the old man leave everything to Children's Hospital? Because he had been brainwashed by the radio. When we went up to his seventy-five hundred square foot cabin after he passed, every day at 10 AM the radio announced an advertisement for Children's Hospital telling people to leave their estates to them in the event they had no one else to leave their estates to the whole time we were there. Every morning this announcement came over the radio and the old man was being brainwashed everyday for over a year living in this place all alone by himself. Now that he had managed to turn all of his sons against one and another we figured that this was his way to get the final laugh by screwing over his kids.

In another situation we met a 72 year old man who was interested in buying some rifles we were selling and it turned out that he was also still working selling LED light bulbs. Since this guy gave us a good discount we had him replace all of our lightbulbs in our home and garage and, eventually, became good friends. Nevertheless, on one of his visits he related that his son had an advertising business and a close friend who worked at a major bank. Now our friend not being very educated, but having a considerable amount of money put away for him and his wife's retirement was invited to this bank by his son's friend, supposedly, to discuss retirement accounts. Again to make a long story short, his son and his friend at the bank were devising a plan to extract one hundred thousand dollars from his father's monies in order to finance his son's business. This exhortation was done behind closed doors and the son got the money by extorting it from his own father.

The sad part about this situation was that this poor old guy was still working in the hope of retiring soon and here is his kid and his friend robbing him of his money so his own son could start his own business. Now for the sad part, this man was a very nice guy even though he had a very bad knee, was way over weight, and would sweat profusely with very little physical movement. The fact that we became friends made this situation even worse because we are not social lites and have very few people that we would call friends. Nevertheless, when we were told about this situation we had to inform this guy that he had been ripped off by his own son. After explaining all of this to him we gave him the name of an attorney because his son had no authority to gain access to his money, but managed to steal it with the help of his banking friend. As of this writing we have no idea of what this guy did, if anything concerning this situation and over time we have lost contact with him.

We could relate several more situations to the readers like the one's we have already related, but we think people will get the idea of what we are talking about when it comes to anyone concerning free money. People will do some very strange things when it comes to thinking about them gaining free money or trying to gain free money from the death of another and their estate. People will bitterly turn into criminals if they even think there is a chance of getting someone else's monies and they will not even think twice about stabbing a loved one in the back in order to get what they think they are entitled to.

The bottomline to this situation for the reader is to make sure that which ever instrument one uses to convey their estate proceeds to that they make sure it is as ironclad as one can make their Last Will or Testament. Again, each state will have their own requirements and that is okay, but how these instruments are drawn up and the wording can have severe consequences if not done properly. It is very important that people go over every area of a Will or Trust making sure it meets your needs because when you are gone no one will be able to second guess you.

# EIGHT

# SECTION V

# WILLS

This is probably the easiest way to transfer one's possessions and distributed the way one wants after they pass. Once you name an Executor who will be responsible for settling one's estate and distributing one's assets, like paying off any debts and any taxes that might be due and payable they will be able to execute the rest of the assets. It is also important to note that a Will, will go through probate and they can assist the Executor, but normally it is not necessary. Once all the designated beneficiaries have been listed and designated to receive or who inherits any assets that have been left to them as named in the Will, one may want to list a charity rather than leaving assets to family members.

One should also include the necessary arrangements for minor children, if any and/or special needs adults or children. In the event of the latter, one should indicate what is required for any physical care as well as any financial support they may be receiving along with their medical background, if any. Even though it may seem basic, if one does not address these basic requirements, the court may declare one's Will invalid and discard it. A will should indicate that one is of legal age and of sound mind and that one's Will states one's final wishes for the distribution of one's possessions. All Wills have to be signed in front of two adult witnesses who would be capable of testifying in a court of law if necessary, and people can use their attorney and their assistance as witness if they can't locate anyone one else.

It is our recommendation that all Wills be placed in a safe place like a safe deposit box, a home safe, or kept at the attorney's office (providing it is allowed) so that one's appointed Executor will be able to locate it when needed. Some Wills can become very complicated depending on one's particular circumstances. However, a court of law will assure that one's last wishes will be and are followed accordingly. One final note, a Will is usually the least expensive estate plan to have constructed because it does not normally maintain as many complications that a trust can have.

# EIGHT

# SECTION VI

# TRUSTS

Unlike a Will where one appoints an Executor, in a trust the "Trustor" appoints a "Trustee" that will be responsible for managing the trust that the Trustor appointed over their trust. The trustee is then responsible for the distribution of the trustor's assets and property to the beneficiary or beneficiaries (if more than one) according to the trustor's wishes. However, there are several trusts available that we will be indicating, but we will not be elaborating on as all of these trusts because they should be handled by a qualified estate attorney.

So, let's get started. First in our list is what is referred to as a "Living Trust." This kind of trust allows the trustor to take advantage of the trust while they are alive and one is usually used to by-pass probate court, assuming the trust is funded. In addition, all property and assets are transferred to the beneficiary(s) when the trustor passes.

Next we have the "Revocable Trust" and like the living trust it is instituted during the trustor's lifetime. This kind of trust is used to transfer assets outside of probate and can be changed or terminated during the trustor's lifetime. Also the trustor, trustee, and the beneficiary are the same person because they can manage their own assets. However, everything will be transferred to the trustee and beneficiaries when the trustor passes.

Next we have the "Irrevocable Trust" which is considerably different in that the trustor cannot change or move assets back and forth like the trustor can do in revocable trust because it cannot be revoked after his/ her passing. Irrevocable trusts are usually very popular because they transfer assets out of the trustor's name and into the beneficiary's name and they are more tax efficient having little if any estate taxes.

There is also a "Charitable Trust" normally naming a charity or a non-profit organization as their beneficiary. However, this kind of trust can also be part of a regular trust, in that the trust's heirs would be entitled to part of the trust's assets upon trustor's deaths, with the rest of the trust going to the named charities or non-profit organizations. Usually these trusts are designed to reduce or eliminate as much taxes as possible concerning gift and estate taxes.

There is also "Funded or Unfunded Trust" that are trust agreements that can either have assets in them or not. However, during the life or after the passing of the trustor these trusts can be funded, but be sure to check with one's attorney concerning these trusts.

Next there is a "Qualified Terminal Interest Trust Property Trust" that is designed to allocate assets to different beneficiaries at different times. This is similar to our Will that we set up, in that, when the first spouse passes everything automatically transfers to the other spouse. Upon the passing of the remaining spouse all assets are to be equally divided amongst the children of both spouses. However, caution is in order here because the remaining spouse has the right to change any arrangement that had previously been agreed to. Therefore, it is imperative that one maintains extreme trust in the remaining spouse that they will not violate the deceased spouse's wishes. Unfortunately, this occurs more often then not, especially, as one ages because one can then be easily influenced by greedy deceptive beneficiaries. In any event, should this be a possible situation, then the next trust will take care of this problem.

This is called a "Blind Trust" and it is controlled only by the trustee without any of the beneficiaries knowledge. In the event that one may believe that they cannot trust their spouse's implicitly, then the blind trust is the way to go as these trusts are designed to avoid any conflicts between the beneficiaries and any trustees.

Another popular trust is the "Credit Shelter Trust" AKA as a bypass trust where the trust fund allows the trustor the right to give the beneficiaries a percentage of the assets including funds up to the estate-tax exemptions in their states. This in turn gives the trustor and the beneficiaries the remainder of their estate tax free. Therefore, even if the estate grows in size the estate will remain tax free forever.

Then there is a "Testamentary Trust," which is an agreement made for the advantage of the beneficiary when the trustor has passed, explaining how the assets are to be distributed after the trustor's passing. This trust is sometimes referred to as a "Will Trust" and is frequently established by an executor, who manages the trust for the trustor's beneficiaries after their testament and will has been created. A testamentary trust is irrevocable and therefore cannot be altered or changed once it has been created, signed, and witnessed.

Lastly there is an "Insurance Trust" that gives the trust the authority to include their life insurance policies in the trust, thereby avoiding taxation on the estate. This trust is also irrevocable and will not allow the trustor the ability to borrow against the life policy or change it in anyway. However, it does give the authority for the life policy to pay for any expenses on the estate after the trustor passes.

As people can now see, there are several more different types of trusts and each one will have distinctive functions and advantages for each one, but we only listed the more popular trusts used in the market place. Therefore, since people are protecting their financial wealth and because certain kinds of trusts help people avoid probate court it is advisable to locate a qualified estate attorney to assist people in selecting and setting up their Wills or Trusts. A Trust or Will have different requirements depending on one's state, but usually the advantage of a Trust will usually avoid estate taxes and gift taxes. Nonetheless, one will need the assistance of a professional who will assist them in establishing and assisting them in proper construction of their Will or Trust.

In our opinion, both Wills and Trusts can serve the majority of the people's needs in our society today, but one never knows what will surface in the coming years that may complicate the division of one's properties, whether personal or private in the future. For an example, in the state of Texas it is no longer necessary for people to setup a Trust unless it is going to require extensive division of various properties.

In Texas, a Will basically, serves the same purpose as most of the above listed Trusts without all of the cost of setting up one of these Trusts.

Even though a Will does go through probate court in Texas, it is a relative simple process where the probate court reviews the paper work to make sure that everything is in order. However, it is important for people in all other states to check with an attorney so they can select the best way to transfer their estates and properties in order to avoid as many complications as possible amongst the beneficiaries that will be involved in a person's final settlement. Finally, it is important to remember that when it comes to monies and properties that are to be divided among people in one's own family, they will do whatever they can to get as much as they think they are entitled to receive. Likewise, don't be surprised to see others come out of the woodwork, so to speak, who will attempt to lay claims to anything that they think they can get for themselves. Good luck when it comes to this situation in one's own family.

# NINE

# GETTING STARTED

# LIVING WITHIN YOUR MEANS

We have all heard the hype about living within one's means, especially, when referring to people going into retirement or those that are already retired, but just exactly what does that mean? In order to accomplish this situation one needs to approach it from a realistic point of view in terms of eliminating unnecessary expenditures. In our experience, the only way to achieve this is to establish a plan, which required establishing a financial budget that would meet one's needs. Naturally, everyone will have different concepts of what they will consider to be important regarding their particular situation, However, everyone will need a base point to start from and establishing a financial budget sheet is the first step to learning how to live within one's means. Therefore, we have included our own personal financial budget sheet that included areas that were important to us as a guideline because everyone will have different requirements depending on what their needs are.

The first thing people need to understand is that living within one's means doesn't mean that one has to deny themselves of life's pleasures. Look at a budget as one would look at dieting and since everyone diets at one time or another they do so in order to look and feel better, but they do not starve themselves to death. The same thought process will apply to establishing a budget so that one has flexibility. In other words, cutting back on foods that are not good for people and consuming certain foods in moderation will lead to successful results when losing weight. This same process should be applied to your budget for one's financial well being.

Living within one's means is similar to a diet in that in the beginning the process may seem strenuous, burdensome, and arduous, but the gratification will come later as one continues on with their diet. The same applies to a financial budget and the gratification, self-satisfaction, and pride will come later if someone loses their job, or when one is able to retire several years earlier because one was able to invest more by living within one's means. Spending moderately is the key to living within one's means. Likewise, spending money just because one has the money to spend does not necessarily mean they should. People are living from paycheck to paycheck and maxing out their credit cards when there are several ways to save money instead of thinking about what their wants are vs. what their needs are and what they can afford.

According to the financial recommendations being made, retirement people should be saving around 20% or more per month. In fact, the majority of working people should be saving the same if not allocating even more towards their eventual retirement. Yes, we know that expecting retired people to save 20% when they are no longer employed sounds a little preposterous, but there are several ways for them to save even more. Ask yourself if you need to go to a gym and pay membership fees or can one workout in one's own home or take a walk around the block or neighborhood? Have people ever tried to workout with the myriad of workout videos on U-Tube? How about cutting back on cable TV, or does one really need Amazon Prime delivery service or Prime video? What about cutting back on restaurants or does one need a new car every couple of years? Do people realize that when they buy a new car and the back tires clear the car lot that their new car just depreciated by one-third of what the car sold for? That is correct and to find out all one has to do is buy a new car, drive it off the dealers lot and drive it back in and ask them to give you a price for your brand new car.

However, this is not the bad part and even though one has lost 33% by driving off the dealers lot their brand new car will depreciate another 20% within the first year. This means that you now own a brand new car and lost a total of 55% of your car's value or your money if you paid cash for it in the first year, but only if one tried to sell the car back to a dealer. In the event of selling to a private party expect to price the car at 20% less or at whatever one thinks the market will bear. So one needs to ask themselves this question, was it really necessary or worth it to have a new car? Only you can answer that question and we could go on and on, but we believe people are getting the point. More on this subject later.

In order for one to start living within their means one needs to have an understanding of their spending habits and with a budget they will be able to get a handle on how much money they are throwing out the window, especially, on holidays like Valentines Day, Easter, and the 4th of July, where people burn up their monies every time they set off a firecracker or fireworks, and don't forget good old Christmas where people can go into debt for the rest of the New Year. Nevertheless, as we progress through this book we will be showing people how they can save tremendous amounts of money and it is not that difficult to do.

My wife and I sat down and made out a budget that was designed for two purposes. The first was to allocate the necessary monies to pay all of the fixed home payments such as the mortgage, taxes, insurance, the trash company, the cable company for Internet services, and vehicle insurance. Next came the variable expenses, such as water, gas, electric, and phones, and the additional variables that included food, gas, medical, vehicle maintenance, personal spending money, and a miscellaneous category. Once the fixed monthly payments were allocated, there would be no room to make adjustments in them, unless of course we paid off the mortgage. However, as far as the variable monthly payments were concerned, we incorporated the following strategy: We took the single largest annual monthly billing in each category from last year, adjusted for inflation and set up the budget accordingly. At the end of each month in which the bills did not meet the maximum established dollar amount in the budget, those monies would go into a savings account. For example, let's say the maximum monthly electric bill was budgeted for $300 and the actual electric bill came in at $150. We would then take the extra $150 at the end of the month and put it into the savings account. This process was applied to each monthly budgeted category.

The second goal for our retirement plan was to spend as little money as possible every month and continue to build the savings account. We also considered other investment opportunities, such as stocks, bonds, and land purchases as another means of adding to our retirement plan, so that we would eventually be living well within our means.

The way we figured things out was based on our desire to know exactly what was going on with our money, and without a budget, there would be no way to assess where the money went each month. Likewise, most people think that the term budget is a foul word because they think that they are being restricted in their spending habits—and, rightly so, because they are being restricted, but only by channeling their monies into productive payments and saving scenario that will benefit them in the long run. Unfortunately, most people don't believe this, so they never manage to stick to their budget, and they always manage to come up with an excuse as to why their budget failed. Trust us on this one: Budgets never fail! Now, you may not like being restricted to a budget, but if you plan to get ahead in this world, you need a financial plan; otherwise you can plan on working for the rest of your life because you can't afford to retire, let alone enjoy retirement. Yes, we realize that this sounds a little harsh, but if you are planning to retire and you do not have a pension (not that that means much anymore) or a retirement plan in place, then you seriously need to consider living within your means as soon as possible in order to have the money to do the things you want later in life. Now, for those of you who still don't believe in budgets, remember this: Budgets can be altered to meet your needs, provided the alterations do not restrict the saving aspects of the budget. Therefore, if you believe that you are being restricted by your budget, then change it, adjust it, or modify it to meet your particular circumstances and then get back on track and stick to your budget.

No one we have ever known has said that budgeting was easy, and we are a classic example. I had never been on a budget until I met my second wife, and when we began living within our means, it still took me over six months to get adjusted to living on a budget. My wife, on the other hand, had been living on and off budgets most of her life, which was also because she never made much more than $50,000 a year until she met me. On the other hand, I was used to making a lot of money off and on over the years that was well over a $100,000 every few months, so I never paid much attention to establishing a budget, as there was always plenty of money available to do whatever I wanted to do when I wanted to do something, and being single that was my way of living. Likewise, I never paid much attention to the idea of retirement and had spent most of my time living large and being well-off and well-to-do financially, but I never managed to save any money, nor did I have anything to show for all the money that I had made over the years. So the concept of being on a budget was a difficult adjustment for me to make, but I was finally able to make the adjustment. Moreover, understanding the reason to live on a budget at this point in our lives made perfect sense as we had to accumulate as much money as we could if we both wanted to retire on a full-time basis.

The suggestions that we have made in this chapter, are designed to show people how to plan ahead for events that they know are coming, and being prepared for the unexpected events to the best of one's ability. The key to a budget is to design a plan that fits one's needs and to be sure to constantly review your plan as it will change over time.

Another thing that is really important is to never get into the habit of trying to live up to the JONES' because this process will put people into serious trouble unless they are already wealthy. People need to learn that they don't need a thousand dollar phone every year, a hundred-thousand dollar vehicle every couple of years, or the newest big screen TV like the Jones' or anything else the Jones' have. Especially, if one wants to live within their means and have any intentions of getting ahead and making life better for themselves.

All of the above is a complete waste of money that could have been set aside for one's retirement, but instead turns out to be wasted monies at their expense. One of the major problems of this situation is that it usually starts when people are in their early working years and they want to live up to their peers, and our question is why? Usually, their peers are older people who have been around longer and have accumulated more simply because they have been working longer and yet for some reason young people never take this scenario into consideration.

Another thing we always hear is people telling others that all they have to do is live below their means and yet no one tells anyone how to go about doing such a thing. This is where we will explain and show people just exactly how they can go about living within their means and not below their means and what it will take to get them to that point. Likewise, we have heard all sorts of scenarios as to how people can achieve living below their means and it usually only encompasses cutting out one or two things in one's life. Fortunately, there are a lot of ways for people to achieve living within their means that we will be covering in the next chapter and some of the major areas such as food, housing, vehicles, and gas, which are some of the most expensive areas that we will be covering among other areas that people can start and continue saving while in retirement.

# NINE

# SECTION II

# SETTING UP A FINANCIAL BUDGET AND PLANNING AHEAD

Now, for those of you who might be thinking of getting ahead, are thinking about retirement, or are approaching retirement age and are not sure whether or not you will be able to retire, you should definitely consider setting up a budget now and start getting used to living on a budget, provided you are not rich. Furthermore, everyone knows that people are living longer and longer these days, and with the advances in medical technology, it is conceivable that you might be around even after you have turned one hundred years of age. If you plan on retiring at the age of sixty-five, that means you could be around for another thirty-five or forty years. So the question becomes, will you be able to afford to live another thirty-five or forty years without a budget? For those of you who do not know how to set up a budget, we have included two examples that we have used and still use to this very day. Also it is important to remember, when setting up your budget, don't hesitate to change it, adjust it, or modify it to meet your particular circumstances, especially, once a year, every year, or until the budget meets your particular needs. And don't stop using your budget, but make it a natural part of your life. What we suggest now, is that you take some time to view the two simple budget sheets that we still use to this day. Each one of these budget sheets can be adjusted to fit anyones concerns or desires depending on one's individual or family needs. Likewise, these budget sheets can be modified and adjusted throughout one's retirement years.

MONTHLY BUDGET

| NET INCOME | AMOUNT | | |
|---|---|---|---|
| | $ | | |
| TOTAL | 0 | | |
| | | ACTUAL PAYMENT | ACTUAL PAYMENT |
| MONTHLY EXPENSES | | | |
| HOUSE PAYMENT | | | |
| CAR PAYMENT | | | |
| CREDIT CARD PAYMENTS | | | |
| | | | |
| | | | |
| | | | |
| | | | |
| SUB TOTAL | 0 | 0 | |
| GROCERIES | | | |
| GASOLINE | | | |
| ELECTRIC | | | |
| PHONE | | | |
| CELL PHONES | | | |
| PROPANE/GAS | | | |
| SUB TOTAL | 0 | 0 | |
| CAR INSURANCE | | | |
| PROPERTY TAXES | | | |
| IRS TAXES | | | |
| SUB TOTAL | 0 | 0 | |
| TOTAL EXPENSES | 0 | 0 | |
| | | | |
| INCOME LESS EXPENSES EQUALS | 0 | 0 | |
| WEEKLY ALLOWANCES | | | |
| | | | |
| | | | |
| SUB TOTAL | 0 | 0 | |
| INCOME LESS EXPENSES AND ALLOWANCES: | | 0 | 0 |
| SAVINGS ACCOUNT | $ | | |

GROCERY LIST

| | A | B | C | D | E | F | G | H | I | J | K | L | M | N |
|---|---|---|---|---|---|---|---|---|---|---|---|---|---|---|
| 1 | PRODUCE | | | PAPER PROD | | | BAKED GOODS | | | SEASONINGS | | | MENU | |
| 2 | LETTUCE | | $1.30 | TOWELS | | $1.25 | COOKIES | | $1.00 | WORCHES | | $1.00 | MON | |
| 3 | TOMATOES | | $1.70 | TOILET | 12 | $9.00 | JELLO | | $0.50 | A1 | | | TU | |
| 4 | CARROTS | | $0.75 | TISSUE | | $1.00 | SHAKENBAKE | | $1.00 | SEAS SALT | | | WED | |
| 5 | POTATOES | | $0.90 | | | | MARSHMELLO | | | TACO SAUCE | | $2.00 | TH | |
| 6 | CELERY | | $1.40 | | | | CAKE MIX | | | SEAS PKTS | | $0.50 | FRI | |
| 7 | GR BEANS | | | | | | FROSTING | | | MAYO | | $5.00 | SAT | |
| 8 | BANANAS | | $0.64 | | | | | | | MUS/CAYSUP | | $1.50 | SUN | |
| 9 | APPLES | | $1.60 | | | | | | | SHRIMP SAUCE | | $1.00 | | |
| 10 | ORANGES | | $1.50 | SOAPS | | | | | | OLIVES | | $1.00 | | |
| 11 | BELL PPR | | $0.80 | LAUNDRY | | $8.00 | | | | | | | | |
| 12 | CORN | | 0.5 | BLEACH | | $2.00 | | | | | | | | |
| 13 | ONION | | 0.84 | | | | | | | | | | | |
| 14 | DELL | | | DOG FOOD | | | CEREALS | | | DRY GOODS | | | | |
| 15 | BOLONGA | | $4.00 | | | $7.50 | OATMEAL | | $1.00 | RICE RONI | | $1.00 | | |
| 16 | BEEF | | $6.00 | DRINKS/SNACKS | | | CHERRIOS | | $1.50 | NOODLES | | $1.50 | | |
| 17 | SH CHEESE | | $2.00 | GATEAIDE | | $5.00 | | | | SPAG | | $1.33 | | |
| 18 | MEATS | | | SODAS | | $4.00 | FROZEN | | | MACRONI | | $1.00 | | |
| 19 | SAUSAGE | | $2.70 | WATER | | $0.70 | POPCILES | | $1.57 | MAC/CH | | $0.50 | | |
| 20 | BACON | | $3.10 | 24PK WATER | | $4.00 | COOLWHIP | | $1.00 | TACO SHELLS | | $1.50 | | |
| 21 | GR BEEF | | $3.48 | CANDY | | $1.50 | RASPBERRIES | | $3.00 | STUFFING | | $1.60 | | |
| 22 | ROAST | | $2.50 | CHIPS | | $1.50 | SHRIMP BAG | | $5.00 | | | | | |
| 23 | CHIC BRES | | | | | | SHRIMP RING | | $4.00 | DRUGS | | | | |
| 24 | CHIC LEGS | | $1.50 | CAN GOODS | | | LASANGA | | $7.00 | TOOTHPASTE | | $4.00 | | |
| 25 | | | | SPAG SAU | | $2.00 | SCALLOP | | $9.00 | HS SHAMPOO | | $7.00 | | |
| 26 | DAIRY | | | ST TOM | | $1.00 | | | | YCOPENE | | $6.00 | | |
| 27 | MILK | | $2.50 | TOM PAS | | $0.35 | COFFEE | | $12.14 | RED YEAST | | $14.00 | | |
| 28 | BUTTER | | $2.30 | TOM SAU | | $0.25 | G TEA | | | GRAPE SEED | | $7.00 | | |
| 29 | EGGS | | $1.80 | ALB TUNA | | $2.50 | | | $3.00 | CHROMIUM | | $5.00 | | |
| 30 | COT CHS | | $2.60 | APPLS SAU | | $1.00 | CAN GOODS CONTD | | | CALMAG | | $6.00 | | |
| 31 | BREADS | | | CH/NDL SP | | $0.75 | FRUT CKTL | | $1.00 | CALCIUM | | $12.00 | | |
| 32 | BREAD | | $2.00 | VEG/BF SP | | $1.25 | MAND ORNGS | | $0.50 | LECITHIN | | $3.00 | | |
| 33 | HD BUNS | | $1.00 | PK/BEANS | | $0.50 | PINEAPL | | $0.50 | BIOTIN | | $4.00 | | |
| 34 | HB BUNS | | $1.00 | MUSHRM | | $0.58 | CHIL BEANS | | $0.50 | BLU ALGE | | $5.00 | | |
| 35 | TORTILLAS | | $1.50 | MUSHRM SP | | $0.68 | | | | VIT A | | $3.00 | | |

89

Now that you have had some time to view the two budget sheets we have included, let's go over each one individually to make sure you have an understanding of how to construct your own personal financial budgets. These financial budget sheets were designed by both of us for our family needs, so feel free to make any adjustments in the categories that will meet your needs and/or your family needs.

In the first column on the left, you will see the category called *"Net Income,"* which is where you would write down all of your household income after taxes, or what is known as take-home pay or spendable income. Note that you can expand the lines in this category to match various incomes such as a spouse's income, pension income, social security income, military retirement income, disable income, etc. Next, we have *"Monthly Expenses,"* which would include all of your fixed monthly payments, which are those monthly payments that are consistent month after month. Next is the *"Sub Total"* category where you simply total the Monthly Expenses. The next area is the area where you would indicate all of your household variable expenses; if you want you can label this category as *"Variable Monthly Expenses"* category as a reference point. As you will note, this category also has a Sub Total area, where you would indicate the totals for this category. The next area covers insurance, property taxes, and IRS taxes and you can add more classifications to this area if you have other taxes to contend with in your budget; again we Sub-Total this category. Note: If you are paying your taxes and insurance on an annual basis, then we suggest that you place these tax monies and insurance monies into separate saving accounts at your bank, so when the time comes for paying your taxes and insurance, the money will be readily available. This is what we do each month, but we add anywhere from an extra $50 to a $100 to these accounts, so they are not depleted when we need to write these checks. To give people another example; we have now built up this account to the point that we could go for ten years without having to worry about paying our taxes and insurance monies. Now we come to the category called *"Total Expenses,"* which is where you would total up all of the Sub Total areas on the budget sheet and put the total in this classification.

The next category is entitled *"Income Less Expenses Equals,"* this is where you find out whether or not you are in the positive or negative side of your budget by simply subtracting the Total Expense area from the Total amount located in the Net Income area.

Hopefully, you will end up with a positive number in the Income Less Expenses area, in which case you can now move on to the *"Weekly Allowances"* category, where you indicate the amount of money that you and anyone else in your household would like to spend each week throughout the month. Note: When we started on this budget years ago as we were struggling just to make ends meet, we used a weekly allowance figure because money was so tight that we needed to know exactly where we were, money wise, from week to week. However, that has all changed, and this category was changed from weekly to biweekly and eventually to *"Monthly Allowances,"* as we are pretty much retired and calculate our incomes on a monthly basis instead of a weekly basis. Nevertheless, you can decide which figure you would like to use depending on your particular circumstances. Again, you will see a Sub Total area for the weekly or monthly allowances, where you can put your figures for this category. Next is the category *"Income less Expenses and Allowances;"* this is where you record your final, bottom-line number. Hopefully, you will still be in a positive cash position. The last category, *"Savings Account,"* is the fun category, as this is where you can start putting your leftover money in a savings account, retirement account, or an emergency account. Also, remember how we showed you to work off the highest amount of a monthly utility bill first? If the next utility bill comes in at a lesser amount, the difference would be allocated to the savings account.

Okay, for those of you who found out after doing your budget that there was no money left over or you ended up with a negative amount showing in the Income less Expenses area, you definitely need to sit down with your partner (unless you are single) and decide what you need to get rid of to get yourselves back into the positive money area. The goal is to move from the *"Red Zone"* to the *"Black Zone"* as soon as possible, as you are technically on your way to bankruptcy or a foreclosure should you continue to stay in the Red Zone. To give you an example, years ago we were having a hard time making ends meet, and that's when my wife suggested making out a budget, so that we would have a better understanding of where our monies were going each month. When she had finished constructing the budget—and even though it was kind of crude and nothing like what we are currently using—we were still able to get a handle on the excess spending, and at the same time we found ourselves in the Red Zone. Therefore, we took some time to evaluate some of our assets, and after a few days of analyzing everything that we had that was of any value, we decided that we had to sell our VW Vanagon to get ourselves out of the Red Zone. Even though it took a couple of weeks to sell the Vanagon, the money that was made was enough to give us the opportunity to pay off some of our outstanding debts, along with the ability to move into the Black Zone. Plus, turning our budget bottom line into a positive cash flow for a few extra bucks allowed us to start a savings account. Moreover, it took us over a year to move from the Black Zone to the *"Green Zone,"* where our monies started to make an impact on our budget and allowed us to be able to take a weekly allowance. Yet none of this would have been possible had we not placed ourselves on a budget.

Before moving on, we would like to point out again to the readers, that if you are serious about getting ahead and staying ahead by living within your means in today's global economy, and especially, if you plan to be self sufficient when you retire and being well-off and well-to-do—then you will definitely need to learn how to live within a budget. Even to this day we live on a budget, and it is because of this budget that we are able to do the things we want to do whenever we want to regardless of what happens in our global economy. Furthermore, we have become well-off and well-to-do and are living very well by structuring our lives around our budget. At the end of every year, we sit down and go over our previous year's budget and make the necessary changes that will allow us to continue living the way we want. As an example, everyone knows that the gas and diesel prices in the United States have been increasing at such a rapid pace (as of this writing) to place the middle class in our society in jeopardy of becoming extinct. Now, we don't know about you or anyone else, but we have no intentions of becoming extinct because of some haywire price gouging that is going on by the big corporations that could care less about what happens to the people in this great country. However, in 2020 the gas and diesel prices have receded recently making gas and diesel fuel very affordable due to the virus pandemic, but there is no telling how long these prices will remain low before going back up. Nevertheless, because of our budget, we simply make the necessary adjustments to compensate for these kinds of events. By doing so, and even though we may have to forego purchasing certain items for a period, we are still well-off and well-to-do— all because of our budget. Let's face the facts people: If you think for one moment that our elected government officials or the major corporations have any intentions of supporting you, your family, and your retirement, or for that matter, supporting you for whatever reason, including this virus pandemic, you are in for a major disappointment. You need to learn how to take care of yourself now, and the sooner the better, especially, if you have any intentions of retiring, which is the reason we have written this book.

Before we move on again, we would like to point out that the Financial Budget Sheet can also be used as a small business financial budget sheet, that will assist anyone in managing their small business finances, if you have or are thinking about starting a small business. In the beginning of your business this budget sheet will serve you well and as time goes on you will be able to afford an independent accountant to deal with your business needs.

# NINE

# SECTION III

# THE

# GROCERY LIST BUDGET

Moving on, you will notice that we have included a *"Grocery List B*udget," as this used to be the single largest monthly cash outlay in our household excluding the mortgage payment; it still seems to be holding up against all prices, as we are seeing major price increases—which makes a budget even more important so you can continue to control the household spending. Looking at the Grocery List Budget sheet, you will see the following categories: Produce, Deli, Meats, Dairy, Breads, Paper Products, Dog Food, Drinks/Snacks, Can Goods, Bake Goods, Cereals, Frozen, Coffee, Can Goods continued, Seasonings, Dry Goods, Drugs, and a Menu category that can be used on a weekly basis or on a bimonthly basis or for a three- or four-week food purchase basis. Currently, we were shopping on a two or three-week basis, where we make out our menu for each week for the two or three-week period, and then we simply buy the items we have listed on the Grocery List that corresponds to the two or three weeks for which we are buying food. The goal here is to make sure that you get everything that you intend to buy without having to go back to the grocery store during the period for which you purchased food. Likewise, you can adjust, modify, or change anything you want so that your grocery list is custom designed by you for your own household. Furthermore, you can add or deduct any items in any category that you do not use or need on a regular basis, and you can also write out the complete categories as opposed to using one word for a category. As an example, look at the category entitled *"Drugs."* As you will note, we do not have anything listed for drugs, as no one in our family uses any drugs so that category is simply shorthand for the grocery store's "Drugstore Department," where we get the items that we have listed on our Grocery List.

As you are viewing the Grocery List, you will see dollar amounts listed to the right in all of the categories. These represent the per-pound price of the items that we are buying and/or the per-item cost of the items. The primary reason for listing the dollar amounts is to allow you to calculate the amount of money that you will need to spend for your household groceries before you even go to the store and to be able to maintain your budget in a set dollar amount each week or for two, three, and even four-week grocery shopping. Once you have established the amount of money you want to allocate to your food budget, you will become a much better shopper and will also be able to take advantage of the bargains being offered at the grocery store and with the use of coupons, you should be able to increase or decrease your grocery spending accordingly. Likewise, by using a budgeted Grocery List, you will be able to adapt to any changes in food pricing immediately by simply observing the price increase or decrease, and recording this information on your Grocery List. Moreover, be sure to total your grocery list before you even go shopping to make sure that you stay within your budget, which will also allow you to adapt your budget to your specific needs. The goal here is to shop only for the period of time for which you are buying food and to avoid having to run back to the store until it is time for your next grocery shopping. Pay attention, as this is a very important lesson that we had to learn the hard way. My wife, was one of those people who used to go shopping whenever she thought that she needed to, and as things would have it, she was constantly going back and forth to the grocery store three and four times or more a week. Now, it's not that there is any problem with what she was doing, but when we sat down and pointed out just how much more it was costing us for her to go grocery shopping that often, she finally realized that she was wasting a lot of money on unnecessary purchases, or what is referred to as impulse buying, not to mention the gas she was wasting and the wear and tear on the vehicles.

Therefore, even before we made out the Grocery List Budget Sheet, we sent her to the grocery store and had her walk around the store in the same way she would when she was shopping and making notes along the way. When she had completed her task, we sat down and made out the Grocery List budget according to the store layout and her direction of travel throughout the store so that she would not have to spend half a day or more in the grocery store. We referred to this process as the *"Economy of Motion Shopping,"* where she could now go to the grocery store with budget in hand and, in a very short period, complete her shopping and be home before she realized what she had accomplished. Furthermore, we pointed out that she was not to go back to the grocery store for the rest of the week (when we were still shopping one week at a time) regardless of whether or not she had forgotten something at the store, unless of course, the item was for me (just joking). As it turned out, it took her about a month or so before she realized how much money she was saving per month by shopping only when it was time to go shopping and not wasting time, money, and energy shopping several times a week.

The next project was to see if shopping for a longer period would save us even more money on a monthly basis. However, before testing this concept on grocery shopping, we decided to test it on gas, as the prices of gas had escalated to the point of being a major drain on the household finances. Normally, we would fill up our vehicle's gas tanks at the halfway mark on the fuel gauge. Even though we thought we were spending less money every month by filling the gas tank up at the halfway mark, it turned out that we were spending more money for gas than if we filled the tank at the three-quarter mark. Now, even though we don't travel much—maybe eight hundred to a thousand miles a month and even less now, we found that filling the gas tank at the three-quarter mark saved us about $75 to $110 each month on our vehicle gas bill. Next, we decided to try running the vehicle's gas tank to the empty mark just to see if we would be able to save more money by filling up only when the gas was empty. We found out that this process ended up costing us even more money than we had been spending by filling up at the halfway mark, though the precise reason for this is still a mystery to us. We now fill up our car's gas tank only when it reaches the three-quarter-empty mark on the fuel gauge, which gives us about seven to eight days of driving before we have to fill up again, and we are able take the extra money we save and put it into our retirement savings account. However, as gas prices continue to escalate out of sight, we realize that our gas savings will dwindle until gas prices stabilize. Likewise, we realize that everyone's driving habits are different, so you will have to conduct your own test in order to determine whether you are better off filling up your vehicle gas tank at the three-quarter mark or when your vehicle is almost empty.

Now that the vehicle gas test had been conducted and recorded, we decided to have my wife run the same test on grocery shopping, just to see if we would be able to cut the cost of groceries. At the time of the test, we were spending anywhere from $300 to $375 or more grocery shopping every week for a family of four, which equates to spending $1,200 to a $1,500 a month on groceries. We started out grocery shopping for a two-week period instead of every week and found that we could save about $300 a month off our grocery bill. Next we decided to try grocery shopping for a three-week period and found that we were saving even more money, as we were now only spending about $350 to $400 on groceries every three weeks instead of the $1,200 to $1,500 a month shopping every week. Now, we don't know about you, but saving between $850 and $1,100 a month on our grocery bills meant a lot of money that we could channel into our various retirement accounts. In our current economy, we have increased our food budget to $650 per month in 2014 that has now been increased to $750 in 2019, which seems to be working just fine for our family and allows us to buy pretty much anything we want or desire and currently has no effect on our retirement funds. And that's still a significant savings over what we were originally spending. Since the three-week grocery shopping savings was so amazing, we decided to try grocery shopping for a full month at a time, just to see if we could realize any further savings. The one month grocery shopping turned out to be a disaster for a couple of reasons: (1) we did not have the capacity to store all of the cold and frozen items that we purchased for the month, and (2) we ended up trashing the majority of the perishable food items we had purchased, thereby wasting a lot of money instead of being able to realize a greater savings. Nevertheless, we continue to shop for a three-week period every month, and we will continue to do so as long as we continue to realize the great savings we are enjoying.

The primary reason that the three-week grocery shopping works for us is that once the basic staples have been purchased according to our three-week menu, it doesn't take much more to buy the added condiments to go along with the three-week menu plan—hence, the major savings we gain. But as we indicated before, you will have to conduct your own grocery shopping to determine whether shopping for a two, three, or four-week period will give you the best savings return on your money. Currently, we are looking at various stand-alone freezer units to determine if the added electric expense will be offset should we decide to buy a freezer and buy volume meat—say, a side of beef—as opposed to buying meat every three weeks and taking up most of the freezer space in our refrigerator, which prevents us from buying other frozen products. Nevertheless, the point we are making is to break the impulse-buying habit, as this process will end up costing you or your family a lot more money than you would spend by shopping on a weekly basis. Update, we decided against a freezer and went with plastic stacking containers that has increased our refrigerator's storage space since our first book.

Here's a little storage tip: We have figured out how to make our produce last and look like new for two to three weeks at a time or longer, which also explains our three-week grocery shopping list. When we buy apples, pears, grapes, bananas, tomatoes, cucumbers, bell peppers, broccoli, etc., we immediately wrap these items individually in *"Viva"* paper towels and put them in an enclosed plastic bag (leave the plastic bag open for tomatoes, peaches or produce that sweats, as the air keeps these from spoiling), and we set them in the refrigerator until we want to use them. However, when you need, let's say, bananas or the other produce two or three weeks from now, just take them out of the refrigerator and they will look and taste like you just brought them home that day from the market. Storage tip two is simple: You can save the paper towels and use them over and over again, thereby saving more money because you are not buying more paper towels all the time. Why Viva paper towels work, and the other paper towels don't, is beyond our scientific understanding at this time.

Now we are going to give you another valuable lesson that we had to learn the hard way: People can save a lot of money by shopping at discount stores such as the 99¢ stores, Aldi's, the Mexican stores like Fiesta, or Elrods, along with Walmart food store departments, just to mention a few. For a long time, we never shopped at these stores because we thought they were for the poor people only—and were we mistaken, as we almost missed out on some major food dollar savings. However, a word of caution is in order: People first need to get past the JONES SYNDROME. The reason most people ignore these stores, thinking the stores are beneath them, is that they still have not managed to kick the JONES SYNDROME. In any case, you will have to do your own investigation on these types of stores in your own areas to find the greatest savings.

To give the reader an example of the savings you can realize at these stores, we will start with the 99¢ stores, where we shop at for our produce and various other items once every three weeks. When we need to stock up on carrots, tomatoes, potatoes, celery, etc., or items like foot power, bathroom spray, antibiotics like Neosporin, razor blades, etc., we buy these items at the 99¢ store and usually save anywhere from 60 percent to 80 percent over stores like Albertsons, Safeway, Walmart, Brookshire, and other major grocery stores here in Texas. Okay, before we continue, let us answer your question: Are the foods and produce any good? The answer is yes, because you have to remember that even though these stores sell their products at a considerable savings, the foods and produce must meet the US Government Food and Drug Administration guidelines just like any other major grocery stores.

Next we go to the Mexican grocery stores to buy more produce, fruits, and vegetables, and some meats, and we save anywhere from 60 percent to 90 percent over the major grocery stores. To give you an example, we just got back from one of our favorite Mexican grocery markets, where we always buy some pink grapefruits. These cost ninety-nine cents each at the large supermarkets, including Walmart here in Texas, and we bought three each for a dollar or fifteen grapefruits for five dollars, for a saving of 67 percent over all the other markets. Likewise, their meats come from the United States, Mexico, or Canada, depending on which country is selling its beef for the best prices, and all the meats are marked as to which country they are coming from, so you always have the choice to buy or not to buy certain meats from the different countries at these grocery markets. Another great thing about these grocery stores' meat departments is that the meats have very little or no fat, as opposed to the American grocery stores' meat departments, which always hide the fat on the bottom side of their packages where the shopper cannot see it. Now we are going to give you another major saving source: These grocery stores usually have printed ads that you can take with you to the major grocery stores and ask them to match the discount store prices. Since most of these major grocery stores are willing to match prices, you can now take advantage of the discounted prices being advertised in the Mexican stores but shop for the items you want at the major grocery stores. We even use these advertised discounts at all the Walmart stores, where we can take advantage of their low prices and realize even greater savings on our food budget. Nevertheless, you must remember that even though you usually avoid these stores because you think they are beneath you and your pride, it is time for you to face reality and learn how to save big and become well-off and well-to-do in your retirement years, living within your means and eating and staying healthy. Since our first book we have stopped using some other stores because we found a better store called Elrods where we can buy Ribeye steaks for $3.79 a pound vs. $12.00 a pound at other stores including Walmart stores for a savings of 68% and save even more on other meats including chicken and turkey.

One more little tidbit to remember, do not waste your hard-earned money on organic foods in major grocery stores, as these are nothing more than the same foods you normally buy in the produce department in the food markets. Not only has this information been proven by the scientific community, but we will now give everyone a lesson that we learned by witnessing an event that occurred in a major supermarket while we were shopping. At the time, we happened to be in the produce section of the market when one of the produce clerks was restocking the lemons. When he had finished stocking the regular lemons, he pushed his lemon cart over to the organic food section and proceeded to stock the shelf with the same lemons and stamping them with an organic label, not realizing we were observing his activities. Furthermore, this was not the only major supermarket where we have witnessed this activity of putting regular produce into the organic food sections. This seems to occur on a regular basis in all major supermarkets; so pass on these so-called organic foods and save yourself a lot of money.

Before leaving the grocery section, we would like to suggest that people avoid food shopping at the major supermarket chains such as Kroger's, Albertsons, Safeway's , Brookshire's, etc., or whatever the major supermarkets are in your state. The reason for our suggestion is due to the fact that these supermarkets are extremely over priced as compared to the smaller discount markets. Just to give people a brief example of what we are talking about: Recently, cherries came on the market selling at $1.99 per pound for two weeks when the people were buying cherries, and then went to $2.99 per pound when the people stop buying the cherries because the price was too high. This type of bait and switch price gouging is the typical tactics of these major supermarket chains as they think they can out think and out smart the consumers. So, instead of reducing the prices of cherries, in order to sell the remaining batches, the major supermarkets do the opposite and raise their prices. Similar to what is currently happening in the food markets today, where people are not buying as much as they used to, because people have been forced from full-time work to part-time work, in order to conserve their money. On the other hand, instead of the major supermarkets lowering their prices to help the people purchase the same or more groceries, so that the supermarkets can maintain their profits, the major supermarkets are increasing the prices of food in an attempt to keep their profits where they were prior to the people reducing their grocery spending money. In other words these supermarkets are gouging the people by increasing their prices to as much as 200, 300, 500 percent and even higher on the different products they are selling, and this now includes the Walmart stores. Walmart stores are becoming just as greedy as the regular grocery stores and they are gouging the people just as bad price wise. So check and compare prices before buying.

Lastly and for some reason people do not take their time to shop around for their food items, but somehow shop at the same stores over and over again. This process will do nothing more than cost people more money than they realize. For an example, when we shop we visit 3 or 4 different stores on the day we go shopping and spend less time actually shopping and yet we save huge amounts of money. We design our shopping route that goes to the furthest store first and then work our way back to the last store closest to our home so as not to waste any more time than necessary and this has worked just fine for us. However, what is convenient is not necessary the best solution for saving money.

# NINE

# SECTION IV

# KNOWING ONE'S FINANCIAL BALANCE AT ALL TIMES

The next order of business to living within one's means is balancing your checkbook every month when your bank statement arrives, to keep yourself up to date as to exactly how much money you will have available to spend or save. This will depend on the balance that you establish to be constant, and any monies that exceed your constant balance should be channeled into a retirement account, investment plans, or emergency funds. However, before we get started, allow us to point out a very critical factor that you will need to take into consideration: Whoever is handling the budget monies may or may not be the person who will be handling the checkbook balancing. Pay attention, as this is very important to remember: You cannot have two captains running the ship. One person should have the responsibility for distributing the family income regardless of who is bringing the money in or contributing to the family's general checking account balance. The way we handle this situation is rather simple. I handle all the money that comes into our household, and then distribute it according to the needs of the person who is doing the grocery shopping for the family; buying gas for the vehicles; purchasing supplies for the home; making the monthly payments for the mortgage, electric, or phone; or making any other payments that keep the ship, so to speak, running smoothly and efficiently. Furthermore, the money that I allocate to the family members goes into their own personal checking accounts, which does not interfere with our primary checking accounts, and any money that they manage to save is theirs to spend as they see fit. So far, in only seven years, My wife has managed not only to keep the pantry full with her monthly allocation, but she has also managed to save over $5,000 in her food budget account, which is hers to spend any time and in any way she desires, and the money just keeps rolling into her account every month. Likewise, we maintain several different checking accounts, all of which are designed to increase in value by $500 to $2,000 each month (a point I will explain later on).

Anyway, after talking to several banks in the Fort Worth and Dallas areas of Texas, as well as California, we were astounded to learn how many people do not know how to balance a checkbook or simply don't take the time to learn. Then they wonder why they never have any money to buy whatever they want, need, or desire. Hence, the reason for credit cards to get people into trouble. This is the area where your financial monthly budget sheet is really going to come in handy because you will no longer have to concern yourself with whether or not you have excess money to save, invest, or spend once you have balanced your checkbook. The nice thing about balancing a checkbook is that the bank supplies you with the balancing setup with your monthly statement, so all you have to do is some minor calculations, place the numbers on the lines that have already been supplied on your bank statement, and either add or subtract according to the directions indicated by the bank in each category.

Okay, if you have a recent bank statement, get it out and we will learn how to balance a checkbook, so there will be no mistake as to whether or not you have money available to spend, save, or invest, and you will avoid ending up in a negative position in your checkbook. Once you have your bank statement in hand, simply look for the page that should indicate *"Balance Your Account"* or words to that effect, and you will see a bunch of lines where you will fill in the appropriate numbers. The first line will indicate that you are to fill in the closing balance shown on the front of your account statement, so go back to the first page and find the closing balance, which should also be in bold type, and then record this number in the line provided to balance your checkbook. The next line is where you will write in any deposits that you have made after the date of your statement. We will say this again: *"any deposits that you have made after the date of your statement."* However, before you record anything on this line, always go to the first page of your statement and check to make sure that the bank has recorded any previous deposits and that you have checked off those deposits in your checkbook. Then look for any further deposits you may have made that were recorded after the date of the statement. You can then add up the amounts of these deposits and write the amount on the line provided.

Next, add the deposits you made to the ending balance and record this number on the line provided. Now you simply go through your checkbook and record all of the checks you wrote that the bank did not record on your account statement. Add these outstanding checks together and record this total on the line provided. In the last step, you simply subtract the checks you wrote from the ending balance and add any deposits that you may have made, and the number you get should match the number in your checkbook. If this is the case, then you have just balanced your checkbook. On the other hand, if the numbers don't match up, then you need to check for any errors in adding up your checkbook, and try not to overlook any money that has been refunded back into your checking account via some vendor refund. Don't forget any electronic transfers that you may have made. It is also possible that the numbers don't match up in your checkbook because the bank cutoff date did not allow the bank to record some checks on time, in which case you will just have to wait for your next statement, or you can go to your bank and have someone assist you with your particular situation. Currently, we do not have any credit cards and haven't had any credit cards for over thirty years, but we do have debit cards. Every now and then, one of us will forget to make the deductions from our checking accounts, but these items usually show up on our bank statement, so if anyone of us is off balance in our checkbooks, chances are that we made the mistake. Now, if you are showing a negative balance, be careful because you have made a mistake somewhere in your calculations. So before you go running to the bank, recheck your numbers and then recheck them again just to be sure that you are not wrong. Should you still not be able to balance your checkbook, than let it ride for a month or so as things have a way of working themselves out in the long run. However, if you are continuously showing a negative balance, go ahead and add the balance back into your checkbook, but keep an eye on it just in case you have made a mistake. The goal to this whole process is to know where you stand financially at all times.

Before moving on, we cannot stress enough how important it is that one, and only one person in the household be in control of the family finances. We have seen time and time again that when two or more people become involved, disruption in the household occurs. Having more than two people attempting to control the family financial situation is definitely not going to work. The way we handle our financing is relatively simple. We both maintain separate checking accounts, thereby eliminating the possibility of commingling funds in the account that we use to pay the household bills. In fact, we maintain a general checking account for gas bills and miscellaneous items, a checking account only for paying household bills, and a separate account just to accumulate incoming cash, and we maintain a tax account as well. All of these accounts, except the general checking account, are designed to increase anywhere from $500 per month to as much as $2,000 a month, depending on how well the economy is doing and our income structure. Likewise, it may not be necessary for everyone to maintain this many separate checking accounts at different banks, but we find it a lot easier to pay our bills at the end of each month by allocating the necessary funds into these accounts. Furthermore, by separating these checking accounts, we are able to concentrate on the bottom line, and if there is a mistake in any one of these accounts, it can be corrected immediately without affecting the other checking accounts.

As was mentioned previously, we always try to increase our various retirement accounts by $500 to $2,000 each and every month by taking our *"Total Net Income"* and automatically putting 25 percent or more back into our retirement accounts. By doing so, we are constantly replenishing our retirement funds, and thereby not having to worry about ever running out of money.

Another interesting fact to this situation is that we use the same procedures with our retirement social security checks. When we look at the total collective amounts of these checks every month we then take 25 percent of these monies and place them in our retirement account. By doing this we are extending and building our retirement account and over the years this has added up to become a significant amount of money that we will eventually use to extend our retirement income over longer periods of time.

To give the readers an indication of what the aforementioned can do for them, we will use our situation as an example. One of us has been retired for 12 years and the other one for 9 years and with our combined social security income and saving only 25 percent each month, we have accumulated almost ninety-thousand dollars in a separate retirement savings account. Now we add this amount to our current cash balances and our current stock balances not to mention our book sales and the monies Joan makes on her Blog since we have been retired and we can remain retired until we are both over a 100 years of age.

Therefore, people can now see why it is important to save even as little as 25 percent of their monies that will benefit them in their retirement years and beyond. However, if people think this is too hard or strenuous they can start with saving 10 or 15 percent of their monies in the beginning and increase as they accumulate more as time goes by. People need to remember that everything can be modified to meet their needs, but it takes commitment to stick to one's financial budget. If people stay on their financial budgets they will eventually, be able to reach the 25 percent figure which is where we stay at so as not to put us into any financial binding situations. Remember, everyone's situation will be different, but saving at least 25 percent of one's income should keep them in the financial safe zone. And remember to add for inflation, as we use an annual 3% inflation figure each year.

# NINE

# SECTION V

# AN ODIOUS NECESSITY

Let's talk about vehicles for a moment. Ask yourself, is it really necessary to buy any new vehicles? One of our goals to living within our means is to avoid any depreciating assets at all cost and that definitely includes buying new vehicles. Unfortunately, over the last 60 years we bought four new vehicles and although we received some great discounts up to as much as 30 percent off on these vehicles, they were never much of an advantage to have because not only did they depreciate in value year after year, but we never paid them off except for the one's that we now own. Once we sat down years ago and figured out what a new vehicle was costing us it made no sense to continue to purchase any new vehicle again and we have owned a lot of them over the years.

Currently we own a 1988 Lincoln, a 2003 Suburban that we built for off roading, and a 2008 Hummer H2 that we bought new and still runs like new. All of these vehicles run like new and they all look brand new, but that was how I was raised to take care of one's vehicle. Nevertheless. the point being made is to avoid deprecating assets at all cost because they never will be able to give one a decent return on their investment. Likewise, unless one owns a business where they can write-off their vehicle then never lease a vehicle and own them outright instead as this will put people way ahead of the rest of the population in terms of financial freedom. Having no vehicle payments when going into retirement or eliminated once in retirement will be a major financial advantage for living within one's means.

# NINE

# SECTION VI

# THE ODIOUS NECESSITY II

The next odious necessity the majority of people think that is a necessity is their living accommodations that can include a house, an apartment, a condo, a trailer, or anything else that would qualify as living accommodations. Thus far in our lifetime we have only seen three of these accommodations that would be considered as having an appreciating asset and that would be a House, a Condo, and a Trailer known as a Mobile Home, but only in the state of California for Mobile Homes where one expects their Mobile Home to appreciate.

Investing in one of these living accommodations is pretty much a standard practice in today's world in the United States, but the question is whether or not one can afford to live in these accommodations because of there pricing? Pricing can be extremely high for housing and condo's depending on where one lives, but the question is, is it necessary? If people buy the right way and only use their net income as an indicator of what they can really afford then the answer would be yes. Unfortunately, people do not use their heads when buying houses and condo's, but rather their emotions and, unfortunately, their desire to live up to the standards of the Jones or at least try to, can end in disaster. This in turn will, eventually, cause a lot of problems, especially, if the economy takes a turn for the worse.

However, since we have already written the most comprehensive book on this subject we will just mention the title called "Home Buying & Financing 101 Second Edition" that can be purchased on Amazon. Not only will this book educate anyone on the process of home buying, but it will educate people on all the in's and out's of loans and the different financing that people can use to purchase their homes. Likewise, this book will instruct people how they will never lose their homes even in the event of a severe recession like the one in 2008 providing they purchase their home or condo the right way.

When it comes to Mobile Homes they too can be a reasonable investment, especially, if one owns the land. However, when it comes to buying a mobile home in a park setting, people will become involved in paying park space rents and there maybe other expenses also, so be sure to check with the park manager to determine what they may require besides space rental fees before buying. Mobile Homes on private lands can be excellent alternatives if one can find some property for sale that will accept mobile homes providing the county or city allows for these units. Again, it is feasible to check with the city or county before purchasing a piece of property to make sure one can place a mobile home on said property. In this situation one will need to establish a water well and a septic system in order to function with their mobile home. Things like a cement foundation, driveway, and walkups can always be added later as time goes on when one has accumulated enough money to install such features if they so desire. All of these added amenities will also increase the value of a mobile home when the time comes for one to sell in anticipation of moving up to a small house or a condo.

As an example, when we were living in Southern California in my wife's condo that was located in Laguna Niguel about a mile or two from the Ritz Carlton, and it was a very expensive proposition for a little 900 sq. ft. place. Although it was a very nice small two bedroom condo the homeowners association fees were exorbitant, the restrictions were ridiculous, and the over all cost were way too much. When we figured out what we were actually paying, it was costing us over $2200 a month to live in this place, so we decided to find something a lot less expensive. Therefore, we started looking around at mobile homes and after a few months Joan happened to be looking in one of the mobile home parks that we liked and found a unit that had a sign in the window that indicated it was for rent. This was on a Friday night and after taking the number down we called the number right away and naturally, no one was available so we left our number for a possible call back.

It wasn't until after the weekend that we received a call on Monday stating that we had been the first callers even though there were over 100 caller inquiries concerning this unit. Therefore, we told the owner that we would take the unit no matter what happens and regardless of the condition of the unit. To make a long story short again, the unit was a disaster, but the park was where every one shared in the land, making the space only 70 dollars a month and that was the only park fee they had because everyone owned their part of the land in this particular mobile home park.

After a day or so we started negotiations concerning this mobile home and after about a week or so we agreed to a sales price of $2,500.00 for the unit. However, when we met the owners they had brought a friend with them who just happened to open his mouth and stated that he thought $2,500.00 was too cheap and we immediately asked the owner, who this guy was? He stated he was just a friend and we then asked him if this guy had any financial interest in the mobile home and he stated that he did not.

Therefore, knowing that something did not seem to be right concerning this situation we told the friend that since he did not have any interest in this property that his comments were not appreciated. Next we looked at the owner and asked him what he thought would be a fair price for the unit. As it turned out the owner needed to pay off some other property they had in San Diego, CA and he needed $5000.00 to do so. Moreover, we stated that we would pay him the $5000.00 for the unit providing that this was the last price we would agree to pay. The owner agreed and we bought the unit from them only to find out that they owed a lot more on the unit then they originally never mentioned. So now we had a different situation altogether and since I love these kinds of deals it was now my turn to negotiate and I had a couple of my own stipulations. First of all, the owners had to agree to continue to make the payments on the unit, but that we would be making their payments, which amounted to only $500.00 per month and that we would pay the annual taxes that amounted to $135.00 a year along with the tax write off.

At that time both my wife and myself were in the real estate business and we owned our own real estate company, a real estate processing center, and a real estate loan company. Therefore, we drew up 2 different contracts where we indicated in a real estate sales contract that we were not going to record because it would make the owners payments all due and payable immediately if recorded. Next we drew up a lease to own real estate contract that basically means that we would be paying the owner current monthly obligations for their mobile home and that we would be responsible for paying the annual taxes. This is similar to an All Inclusive Trust Deed also known as an AITD wrap-a-round real estate transaction. In essence, this type of real estate transaction prevents the owners outstanding loan balance on said property from being called by their lender as being all due and payable immediately. However, in order to protect our position we recorded this AITD real estate contract agreement that can also be used for credit purposes along with Tax write-offs. The readers should also note that an AITD is an excellent way to purchase property in the event the owner or owners do not need the money from the outright sale of their property.

Lastly, there are apartment rentals, housing rentals, and mobile home rentals where one definitely does not want to splurge on unless they have plenty of money to throw away. Rentals are good in the beginning of one's life, but in the long run they are not satisfying anyone's needs for living within or below one's means, because people are wasting their monies. The sooner one can buy a place to live, the better their chances are for gaining financial freedom in the long run. Remember, when you own you can always move up, but when one rents it is a losing proposition.

All in all we have covered an awful lot of information in this chapter so feel free to read it over again as many times as one may need to log this information into one's brain matter as it will pay dividends when the time comes when you need it. Understanding one's financial situation at all times is critical not only for one's success, but also for designing one's retirement plan. We have seen several retirees over the years have nothing but problems because they never made a plan concerning their retirement, and a lot of them end up filing for bankruptcies simply because they did not have a written retirement plan. On the other side of the coin we have seen very self confident retirees who not only had a plan, but they followed their plan accordingly and adjusted it annually or whenever they needed to in order to conform to their particular situation.

One thing people will learn about being in retirement is that it is always changing and retirement will never remain the same from year to year. Likewise, having a written plan that one can adjust or modify as needed will make life a lot easier as time goes by. This also applies to one's financial budget as well as one's grocery list budget that will always be changing as time goes on. In our situation we even have a vitamin shopping list that we use all the time and we adjust it according to the changes that each company makes on their vitamin prices. The advantages of having these lists is that we do not waste anytime in supermarkets or anywhere else we go because we know exactly what we want and need at all times unlike a lot of other people we see in these markets. It's as if they don't know what they are doing and they look lost. Whereas, if people had a list be it financial, grocery, vitamins, or any other kind of list they could follow, it would immediately simplify their lives and increase their free time to do whatever else they wanted to do whenever they wanted to.

# TEN

# A TEST TO SEMI-RETIRE

One of the advantages of living within your means is that you will start accumulating a lot of cash over a short period of time, to the extent of having excessive money available to you at any given time. The problem with accumulating a lot of cash is that you will reach a point when you will want to spend some of it, and that is all right, providing you don't go overboard and spend more than you have accumulated. As a rule of thumb, go ahead and spend some of your accumulated cash, but only to the tune of 10 percent of your proceeds, as your goal is to eventually become well-off and well-to-do in the long run and be able to live the way you want in retirement. If done properly, living within your means will allow yourself to do what you want whenever you want, and at the same time, assist in compensating you for your efforts by constantly putting money back into your retirement accounts. Likewise, living within your means simply means that you will be living within your means until you feel that you can capitalize on the savings you have realized over time. You and only you will then be able to make that determination of when you have reached that point based on your future plans. In our situation, we only had approximately seven years to get ready for retirement. By saving our money and living within our means, we somehow managed to make it work out even though neither one of us wanted to admit that we were living way below our means. It was nice to know that we had accumulated plenty of money and continued to do so until we eventually reached a point seven years down the road where it was time to semi-retire. When we use the term semi-retired, it simply means that one of us stopped working altogether to see if we could live on the money that we were accumulating—sort of like testing the waters for another year to determine if both of us would be all right to retire completely when the other person also quit working. Looking back, it took us eight years to know that we could retire without ever having to go back to work for the rest of our lives.

The bad part about living within your means is that you have to sacrifice a lot in order to get ahead, and that means sticking to your budget whether you want to or not and not going out whenever you want even though you have the money to spend. If people have made the decision to live within their means in order to become well-off and well-to-do, then one must learn to do without all the frills that go along with the basics. To give the reader an example: We had a basic phone service without call forwarding, call waiting, or caller ID and a lot of other features that the phone companies were offering, and we negotiated for flat rates. However, we were still spending around $130 a month on phone service. So we decided to switch to Basic Talk phone service, which used to costs us about $12 every month, but has now increased to 15.00 per month thereby now saving us about $150.00 per month. Again this may not sound like much, but over a year, we are now saving over $1,620 a year, which goes into our retirement accounts. Next, we canceled our basic cable TV service and switched to Netflix and canceled the Dish Satellite service, for which we were spending around $115.00 a month. Furthermore, Dish Satellite managed to increase our monthly fees every year or two. When we originally started with Netflix we spent $8 a month and they offered all the movies one could ever want to watch without any commercials, and we were saving a minimum of $47 a month, or another $564 a year that was going into our retirement accounts. Now, seven years later we are still with Netflix even though they increased to $14.00 per month we are saving over $1025. 00 a year thereby increasing our retirement accounts. What about the regular news, you ask? Simple: we just listen to the radio if we want to know what is going on in the world, or we spend our time on the Internet exploring the news. So, we will never have to go back to Dish as long as Netflix stays in business. If you add up all the savings from making these changes, one will realize that we are now saving around $2,645.00 a year, which is now going into our retirement savings accounts instead of someone else's pockets.

Next we cut down on our social events, and we even cut down our car expenses by buying used cars and making these vehicles last as long as possible. When we need another car, we buy used vehicles instead of financing new ones. Another thing we do when buying used cars or trucks is to pay cash for these vehicles and then set up our own monthly car payment loan. We double or triple the going car or truck loan interest rate and pay ourselves back until the car or truck is paid off, which can add up for our retirement accounts. When you become your own bank, not only will you make money on your vehicle loan, but you will never have to worry about your vehicle being repossessed if you decide to miss a payment or two. As an example, let's say that you want to buy a new or used vehicle and want to finance $10,000 for three to five years at the going financed interest rates, which are currently running between 2.5 percent for people with excellent credit and as high as 12 percent for people who have questionable credit; these rates are for Texas, and other states will vary in their rates. For this example, let's finance a car or truck loan for three years at 3 percent using the $10,000 figure on the cash you put up to buy and finance the vehicle yourself. The monthly loan payment for you will be around $291 (rounded), including the interest rate payment at 3 percent per year for three years. Therefore, at the end of three years, you will have made back your principal of $10,000 and an additional $476 (rounded) in the form of interest for a total of $10,476.00 that you charged yourself, since you are the bank. Now, had you charged yourself 6 percent interest on your loan, you would have made your principal back plus an additional $952 (rounded) for three years. If you had charged yourself 12 percent interest on your loan, you would have made an additional $1,957 (rounded) in interest alone in addition to your principal for the three years. By acting as your own bank, you could finance for whatever number of years you wanted to and for a lesser monthly payment and more interest or vise versa. Also, for those of you who do not want to learn how to amortize a loan, just call a bank and ask them to do it for you, and be sure to give them the interest rate you want to charge yourself—but don't tell the bank what you are doing. Likewise, be sure to set up a separate bank account for your car or truck loan and try not to touch these monies until you make the last payment to yourselves.

Because our goal was to be well-off and well-to-do in retirement and not want for anything, living within our means eventually became a way of life for our family. Furthermore, when we saw an opportunity to cut expenses, we would make the adjustment and save even more, and we continue to make adjustments anytime we believe we can live without something.

We looked at different investment vehicles in which to place our money, but most of the investments came with large penalties for withdrawing money before the investments had run their course. IRAs and Roth IRA's were a complete waste of time as an investment vehicle, even though you could use your IRA funds to invest in the stock market. As we have noted above, after doing some research on IRAs, we came to believe that our wonderful government created the IRA just so they could extort more money from the people, knowing full well that sooner or later most people would not be able to let their IRAs ride for ten, fifteen, or twenty years without touching their money. And then—BAM—they would get hit with heavy fines, and our illustrious government would reap the rewards in the form of free money. Next, we considered 401K programs, but like the IRAs they too were a waste of time, so we put our monies into brokerage accounts, as they were guaranteed up to $50 million. Likewise, our accounts were placed into high-yield money market fund accounts, and if we had to get to our money, we could do so without suffering any penalties.

Toward the end of 2001, we were reaping major dividends by living within our means, so we decided to purchase a motor home and move to the mountains in Julian, California, which was located northeast of San Diego. We set up shop selling homes, as the area had experienced some wildfires that had burnt down about fourteen hundred homes. We paid for a dealer's license with an outfit located in North Carolina to sell their pre-made homes, which were superior to the homes that had burnt down in the Julian area.

Since we were making a considerable amount of money each month living within our means, we would visit the Julian area every weekend looking for a place to rent that would not cost us an arm and a leg. After going back and forth to the area for a few months, we finally located a place that was about five hundred square feet in size and was already split into two offices for our business, which was perfect for us. After negotiating with the landlord, we finally agreed on a dollar per square foot, provided we were able to park our motor home on the property and we could hook up our unit to be self contained. The landlord agreed and offered us a space behind the main building that had water. All we had to do was bring in a plumber to install a line from our motor home to the septic system, which was already in place. The plumber charged us $250 to do the septic installation by connecting the lines, and we were ready for full-time living in our motor home in the mountains of Julian. Next we had to set up the office, so we took several phones and desks from our other business locations in Irvine, California, and brought them up to the Julian location in order to furnish the office. Since we already had a real estate office, we simply used the new location as a satellite office. Next we placed ads in all of the major papers and ordered a thousand brochure booklets to hand out to all the locals who had lost their homes. Then all we had to do was wait for all the business to come in, or so we thought. This adventure turned out to be a complete waste of time and money so we packed up and moved to another state.

Okay, let's get back to "living within your means." We were now going into the year 2006 and getting extremely close to wanting to retire, so we talked it over and considered selling our mobile home in San Juan Capistrano and having my wife move up to Julian in the San Diego mountains until we could find a reasonable state to retire in. Since we were still in the high-selling home market in California, we decided to list our mobile home and start looking for another home to buy for our retirement. It did not take long for us to sell the mobile home in San Juan Capistrano, and for an amount that people only dreamed about when selling their homes. If you remember, we had purchased this mobile home for only $5,000 and took over the payments and taxes. We ended up selling the unit eight years later for a whopping $330,000. Talk about buying low and selling high! This was the best deal that we had ever made in our lifetimes so far, as we ended up with a little over $300,000 in cash after everything was paid off.

Now that the mobile home was sold, we moved all of our stuff into a storage unit up in Julian and started living out of our motor home located next to our business. As we continued to look throughout

California for another place to live, we were not able to locate a home that we could afford, as the prices all over the state were higher than we could even think about paying for another home and at the same time be able to retire. The cheapest home we could find on the mountain in Julian was not quite a hundred years old, was eleven hundred square feet on a quarter acre with two bedrooms and one bathroom, and was selling for $695,000. And the only other place we found was located up near the California and Oregon border in Crescent City, where we found a single-wide mobile home on three acres for $225,000, but the mobile home itself was not habitable and needed to be hauled off the land and replaced with another home. Needless to say, we did not want to spend all of our money on another mobile home out in the middle of nowhere that we could not live in, so we decided to look in other states. Likewise, having been in the mortgage loan business most of my life in Southern California, I knew the mortgage market was headed for another crash, and I did not want to be left holding onto a mortgage loan that might go upside down when that happened.

We started looking in other states, and most states in which we were looking at real estate were just as ridiculous in price as California was—and even worse in some states, such as Nevada. We continued looking for a home in Arizona, Idaho, Montana, Oregon, New Mexico, and a few other states, only to discover that we still could not retire and be well-off or well-to-do any time soon, even with the amount of monies we had accumulated from the sale of our mobile home and even after adding our other accounts to those monies. However, a few days later, Joan heard from one of our loan officers, who told us that he was showing a lot of families homes for sale in Texas because the prices there were still reasonable. When Joan informed me of this situation, we decided to investigate and ended up spending the next twelve hours on the Internet viewing unbelievable homes at unbelievable prices in Texas compared with California prices. The next time I spoke to Joan, I told her that we would be packing up and heading for Texas the following week and that we would be spending approximately a month or so there looking for homes and a place to live where we could retire. This, incidentally, is just an example of what you can do when you live within your means.

Since September was almost upon us, we decided to take the last few days left in August and travel to Texas in search of a new home. However, before we left we decided to view the California map we had, and measured the distance between Julian in San Diego County and Crescent City, which was the farthest distance we had considered moving to in California. According to the map, the distance was a little over eleven inches. So we then turned the ruler sideways, and when we viewed the eleven inches to the right of Julian, we found that we would be located about twenty to thirty miles west of Fort Worth, Texas. Since we did not know anything about Texas, we decided to call a realtor who might be interested in showing us homes in the surrounding areas. After several calls, we finally settled on a wonderful real estate agent by the name of Dee-Dee Jones, located at the Century 21 office in Glen Rose, Texas. When we first arrived, we ended up in a place called Lake Whitney, where there was a motor home park for us to stay in while we made arrangements to contact Dee-Dee.

Little did we know at the time that Dee-Dee was traveling from Glen Rose, Texas, to Lake Whitney, Texas, a distance of approximately forty-plus miles, every day to pick us up and travel to other counties to show us homes. To say the least, we were impressed, as we were looking at approximately ten homes a day, seven days a week, and covering a lot of territory. At the same time, we were learning a lot about Texas and Texans. Did you know that 75 percent of all people who are born in Texas live, work, and die in Texas? Right now that is the highest rate for any state in the United States. It is relatively easy to become a Texan because you simply keep your mouth shut and vote no on everything. Moreover, Texans seem to be very religious, since they are part of the Bible Belt, so attending or affiliating with a Church group would put you in good standing in any community—and trust us, you will never have a problem locating a place of worship in Texas. However, there are a couple of downfalls that most Texans indulge in, just as the rest of the people do in the United States. For example, they drive too fast and they are never wrong in an accident or close call, unless proven wrong in a court of law. Texans really don't pay attention to the way they are driving; especially during deer hunting season or when they are on the telephone in their vehicles. Nevertheless, we have found Texans to be some of the most generous and wonderful people to be around, and they will go way out of their way to help other people, making Texas a great place to live as long as you don't drive with Texans.

Anyway, we continued to look at homes for another couple of weeks before making our first offer on a home located in Lake Whitney. We offered the owners $150,000 for their home, which happened to be $3,000 more than the highest comparable (comp) in the area. However, the owners responded by indicating that they thought our offer was an insult. After informing them that our offer was in fact $3,000 above the highest comp in the area, we then informed them that they could keep their home for another ten years or so and left. It was now approximately three weeks that we had been escorted around by Dee-Dee looking at approximately two hundred homes, and we were getting tired. So we told Dee-Dee that we were going to take a break for a day and go look at a lake we heard about called Eagle Mountain Lake somewhere up north of Lake Whitney. The next day we headed off to find Eagle Mountain Lake. Roughly 170 miles later, we finally found the lake, and it was everything that everyone had told us it was. It was big, wide, and deep, with great fishing, and was very well maintained. After a while of driving around one portion of the lake, we finally decided to head back to Lake Whitney in a leisurely manner and take in the sights as we drove.

After an hour or so of driving, we agreed that we were lost and out in the middle of nowhere. Then we came upon a road called Confederate Highway, also known as Farm Road 1886, and we decided to follow the road west. Having gone about seven or eight miles, we came upon a road called Church Road going north, which was canopied by the trees on both sides of the road. Both of us, along with my son, thought Church Road might be a good place to look around for a home, so we made a note to ask the real estate agent about the possibility of looking at developments in this area. As we continued west on Confederate Highway, we came to another Farm Road called FM 730, and since we knew that Lake Whitney was to the south, we made a left turn and headed south, hoping to pick up Interstate Highway 20 or 30, so that we could find our way back to Lake Whitney. We managed to find our way back to Lake Whitney, but we definitely wanted to go back to where we got lost to look at homes with Dee-Dee the following day.

The next day when Dee-Dee arrived, we told her about our little adventure, and because we could not remember the Farm Road number of Confederate Highway, she said she would not know what direction to go unless she had the Farm Road number. So we asked if she knew where White Settlement Road was located, and she said she did, so off we went. However, apparently Dee-Dee had another area that she wanted to show us first, in a place called Aledo, which was located near Interstate Highway 20 and about thirty miles west of Fort Worth. We agreed to go take a look at the homes in Aledo, as Dee-Dee seemed to be excited about the area. When we arrived at the first development and were looking around, both of us looked at each other. Still thinking in terms of California housing, we both figured that these homes had to be anywhere from $2.5 million to $3 million each. We immediately informed Dee-Dee that there was no way we could afford even a garage in this area, let alone a home. Dee-Dee started laughing and replied that these homes were going between $280,000 and $350,000, and we were in total disbelief.

We decided to take a look around and viewed a few homes until we came across a home that caught our attention. Apparently, the builders had someone make a custom fireplace suppresser for the top of the outside chimney, which was made out of hammered copper and bronze that was magnificent in its Aztec design. We asked Dee-Dee if we could view the home, and as she was showing us the home, we became more and more impressed with all the details the builders were adding to this beautiful home. The home was a little over three thousand square feet, with four bedrooms, three baths, and a great three-car garage that even had real cedar wood doors. We asked what the builders wanted for the home, and they said $320,000. So we offered them $250,000 for the home, as I did not want to blow all of the profit we had made on the mobile home back in California. The builders came back with an offer, and we again countered, and so on, until we finally settled on a price of $300,000 pending an inspection. Now, we don't know about the rest of the country, but in Texas all a buyer has to do is pay $100 to the owners or builders and request an inspection of the home, and even though you have made an offer on the home, you still have the right to walk away from the deal if the inspection does not meet your requirements. What a deal!

Right away Dee-Dee placed a call to the inspector, and we all agreed to meet at the house the next day. When the home inspector arrived, he introduced himself to everyone and began inspecting the home. After about three and half or four hours, the inspector indicated to us that the house was in excellent condition and was well built. Next came the roof, and that is where we encountered a major problem. The builders apparently started building a wood chimney, and once they reached the roof, they decided to change to an all-brick chimney. However, the builders started building the brick chimney on top of the roof line and attempted to mortar the bricks to the wooden structure. Likewise, there was no flashing on the top or bottom of the chimney, and the bracing for the entire chimney consisted of three four-by-six pieces of wood nailed under the chimney in between the roof trusses. We asked the inspector what would happen over time if we just accepted the home as it was. He informed us that it would just be a matter of time before the chimney ended up in our living room after a good rain or snow fall. Next, we approached the builders and told them what the inspector said about the chimney, and they asked us what it would take to make the deal and sell the home. We informed them that they would have to tear down the chimney and rebuild it the right way, with the proper metal bracing in the attic and the proper flashing installed in the roof, and then build the chimney to the proper height according to the State of Texas building code. To make a long story short, they refused to rebuild the chimney, and we refused to buy their newly built home. After this incident occurred, we asked Dee-Dee what the building requirements were in the State of Texas for someone to become a home builder. Dee-Dee's reply was *"A baseball hat, a hammer, and a pick-up truck."* In other words, anyone can become home builders in the State of Texas, provided they ply their trade outside any of the city limits. So the word is "buyer beware" if you happen to be looking at homes outside any of the city limits in Texas.

We never did find anything we liked in this area and Dee-Dee got the idea to move on to White Settlement, and we looked at houses for the rest of that day in this area. Now that we were quite a ways from Lake Whitney, we decided to move closer to the area where we were looking at homes, and we told Dee-Dee that we would inform her of where we were going to be located if she still wanted to continue to show us homes. Dee-Dee agreed, even though we were going to be located over seventy miles away from her office. Talk about being relentless—Dee-Dee was turning out to be the epitome of what a real estate agent was supposed to be. Anyway, we ended up going to a place right off Interstate Highway 20 called Weatherford, Texas, which turned out to be a nice little town that we visit and shop in to this day, even though Weatherford is no longer a little town.

The next day we finished looking at homes in White Settlement, and we actually managed to find Farm Road 730, so we proceeded north in search of more homes, when we accidentally came to Farm Road 1886, otherwise known as Confederate Highway. To say the least, all of us were excited, as we had finally found the missing Farm Road and now we could start looking for Church Road. We could only go east, as Confederate Highway ended at Farm Road 730. So away we went until we found Church Road again. Getting even more excited, we headed north looking for homes or home developments in the area that we might be interested in buying. Now, for those of you who are not familiar with the rural areas of Texas, but happen to be looking for a home to purchase, let us enlighten you a little. Once you have traveled out of the city areas, finding home developments can be a daunting task, as the distances between developments may be several miles. Therefore, we recommend that you find a real estate agent familiar with the area you're looking in and the surrounding areas, even if the developments are several or so miles apart. Anyway, after a couple of hours of getting lost, we finally located some homes for sale. We took our time looking until we found a great-looking home located on three acres of land, with RV parking and hookups and three additional buildings to do with as one pleased. The home was approximately 3,700 square feet and was located at the end of a cul-de-sac and listed at $275,000, so we decided to take a look.

The entryway was really poor, as it led into a very small area; you really could not figure out what it might be used for, and neither did the current owners, as the room only had three chairs in the center. Nevertheless, we continued throughout the rest of the house only to discover that the kitchen was very large as were the rest of the rooms in the home. Then we ventured out onto the patio area to discoverer a fruit tree orchard, which really appealed to my wife. Next we went out the side gate to discover that the backyard was a little over two acres, and that's when it hit me: it would take me several days just to cut the grass of this well-manicured lawn, so we decided to keep looking. Next we went to Hidden Valley Estate, then Deer Plantation Estates, and then Windy Hills Estates I and II, where we found nothing that piqued our interest in the way of homes we would consider buying. But then we passed Windy Hills Estates III, and the main thing that caught my eye was the trees in the estates, as the rest of the estates that we had looked at did not have any trees around any of the homes. So we asked Dee-Dee if we could turn around and go back to Windy Hills Estates III and take a look around, and again she was more than agreeable with our request. Incidentally, just about everything in Texas is called an estate, which really doesn't amount to much except to the Texan ego. Basically, these are just community housing developments situated on some land having anywhere from a half acre to as much as three to five acres or more, with the average home having at least one acre. Also, some developments have gates for entry while others do not. However, the gated housing communities will usually have association fees, which you want to stay away from, as these fees are nothing more than a waste of your hard-earned money, and you usually get very little in return for your association monthly dues. Moreover, one should know that in the event the homeowners' association should go bankrupt, everyone in the community will become responsible for the debts and future lawsuits that it incurs. Likewise, people should understand that the homeowners' association will be made up of the homeowners in the association, who may or may not be qualified to be on the board of directors. This means that the board members could drown everyone in the association without anyone in the community knowing what is going on until it is too late, or when one is notified that the association is bankrupt. The point we are making is that everyone in the association community should know the qualifications of all people who would like to be elected as board members of an association. The easiest way to do this is to have all future board members submit their resumes to the current board members and also post these resumes in an open area for the rest of the association members to review. Furthermore, there is one more item everyone should know about: in today's society, people may or may not be what they seem or pretend to be; therefore, it would be advisable for the board members to run background checks on board member candidates to verify that the candidates are really who they say they are and have the best interests of the association and the community as their upmost priority.

Upon turning around and entering Windy Hills Estates III, the first thing Joan and I noticed was that the homes were similar to the Aledo homes, but instead of being on a half acre or less, these homes were being built on a minimum of one-acre lots, and some lots were even a little larger. Again, in California these homes would be selling for $2 million to $3 million, but in Texas they were in the $300,000 to $400,000 range and between 2,500 and 4,500 square feet in size. After we first drove through the housing development, something in the second cul-de-sac caught our eye. We couldn't figure out what it was, but we knew something was wrong with the way it was developed. Nonetheless, we started looking at the homes. At that time, only three of the homes had been sold, and only one custom home was being built by another builder. Other than the homes that were sold, all the others were in some phase or other of being built. Taking our time we went through every home and rejected them for one reason or another. We were finally getting tired and started to have Dee-Dee take us back to get our rental car when we again passed the second cul-de-sac and again we noticed something was wrong with the development. But we still could not figure out what it was that was bothering us. So we asked Dee-Dee if she would turn around and take us down this cul-de-sac, even though there were no *"For Sale"* signs on any of the properties we could see, and only one house had been sold.

Again Dee-Dee agreed, and we turned around and went down the cul-de-sac. As we were approaching the end of the cul-de-sac, we realized what had been catching our eye every time we passed by. It turned out that there were only two homes being built at the back of the cul-de-sac instead of the normal three homes that are usually built in that spot. Moreover, the house being built in the cul-de-sac was by the client who was having his home custom built by another builder; he had decided that he wanted to have a little larger lot, thereby also making the other cul-de-sac lot larger than the one-acre lot. Since the client was having his home built by another builder, we glanced at the only other home in the cul-de-sac and noticed it just had a builder's sign on the property and was in the final phase of being built. Since we had nothing to lose, we again asked Dee-Dee if she would be kind enough to call the builder whose name was on the sign. Dee-Dee agreed and called the builder. He had just placed his sign back on the property because the property had been sold to a couple in Florida, but they had forgotten to tell the builder that the sale of the home would be contingent upon them selling their home, thereby misleading the builder and falsely hindering the sale of the builder's property. This forced the builder to go to court to get an Injunction of Release against the would-be buyers. However, none of this information was related to us until several days later, after we'd had a chance to view the home with the builder. Anyway, Dee-Dee had made contact with the builder, and he said someone would be at our location within thirty minutes, so we sat down and waited.

The person showed up on time, and after all the introductions were over, Dee-Dee had him sign her sales agreement so that if we bought the place, she would get her commission. The person introduced himself as Andy, and he began showing us around the house and answering any questions that we asked. When we came to the third bedroom, which would eventually be our son's room, it appeared to be too small for him and all the things that he would want to put in his own room. Andy made the comment that it was only plaster. Not understanding what he was talking about at that time, we continued viewing the rest of the home, and when we came to the living room, we noticed another room located way back in the house where the fireplace had been installed. When we asked Andy what the room was for, Andy told us it was the family room, and we immediately asked Andy why anyone would build the family room right next to the living room, with both rooms maintaining the same open entry and exit way? We then indicated to Andy that someone had to be off their rocker to make such a mistake in building. Andy stated that he'd thought it was a good idea at the time he was building the connecting room. Again, I had managed to stick my foot in my mouth, so to speak, because we now realized that Andy was the builder. Again he told us it was just plaster, only this time we got it, so we started redesigning the back portion of the home with him.

We asked Andy if he could cut an archway in the wall between our son's room and the family room that would match the rest of the archways in the home, and he indicated that it would be no problem. Next, we asked if we could remove the fireplace in back of the house and move it up to the fourteen by sixteen opening connecting the family room with the living room, and he said that it would be no problem. Next we asked if it would be possible to soundproof the wall that was going to separate the two rooms so that we would not be able to hear anything from the rear room, and again Andy agreed. So now that we were adding a complete and separate family room just for our son's use, the size of the third bedroom did not matter. Our handicapped son would now live in his own home with his own entrance and exit door, not realizing that he was still living in the same home with his dad and his best friend (my wife). What a deal for our son! After asking Andy a few more questions about the house, I asked Joan what she thought, and she responded in total disbelief simply because she had never lived in such a wealthy environment. I told her to get used to it, and I made Andy an offer for the home. I offered him $250,000 for the home, and he countered with $5,000 more, for a total of $255,000 on a home that had a listing price of $320,000—a 2,500-square-foot home on 1.2 acres of land. I accepted his counteroffer, contingent upon a home inspection. Talk about being at the right place at the right time! Because the house had been in ligation for such a long time, causing Andy to lose money as the home just sat there, he needed to get it sold as soon as he could so he would not continue to lose money and he could move on to building more homes.

Andy had no problem with the request for a home inspection and actually thought it was a good idea, which told me that not only was he confident in his building abilities, but he also had nothing to hide. The next day we met with the same home inspector who had inspected the Aledo home, and again he proceeded to take the next two or three hours to do his job. After he had completed the inspection, he proceeded to the attic first before inspecting the roof of the home. Approximately an hour later, the inspector told us and Dee-Dee that this was an extremely well built home and that the level of insulation was exceptional in the attic area of the home. The inspector then informed us that he would have his written report for us within the next few days. Since we had to get back to California, we asked him to send us a copy and at the same time give a copy to Dee-Dee, just in case we had any further questions.

After approximately thirty-one days of looking at more than three hundred homes, we had finally found the home that we wanted and were willing to purchase. Everyone was happy, especially Dee-Dee, as she was no longer going to have to chauffeur us all over Texas looking for a home. How she managed to put up with us, I'll never know, but I will say that she was the best and most polite real estate agent we have ever had the pleasure of knowing. Dee-Dee had the patience of a saint, the tenacity of a pit bull, and the elegance of a true lady. She was always kind, courteous, and polite, regardless of the request we would make of her and the situations we would get her into by venturing way out of her geographical area. In our opinion, Dee-Dee was a superstar real estate agent.

The main emphasis of this chapter is to indicate to the reader what can be accomplished by having a plan, learning to budget, and establish a saving pattern by living within their means. Also, we are pointing out to the readers, that if you have to move to another state in order to retire comfortably, take your time and pick the states that you would consider retiring in, and narrow the states down to the one you would like to live in. Your next order of business would be to go to that state you decided you want to live in, in order to confirm your selection and then rent a place for a week or two in order to confirm your convictions that this is the right place to retire in the state you have chosen.

# ELEVEN

# THE RELOCATION MOVE

It was now the end of September of 2006, and since we had finally found a home to purchase in Texas, we had to head back to California to figure out exactly how much money we needed to put down on our new home. We wanted to keep our ratios low enough to live within our means and be well-off and well-to-do when we made the move to our new home in another state. Since the home would not be ready to move into until January of 2007, we had a little time to get our affairs in order for the move to Texas and to plan the move itself with the movers. The ratios that we are going to be using are the same ratios that lenders use in the mortgage loan business to establish one's ability to make a monthly mortgage loan payment and still have sufficient monies left over to pay one's outstanding debts. The ratio is 28/36, also known as twenty-eight over thirty-six in the mortgage industry, where the 28 percent figure is the amount of one's gross monthly income that is allocated toward the home's monthly mortgage loan payment of principal and interest along with taxes and insurance—otherwise known as PITI. The bottom ratio of 36 percent represents all of one's outstanding debts, which means that a person should not maintain outstanding total debt that exceeds 36 percent of one's total gross income when added to the principal, interest, taxes, and insurance.

Since this is such an important mortgage ratio to understand as opposed to the consumer retail ratio, which we will talk about later, We will use our own situation to give you an idea of how to calculate this ratio. We had planned on putting down more than 20 percent as a down payment on our home because we wanted a No Documentation, No Income Verification, Adjustable Negative Loan, which used to be the best loan in the mortgage marketplace at the time this loan was still available, so we were still able to get it. However, because of the subprime mortgage debacle, the negative adjustable mortgage loan, along with a myriad of other great loans, has disappeared from the mortgage loan market, but hopefully, it will eventually reemerge. Now, for those of you reading this book who would like an extensive education into mortgage loans and want to have more financial knowledge than the bankers, you can read our other book entitled *Home Buying and Financing 101* Second Edition at amazon.com. Nevertheless, we figured that if we stayed with the 20 percent down payment figure, we would have to come up with $51,000, which in turn would give us a figure of $204,000 that we would be financing. We would need to have an income of approximately $9,398 a month in order to satisfy the front-end ratio, thereby giving us a front-end ratio of 14 percent for the principal and interest payment and 27 percent for the total PITI payment. Now, for the back-end ratio, based on the $9,398 in gross monthly income, we simply multiplied this number by 36 percent, which told us that our outgoing monthly debt payment should not exceed $880 a month in addition to the PITI payment. However, we decided that we did not want a house payment to go much higher than $600 a month, and therefore, we had to calculate exactly how much of a down payment we were going to have to make in order to keep the monthly payment around that mark.

We started by making a paper down payment of $150,000 and adding the $5,000 that we had on deposit, and we figured on financing $100,000 on the home. Next, we amortized the $100,000 over thirty years at 6.29 percent and got a figure of $618 as the monthly mortgage principal and interest figure and to think that people today complain about 3% interest rates or less as being too high as of year 2020, we have to laugh because these people do not know just how fortunate they are. Anyway's, we figured the taxes at 1.87 percent based on our tax area in Texas and got a figure of $4,769, and we then divided this figure by twelve months to get a monthly figure of $397 (rounded). Next, the homeowners insurance was figured at 3 percent and came to $3,000, and we again divided by twelve months to get a monthly figure of $250. Then we added these figures together in order to get the total monthly payment figure of $1,265. Next, we multiplied this figure by 3.75 percent and got a figure of $4,744, which was the minimum amount of monthly income we had to make in order to afford a $618 monthly mortgage loan payment that included the entire PITI. Then we took the figure of $1,265 and divided it by the monthly income and got a figure of 27 percent for the PITI payment. Next, we multiplied the monthly income by 36 percent, and we knew we could afford an additional monthly debt up to $443 if we wanted to buy something using monthly payments and assuming our monthly income was $4,744 per month. Okay, so everyone can understand how we are getting the figure for the additional outgoing debt: we are multiplying the monthly income by 36 percent, which gives us a figure of $1,708 (rounded), and then subtracting the PITI monthly payment of $1,265, giving us the figure of $443—that's what we could afford to have in additional outgoing debt to the PITI and still qualify with perfect mortgage loan ratios. However, you should know that these loan ratios are just guidelines for the bank lenders and they will fluctuate from bank to bank and may go as high as 45 percent on the backend ratios, depending on one's creditability and the stability of the financial markets in the housing industry.

In our situation the above figures should represent the perfect borrowers to a lending institution and, technically, if these figures are correct, they should put one in the priority column at any mortgage lending institution. But this was not always the case. As it turned out, the more qualified one was, the more difficult it was and the longer it took to get approved and funded for a mortgage loan. Our situation was the exact scenario we outlined above, yet for a mortgage loan that should have taken less than thirty days to fund, it took almost two months. We were having a hard time understanding why, as both of us were in the real estate and mortgage loan business. It wasn't until the following year that we understood why it took so long for the institutional lender to fund our mortgage loan. It was because the banking institutions were trying to put as many borrowers as they could into subprime mortgages, making it almost impossible for the perfect borrowers to get funded. The lenders were looking for some kind of glitch in order to force borrowers into subprime mortgage loans, as that was where the money was being made at the time in the mortgage loan business. Nevertheless, we prevailed, and we got our mortgage loan for our new home in Texas.

In the beginning of this chapter, we mentioned that we would take a look at *"Consumer Retail Ratios"* and how they work, not so much for you, but against you if you don't understand how they function. The guidelines for the Consumer Retail Ratios are set at 45/75 percent of gross monthly income, thereby giving people greater latitude when it comes to how much credit a consumer retailer is willing to extend. The credit card companies—along with all the major and minor retailers that are willing to send you credit cards or extend credit to you as install-ment payments or car loans for whatever you are buying—don't care about you one way or the other, but they do care about maximizing your front-end ratio so you can buy what you want even though you techni-cally can't afford it. The Consumers Retail Ratios are very important to understand, especially, if you are planning on purchasing a home any-time in your future.

Remember, the mortgage loan ratios are always set at 28/36 percent and will vary depending on your credit score and the amount of risk the lender is willing to take for you. Now, since the Consumer Retail Ratios are set at 45/75 percent of gross monthly income, we can now see how much additional debt we will be granted by the retailers by subtracting the 28 percent figure from the 45 percent figure. We get a figure of 17 percent that we can afford to carry in the form of debt in addition to our monthly mortgage payment. Now, if you look at the Consumer Retail ratios, hope-fully, the reader can now see why it is so important to understand the difference between Consumer Retail Ratios and Mortgage Loan Ratios, what they mean to you financially, and how they can affect you right now and anytime in the future. Living within your means, and becoming well-off and well-to-do will eventually determine how well you learn how to process financial information and how to use it to your advantage. Like-wise, understanding how to use credit to your advantage will become very important when you are trying to purchase a home, and for those of you who want to learn about credit we also published a book called *"How To Establish Your Credit"* and was designed for personal and business needs that can be purchased on Amazon. This is a great book for young people as well as everyone else who would like to know what bankers are look-ing for before they approve or deny anyone's credit decisions. Another thing that people need to understand is how to play the credit game and learn how they are rated by the credit companies. People are issued a FICO score, which runs from 300 to 850 and is based on five main areas. The rating system was designed by the Fair Isaac Corporation using a statistical model to determine one's ability to borrow money and repay it in a timely manner. However, we are not going to go into detail at this time explaining all the ins and outs concerning credit scoring. If anyone is interested they may purchase our other book, entitled *Home Buying and Financing 101 Second Edition or "How To Establish Your Credit"* which will teach people about credit scoring in more detail.

Before leaving the subject of credit, we would like to point out that credit card companies have established a relationship with the mortgage lenders, and both of them have been involved in a catch-22 scam with the public. They insist that people maintain a minimum of three active credit card trades carrying outstanding credit balances in order for the people to be granted a credit score that the mortgage lenders can use to qualify a potential homebuyer for a home loan. This is a bunch of baloney and should be against the law, as this scam that has been forced on people has caused and continues to cause serious financial consequences for the multitudes of people who believe that they have to maintain lines of credit to get a good credit score. But they do not understand how the credit card companies and the mortgage companies function. As far as the credit card companies are concerned by themselves, no one should be forced to maintain an outstanding balance on their credit cards in order to be able to retain their previous credit score. Likewise, when people maintain a high credit score and then decide to pay off their credit card debt, their credit score should remain high regardless of the length of time they go without making another credit card purchase. People should not be subjected to higher interest rates or require co-signers just because they decided not to use their credit cards for long periods.

For retirees and future retirees this chapter has pointed out the importance of understanding basic financing. If people don't have any sufficient knowledge of financing and how it will affect people for the rest of their lives, it is vital that one finds someone who they can trust and rely on for accurate financial information.

Another important subject that people should be made aware of is that there are a large number of people on the internet who are spewing out information that may be viable, but the majority of their retirement information is nothing more than *hogwash*! First of all, the majority of these people are not retired, therefore, they are putting out would be, might be, could be scenarios designed to scaring the heck out of retirees or soon to be retirees for no logical reason. Example: They attempt to tell people to stall their retirement until the age of 70 telling the people that they will gain more in retirement money? Technically, that is correct, but what they don't tell you, is that you will be way ahead of these people if you were to retire at 62 or at 65. If you retire at 62 collecting a $1,000 a month with annual increases you will have collected a minimum of $96,000 and at age 65 a minimum of $60,000 while the other people wait until they turn 70. In other words, retiring at 62 as opposed to age 70 will put you six years or more ahead in income of those retiring at 70. Likewise, at age 65 and depending on what your Social Security income is, you should be a minimum of four years ahead in income of those waiting to retire at age 70. Therefore, it will take at least six plus years for the 70-year olds to catch up to the income you have already received, and depending on your Social Security income at age 65, it will take at least four years or more for the 70-year olds to catch up to the income you have received. Moreover, by the time the 70-year olds catch up to you in income, a person will have bridged the income gap and they will be receiving just about the same as the 70-year olds, who will now be pushing 76 or 77 years of age at the same time as you.

Another thing that people need to be aware of is the way these so-called retirement financial experts want to convince everyone that they need 70 percent to 80 percent of one's working income to maintain the same standard of living after one stops working. What we want to know is where do these so-called experts get this disinformation? When one retires, one's income will be reduced to about 50 percent or less of what they were making working full-time, and even if one maintained a part-time job, one might be able to supplement their retirement income to 70 percent. So, what is wrong with retiring on 60, 50, or 40 percent or even less of one's previous working income if you are happy and can get along with what one has? In our opinion, these so-called financial experts and others are nothing more than propaganda experts who are trying to take as much money as they can from people if they can get away with it. What about the experts who misled and hyped that people need to have at least $500,000 in order to be able to retire? This is absolutely ridiculous, for the simple reason that they don't take into consideration all the variables that can effect one's retirement, and that they don't want to tell you about. In this situation the so-called experts either don't know what they are talking about or they don't know themselves. Figures such as the above are nothing more than pure nonsense as they are strictly guesstimates that mean nothing. For example: Are you going into retirement with a home or other debit payments? How is your health holding up? What kind of standard of living do you want or expect to maintain? What kind of living style do you want or expect? How long are the longevity lines in your family? Therefore, how these so-called fickle financial experts manage to come up with how much money one may need to retire on, puts them in the category of fortune tellers! How much one may need for retirement, as stated before, is nothing more than a guesstimate that you, and only you will have to decide for yourself once one is retired.

Based on the above aforementioned, one might retire on 40 percent or less with just $75,000 or $100,000 to start their retirement as long as they continue to grow their retirement accounts. Then others may want to have at least half of their working income when they retire, having $150,000 to $250,000 in their accounts, and others may want more or less depending on their particular circumstances. Likewise, and regardless of their requirements, all retirees will need to continue to add and advance their retirement accounts with some sort of income. Nevertheless, the decision will be yours and yours only and not the fortune tellers. Think about this for a minute: According to government's statistics, and based on our current income, we are living just above the poverty level, but because of what we have related to you in this book so far, we are living like Kings and Queens. Likewise, after reading this book, people will understand why *Anyone Can Retire* providing they establish a realistic plan and financial goals that they can continue to achieve during their retirement. Let the so-called financial experts fend for themselves when their time comes to retire. In fact, the experts may be asking the retirees for retirement advice. Therefore, knowing what one's expenses are before going into retirement or people who are recently retired becomes extremely important.

Now for the not so good news, it will take anywhere from two to three years being in retirement before people will actually find out what retirement will really be costing them, especially, the younger they retire. This is why we recommend that people design a retirement plan to follow when they enter retirement and keep accurate records of all of their expenditures. We use spreadsheet every year when we first retired when one of us was 42 years old in order to track our expenditures to get a better handle on our yearly cost. The funny thing about this process is not only did we learn a lot about our spending habits it also taught us about all the things we never knew we could do without that turned out to be completely unnecessary and a waste of money.

As it turned out, keeping and using a yearly spreadsheet has been one of the best things we ever did and we use one every year to track our spending habits. This in turn allows us to regulate and adjust our financial and grocery budget sheets accordingly and allows us to determine precisely what we can and cannot save or add to our retirement accounts. An annual spreadsheet can be a very valuable tool when one is planning for retirement or already in retirement and it seems the longer we use these annual spreadsheets the better off we become in our retirement years financially. One of the major keys to our retirement was entering retirement debt free which we had to learn the hard way. Since we had just bought a new home and a new truck we found that attempting to live within one's means was extremely difficult to do. Therefore, we concentrated on paying off our home, which we did in only five years and then the new truck six months later. Our only payments now are taxes and insurance for the home and vehicles. Granted one will encounter other expenses, but they should be minor providing one has a retirement plan and can put all that extra money into their retirement account.

Some additional advice and suggestions people may want to consider. Start planning early for one's retirement, but remember everything will start to change once in retirement and as time go on. No one will really understand what one needs financially to live on in retirement until they have been retired for at least 2 to 3 years and can tract and trace their annual expenditures. Pick an age in which one would like to retire and don't be afraid to change it if need be. Don't listen to what other people tell you as it is your retirement and not anyone one else. Keep one's self informed and continue to learn, be healthy, and keep active in one's retirement. Remember, as long as one is happy and content they can get by on just about anything financially providing they have a made out a retirement plan that can be changed and adjusted as needed throughout one's retirement.

# TWELVE

# THINGS RETIREES SHOULD KNOW

Naturally there are all sorts of different things that all future retirees and current retirees need to be made aware of and we will be relating several areas that we have encountered over our years of being in retirement. Hopefully, people will find these suggestions of some value to them as we progress through these items, and don't get discouraged even though we may have touched on some of these items throughout this book in more detail along the way.

# DESIRES, WANTS, AND NEEDS

When people enter retirement or are thinking about retiring they should first think about what their desires are concerning retirement. The second thing people should consider is what their wants will be or what they expect when they become retired and thirdly, what will be their actual needs before retirement or when they become retired. For example, what will your goals be and what does one plan to do when they retire? Writing these goals or plans down will assist people when they retire even though they may change as time goes by. What does one want to do once they are retired? Travel, seek adventures, if they are young enough and in good shape in their early sixties, or do they want to hunt, go fishing, explore the world or the USA, or explore several other endeavors? How about one's needs they will have when they retire? If people have some sort of medical problems, what will be their requirements or restrictions be once they are in retirement? Will people be happy or elated once they are in retirement or will they need or have the desire to work and stay active? Everyone needs to be thinking in these terms when planning their retirement or are already retired. Retirement is not a time for one to become depressed because retirement should be a time of excitement because one has survived in order to make it to retirement. Just think, no more work, no more worrying about a boss, no more worrying about meeting a timeline, no more worrying about getting up in the morning. This is a time to relax, to enjoy one's life knowing that no one or anyone is going to tell you what to do for the rest of one's life and it doesn't get better than that. Now is the time to satisfy all of one's dreams and there are no restrictions or limitations to one's thought processes. That is why we recommend that all people entering retirement take at lcast 2 to 6 months off or longer and do nothing but think about what one wants to achieve in their retirement years. Also remember that everything will change the older one gets, so be sure to plan ahead for these changing events too.

# THE FINANCIAL PLAN

People need to make out a financial plan even if it is relatively simple in design in the beginning because it will start people on their way to continue to modify, construct, and add more and more details to their financial plan once they are in retirement and they gain experience being retired. Also remember to make out an annual spreadsheet where one can keep tract of all of their outgoing expenses. And remember to itemize everything concerning out going expenses that one can total at the end of every year that will give all retirees a better understanding of where they stand financially at all times while one is in retirement. As we have already mentioned earlier in the book, having an understanding of one's financial situation at all times will be extremely beneficial to all people once they retire because they will know exactly where they stand at any given time.

# ADAPTING TO CHANGES

Once in retirement things will always be changing as one ages and having the ability to adapt to these changes can mean the difference of having a good retirement as opposed to a bad retirement because one was not able or willing to change as time goes on. To give people an example, we have always been in excellent physical condition and as treasure hunters we were and are always on the go traveling all over the place every week or so. However, even though we still go treasure hunting because that is our retirement hobby, we have both aged over the years and even though we are still in great shape for our ages, we may now only travel to 1 or 2 different states a year to treasure hunt. Nevertheless, we had to learn to adapt to our abilities according to our changes in age where we used to travel to 15 or 20 different states each year, we are gradually cutting back and adapting as we are getting older. Don't get us wrong because the desire, want, and needs are still there, but because of the changes in our abilities as we age we had to learn to adapt to these changes. We are now down to hunting just buried gold and diamonds instead of all the other items we used to hunt, but that is okay with the two of us.

As people can now understand that adapting to changes whether it be caused by aging or by some other event that has taken place in one's life there is no reason to become discouraged as this is just the natural development of things to come as one ages. Being willing to adapt and adjusting to changes, whenever and regardless of what the changes may be, can make all the difference in one's remaining retirement years.

# DOLLAR COST AVERAGING OR RAVAGING

We have all read or heard of "Dollar Cost Averaging," but we, as well as others, refer to it as "Dollar Cost Ravaging." In our opinion this is just a waste of time and can cause more problems than one can imagine. Everyone hears and reads about dollar cost averaging that is based on a specific amount of one's retirement monies, but the problem is that the majority of people do not fall into these categories. For anyone to suggest that someone should withdraw a certain amount from their retirement savings account is probably the most ridiculous things we have heard of over the years from these so called experts of which there is no such thing as an expert in our society.

In our opinion anyone can become an expert providing that they have a sufficient amount of experience, training, or knowledge in any given area of their endeavor or one may have obtained a particular skill over a period of years. In other words anyone can call themselves an expert in any given field, but the question is whether or not they are proficient at what they say or do? From our experience no one is an expert even though they think they are unless they know something or can do something that no one else knows or can do.

For an example, as the writer of the ***"Home Buying & Finance 101 Second Edition"*** book, technically, I could call myself the foremost leading expert in the world concerning the Negative Adjustable Loan and that would probably be an accurate description of myself, but would that be accurate? My answer would be no because now thousands of people also maintain the same knowledge as I had before they bought or read my book themselves thereby disqualifying me as the leading expert concerning this particular mortgage loan. Okay, enough about the semantics relating to so called experts. Let's just say these so called experts may or may not know what they are talking about when it comes to the accuracy of any given subject matter when it comes to reality. A classic example would be the so called pandemic experts who knew absolutely nothing, but they pretended they did when all of them were wrong. Need we say more?

Anyways, attempting to set a certain percentage figure and telling people that this percentage figure is the figure one should use to regulate their retirement income on does not make any sense. The reason it doesn't make any sense is due to the fact that these so called experts have no idea of what any one person's particular situation may be when they retire. However, if these financial people indicate that using a 4 percent figure would be a reasonable figure, one might start with that figure as a reasonable figure knowing that one may find they need to use a greater or lesser figure in which to withdraw from their retirement accounts.

Whereas one could start with a 2 or 3 percent monthly figure and others might be able to consider that they could withdraw 5 or 6 percent or more from their retirement accounts as it all depends on one's financial capabilities. What we are trying to point out is that everyone will have a different financial situation and therefore they will require different strategies based one's needs and requirements.

To give people and example, in our particular situation when we finally reached retirement age at 62 and even though one of us had retired twenty years earlier, things had changed financially for us that we now had to consider refiguring our financial situation and started living on 20 percent of our savings in the beginning of this change. However, when the other one of us retired at age 65 and started drawing their social security monthly checks, a few years later we were able to withdraw more because our financial situation had changed again. Therefore, we again refigured our withdrawal figure and ended up withdrawing 45 percent from our retirement accounts because we had an extra four years of savings that we had added to our retirement funds. And here we are today 11 years later and we have stayed at the 50 percent monthly withdrawal rate and we just save the other 50 percent and keep extending and adding to our retirement accounts.

Now, let's talk about the hazards of dollar-cost ravaging that can effect one's retirement. If retirees have established unrealistic income goals and they use the wrong percentage figures as a withdrawal rate figure, people could have disastrous repercussions as opposed to dollar-cost averaging where people constantly are draining their retirement account or accounts and not paying attention to what they are doing. If people do not have a financial plan at the beginning of their retirement they can end up with disastrous results down the road simply because they have unreasonable income expectations. There are many factors that can come into play in one's retirement that can add or deduct from a retiree's financial longevity in their retirement.

Likewise, some will try to convince people that they are living longer and therefore they should plan accordingly, but that statement is incorrect because people are not necessarily living longer according to our government's death statistics. Currently, the majority of men pass by 78 and the majority women pass by 82. Granted some will live into their 80's. 90's, and even into their 100's, but very few will survive that long. Therefore, it is not necessary for retiree's to try and take on more and more financial risk in an attempt to gain more wealth whether it be in terms of money or other investments like stocks and bonds. However, we have not known anyone having an insight into one's demise where they can determine when they will be called back home, so to speak.

For retirees who invest in the markets, they should be prepared for the ups and downs that all of us have been exposed to and how something like this can affect their portfolios, but one needs to be prepared in the event of a larger than normal turndown in the stock markets. Nevertheless, when retirees have spent more money than what they are taking in, it is referred to as dollar-cost ravaging and this will make it harder for retirees to recover from their losses, be it stock market losses or their personal financial losses from their retirement accounts. Nonetheless, it is important for retirees to constantly keep an eye on their investments whether they are in cash, stock, or bonds and continuously adjust them as necessary as time goes on.

One final item retirees should be made aware of is to make sure they maintain the correct balance between their investments and their bank accounts because one's financial wellbeing is probably the largest investment in one's retirement in the short or long run one will have to deal with other than their health and medical care. In our opinion, these are probably the two most important areas in anyone's retirement because neglecting any one of these areas can have a disastrous outcome for anyone planning to retire or who are already in retirement. When people are younger they have years on their side to recover should something occur that affects their portfolios. However, as people get closer to retirement or are in retirement they will not have the luxury of time on their side and conserving their finances becomes more important. Adjusting one's portfolio when they are close to retirement or in retirement will be crucial. Likewise, making sure people's portfolios are diversified among different investments such as stocks, bonds, and other financial assets can assist people should the markets take a turn for the worst. It is our recommendation that one reviews their portfolio every six and 12 months to make sure they are up to date to meet their needs. The goal of this situation is to make sure that one is maintaining preservation of one's financial well being throughout their retirement years so as to not end up in a wanting or needing situation as long as they remain in their retirement.

# NEVER MAKE INVESTMENT DECISIONS BASED ON EMOTIONS

This is an area that we learned the hard way and we ended up losing a considerable amount of money all because we did not control our emotions. Investing in a particular stock that had amazing write-ups caught our attention and we began our research into this particular stock and it appeared to get better and better as we read. Not only did the stock look appealing, but this particular stock had the backing of a major foundation with the owner's being people that we had been aware of for sometime listening to the business news reports. Not having found anything wrong with this company we decided to buy 5000 shares of stock, then another 5000 shares and the information being put out by this company indicated that this stock was about to break wide open very soon. So, like a dummy, letting our emotions run-a-way, we bought 5000 more, then 5000 more, and finally 5000 more shares all based on emotions and the thought of becoming well off enough to do anything we wanted anytime we wanted in a very big way. Unfortunately, things did not turn out the way we expected and instead of this stock breaking out big time, the company announced it was going do to a 20 to 1 reverse stock split.

Needless to say we managed to exit the stock before the split thereby salvaging what we could financially. In addition, we had learned a very valuable lesson and that was to never again buy stock based on believing all the hype and getting emotionally involved in any stock again. Yes, we lost a lot of money on this stock that was originally bought for our kids to inherit when we passed, but unfortunately, this event did not turn out the way we had expected. The moral of this event taught us to never buy more than 10,000 shares of any stock again, never buy based on emotions, and never become greedy based on any company no matter how much advertising hype they put out and to discard their backers no matter how many millions they have or have invested in any particular company because they are just gambling like everyone else.

# NEVER PANIC IN A BEAR MARKET

We hear this all the time and we see this happen all the time and yet we have never been able to figure why this occurs until recently. Why do people panic when they hear or suspect there might be a bear market the same as they do when they hear of a possible recession? Simple, it is a matter of emotions caused by the creation of negativity by the media or someone else who is supposedly a so-called expert who got lucky at one time or another picking a stock or calling the DOW or some other ridiculous situation that occurred in which they were lucky and were correct, and such an event makes them an expert? People should understand that they can all be experts doing the same thing these so called experts do, providing one gets lucky and is correct in their forecast or forecasts providing they come true.

That being said, people should just ride out a bear market because bear markets usually do not last that long. Looking back at 1929 when the stock market crashed and people were panicking and some of them off themselves for no other reason, the stock market rebounded in only six months. Granted the Great Depression lasted a lot longer, but the point being made is that one should never panic and sell off in a bear market. We have gone through a few bear markets in the last fifty plus years since we were in our twenties and the stock market has always come back stronger than before. The same scenario has occurred over and over again and the last bad recession we had was the financial recession starting in 2008 and still having repercussions even to this day in 2020, but the stock market rebounded and is stronger than ever. The bottom line is to stay in the stock market should we enter a bear market and don't panic because it is just a matter of time before we will come out of it again in time. Now, for those of you who invest, you already know that investing in a bear market is to your advantage because one can find some very good deals that will allow them to become wealthier in the long run. However, we found that trying to time the bear market is a complete waste of time and one is better off dollar-cost averaging their stock picks until the bear market ends.

# VIEW MONEY AS A TOOL AND NOT AS A NECESSITY

The main problem we have encountered, especially with the younger people and the newly retired people, and those who retire earlier than 65 is that they don't view money as a tool, but rather as a necessity. It is true that everyone needs money to buy things, but is it necessary to indulge in wasteful spending? To give the readers a better idea of what we are talking about we will give them another example. We are health nuts and buy various vitamins all the time, but we restrict ourselves to spending no more than $200.00 in any one month period. My wife and I sat down and discussed this situation and agreed not to spend more than the $200.00 mentioned above on anything over two hundred dollars as we would have to rethink our ordering process.

Just recently my wife and I looked at our vitamin inventory and we each indicated the vitamins that we needed to repurchase to maintain our requirements to replenish our inventory. After totaling everything, she came up with a little over $400.00 dollars worth of vitamin cost, which was way to much to spend on vitamins in one month. Nevertheless, we went through our list again and cut back on the quantities of vitamins and ended up with $137.00 dollars worth of vitamins and then found out that she had already spent another $119.00 that she didn't tell me about. So we ended up spending $256.00 dollars instead of $137.00 dollars. Even though that does not cause a problem financially, it does cause a problem because now we can only spend a total of $144.00 next month on our vitamins less the $56.00 that was over spent this month that will then level out our out going vitamin expense back down to our normal $200.00 per month limit. It is true that some people have to learn the hard way and trying to hide things is not the right way to run a house-hold. I told my wife that had I known this before hand we could have made the necessary adjustments instead of having to overspend on our budget. After all that is what a budget is all about and it is called conservative spending, which is our next subject.

Because we view money as a tool in order to buy the things we need instead of wanting, desiring, or impulse buying items that we may only use once or twice and then discard them because we no longer need or want whatever it was that we purchased can make all the difference in the world, especially, to retirees. Nevertheless, we have found that the older we get the less money we require and instead of buying more things we are now selling certain items that we no longer use or need and all of this money goes into our retirement accounts. Eventually, we may sell one of our three vehicles, but we are not tired of them yet and as long as they work, we are in no hurry to get rid of them and we have no desire to buy any new vehicles because they are a waste of money. Viewing money as a tool and not as a necessity or as a luxury will change a person's perspective about money simply because money will no longer run one's life.

# SPENDING CONSERVATIVELY

We kind of hinted about this all throughout this book, but learning to spend conservatively can become a major factor for any and all retirees, especially, as they age. However, the trick will not necessarily require spending conservatively, but rather conserving their money as more and more people attempt to con or extort money from the elderly. Having a plan will also assist people in conserving their wealth. A particular situation of aging is not being aware of what is going on around people all the time whereas when they are younger people pay attention to what is going on most of the time. On the other hand the aging retirees will have the tendency to forget, ignore, and may overlook several things when it comes to spending conservatively, and unfortunately, that may lead to major financial setbacks if someone is not looking out for them. Not only is it too bad for the retirees, but it is also sad to have to give up someone's rights to do what they have always been accustomed to doing for themselves all their lives. Nonetheless, it is to their advantage to have planned ahead and selected someone that is honest and can assist aging retirees so that they don't lose their financial retirement incomes that they worked so hard for over the years.

The big question that all retirees need to ask themselves when thinking conservatively is whether or not they really need what they are about to spend their monies on? In our particular situation we always look over whatever it is that we are thinking about buying and then wait a week or so and then decide if we really need any particular items we maybe contemplating buying. After a week or two if we decide that whatever it was that we were looking at will satisfy a need, then we will search for and negotiate for the best price. On the other hand, if we decide after a couple of weeks that we really don't need whatever it was that we looked at to buy, then we just keep our money for another time. In other words, don't buy on impulse because it is just a waste of one's money and learn to spend conservatively and do without some-thing that one never needed in the first place.

Retirees need to discuss their needs and wants before spending their monies and the best way to do this that we have found is by writing down certain questions that will address these situations. Once we have a clear understanding of what we need or want then we weigh all of the pro's and con's concerning our subject matter, then we decide whether or not to purchase this item through negations if it is expensive, over a thousand dollars, or do we buy it outright if it is under a thousand dollars. We use this process every time when we decide to buy anything because it has become a habit for us, having used this process for over 50 years. Our process is simple and to the point and does no require major time for us to reach a decision concerning anything that we buy or don't buy and it all revolves around spending conservatively.

# DON'T LET CHILDREN RUIN ONE'S RETIREMENT

Kids can become a major drain on their parents retirement, especially, if their kids are still in college, if they go to college, and the parents took out 10, 15, or 20 year loans in order to finance their kids college education, they may want to rethink their decision. In this event it would be wise to try and payback these loans before one reaches retirement age in the event that one's kids are unable to pay back these loans. Therefore, it is wise to have your kids sign for their educational loans and not the parents and never co-sign for these student loans by leveraging one's home. In our opinion, kids should learn responsibility on their own and not encumber their parents if at all possible because this can cause several problems down the road. If kids want to go to college they should go to a local junior college and then transfer to a college of their choice that they can afford, if they qualify. This is exactly what we did with our daughter and she graduated from a major University in Southern California two years later and she paid all of her bills by working in summer working part time while going to college. Question, was it worth while for her? Not right away and it took about 1.5 to 2 years for her to get a good job which has led to a fantastic position with a major company and she has made major advancements since then, telling us that we did our jobs well as parents.

Another reason people may delay their retirement is because they had their children later in life and their children may still need their assis-tance. If at all possible avoid this situation at all costs because kids that still require assistance will be throwing up a major road block to one's retirement. If people raise their kids properly, kids will have the ability to take care of themselves, especially, if they start their own families. There is also another great book that we published that deals with these situations and more called *"Making Parenting Simple Handbook"* also available on **amazon.com** if people are interested.

# BEWARE OF TOO MUCH DEBT GOING INTO RETIREMENT

People thinking about retiring or who are already retired and have not paid off their home can be in for a difficult time once they are in retirement, along with carrying credit card and other debt in the way of vehicle payments along with other debts. Unfortunately for us, when we retired we had moved to another state and bought a newly built home on an acre of land and even though we had made a considerable downpayment we still had a 30-year loan to deal with. Nevertheless, we made it our first priority to pay this loan off as soon as possible. Even though it took us five years to pay the home off we had also bought a new vehicle that we then made our second priority and 6 months later the vehicle was paid off too. Once we became debt free we no longer had to concern ourselves with any debt and since we had been using debit cards for several years instead of credit cards we were pretty much debt free except for taxes and insurance that we now pay once a year in full.

When we thought about it we were only 58 and the other one was 65. So technically, having a 30-year home loan would have made us 88 years old and the other 95 years old by the time we had paid our home loan off. Now, maybe one of us could have lived that long to pay off our home loan, but rather then take the chance we elected to pay the home loan off as soon as we could and that turned out to be a great decision. Not only are we not big on having debt, but now we can see the results over the years of being debt free. What people need to realize is that debt held by 50-to-85-year-olds has been on the rise and retirees have been filing for bankruptcies in massive numbers. According to the Center for Microeconomics Data more than 60 percent of retirees are in debt that they can't get out of simply because they did not have a financial plan to follow in their retirement years. Having a debt free environment in retirement can make one's savings explode to heights that one can only hope for while in their retirement years.

Now we come to the people who are afraid they won't have enough money to retire on and one would definitely not be alone if one does not have a written financial plan they can follow to let them know how far their retirement monies will take them in certain situations. On the other hand, this is kinda of a misnomer because no one can predict the length of time one will live in their retirement years. Therefore, people can only project for the future and hope and pray that they will live as long or longer than they estimated. In this situation one can figure what their cost of retirement will be and if that does not become true for them, then they should make sure they have made a Will or a Trust that they will be able to leave their remaining assets to in the event they pass away before their calculated time factor runs out.

People, the variables one will face in retirement are unpredictable and will constantly be changing and if one does not have a financial plan it is very easy to fall into a maze. Likewise, getting out of this maze will require planning, fortitude, persistence, and one's desire to be able to change their situation around because the only alternate is to join the other 60 some percent of retirees in bankruptcies. Don't be afraid to ask for help from one's banker, stock broker, or find someone who knows what they are doing and ask them for help. Some people may want to talk to an advisor, but we are against this because the majority of them just want control of one's monies. Bankers or stock brokers can offer one very valuable information at no cost once one has established a rapport with them. However, this has all been discussed in our other book on "HOW TO ESTABLISH YOUR CREDIT" and can be purchased on Amazon. Nevertheless, the bottom line is to try to enter one's retirement as debt free as possible, which will make one's retirement much more enjoyable and allow them to do the things they need, want, or desire for themselves. By becoming as debt free as possible in one's retirement will also allow them to be able to recalculate their funds much more easily because the less debt they have the more money they will have to spend the way they want.

# AVOID BUYING DEPRECIATING ASSETS

This is an area of retirement that has been way overlooked by just about everyone and is a major cause that can lead to several retirement financial problems. For example, how many people ever looked at all those motorhomes that are on the roads of America? How many ever noticed the people that are driving these units? The vast majority of these people are retired seniors who believed they would travel the country once they retired. Do people know how much these motorhomes can cost? Do people know how much the up keep can cost yearly? Do people realize that they will be required to empty their black and grey holding tanks when they become full and be required to refill their water tanks? Now people may understand why these motorhomes are constantly being resold with very little milage on them and little to any wear and tear on these units. The reason being is that seniors and other people are only told by a sales person that these are your black and grey tanks, but neglect to mention what is required to keep these holding tanks clean and fresh. Unfortunately, retirees have to learn the hard way and when the majority of them find out what is involved after their first one or two trips they become frustrated and fed up with their new motorhome and end up taking a bath on the resale of these coaches.

The bad part about this is that all the while they were figuring out how these motorhomes work and function, their units were depreciating big time and no one told them about that either. In other words, the retirees bought a huge depreciating asset and didn't even realize it at the time. As time goes on for them their dreams of traveling the country fade away along with their monies until they take a bath trying to sell their motorhomes back to the multiple dealers that are on the market every year just waiting to take advantage of them as they steal these units for peanuts.

To give the readers another example, we bought a new 35 foot 2001 motorhome in 2002 when we were 53 and 60 years old because we needed room for our treasure hunting equipment. However, the first problem we had was to find a place where we could park our motorhome. The next thing we had to do was outfit the unit the way we wanted and that was expensive. Even though we used the unit for eight years and we drove it to our new home in Texas in 2007 where it sat for the next 3 years until we turned it back to the lender even though we had listed the unit for sale for 3 years. Naturally, the lender tried to collect our outstanding balance even though the unit was now valued at $22,000 and we had paid $68,000 eight years ago. Since it was a new year and the lender was still trying to collect on the outstanding balance, we wrote a letter to the lender stating that we were not going to send them anymore money for the motorhome. On top of that, we told the lender that if they had already written off their loss on the motorhome that we would report them to the IRS for extortion if they insisted on bothering us anymore. We also stated that if they attempted to ruin our credit rating that we would then have them investigated by California's Attorney General office. Needless to say, we never heard from them again nor anymore collection companies and our credit remained just fine as the lender reported that we had paid in full. It is also nice to know a little about the law.

In other words people, think about what you would want to do and then check it out before one makes a final decision to buy a depreciating asset. That goes for all new vehicles regardless of what they are, jewelry and anything else that might be considered as a depreciating asset. If an item loses money, it is a depreciating asset and retirees definitely don't need to lose any more of their finances while in retirement. Granted that there are a lot more things that retirees need to be aware of, but we will only be indicating one more that retirees need to be on the alert for in their retirement which is listed in the next chapter.

One more thing that seniors should know about motorhomes before they decide to purchase one is to rent one and take a trip. By doing this seniors will learn and find out if they really want to buy a motorhome for themselves. Granted it will cost to rent a motorhome, but it will be well worth it rather than taking a chance of losing a lot more of one's money on a major depreciating asset that one knew nothing about in the first place just to live up to the "JONES." We had a reason for buying our motorhome and needed the extra space for our equipment at the time for treasure hunting, but we had to learn the hard way about the massive deprecation these motorhomes are subjected to in the market place. Even though we had bought a brand new motorhome and used it for a little over eight years the unit had depreciated by 46 thousand dollars or by 60 percent of its purchase value. Had we bought the motorhome at the original price we would have lost a little over 84 percent just in depreciation alone, not to mention the cost of the up keep for 8 years. In other words, unless one really needs a motorhome for some purpose, they need to realize that a motorhome is a total waste of one's monies, but if one has money to throw around in retirement and they want a motorhome then feel free to buy one.

Motorhomes are not an investment, but rather it is an investment as well as a large money losing investment as long as one owns their motorhome. Therefore, one needs to take their time and investigate and determine if they are interested in spending large amounts of money buying one of these major depreciating losing assets in the way of a motorhome. The chances of anyone getting their money's worth back when it comes time to sell their motorhome is slim to none and one should be prepared to take a major loss regardless of what they may think. However, if one still wants to buy a Class "A, B, or C" motorhome, buy as cheap as possible, buy used, and sell cheap when one is done with their motorhome and hopefully one will not lose too much money and will have enjoyed their motorhome adventures.

# THIRTEEN

# BE ON THE ALERT FOR SCAMS

Scams can be one of the biggest downfalls for retirees because they are responsible for taking billions of dollars away from unsuspecting retired seniors every year. A lot of the scams are the same scams used over and over, only with a new twist and new scams are always in the making. Therefore, retired seniors need to be on alert and be able to detect a scam when or if they recognize one. Granted that scams are becoming more and more sophisticated each year, but they all have the same common denominator and that is to take as much money away from people as they can. Even though most scams are targeting people over the age of 62, everyone is at risk of being scammed, especially, when it comes to telemarketers and computer scammers.

All people need to be aware of these diabolical scammers and even though they are not unintelligent, they will prey on anyone, especially, the seniors because they may be lonely or feel isolated making them trusting, or their thought processes may be dwindling that can impair their judgement. Scam criminals are always looking for and using old and new scams all the time in order to relieve people of their hard earned monies and they are largely targeting the seniors. The reason they target the elderly is because they usually maintain most of the money in our society and for a variety of other reasons. Unfortunately, the biggest targets are the elderly widows because they are usually lonely and they get the immediate attention of these con artist even to the point of showering them with simple gifts in order to gain their trust and attention. Therefore, it is imperative for family members to stay in touch with their aging parents and be involved in their lives if possible.

Let's look at some of the areas where seniors lose billions of dollars every year to IRS scams, home repair scams, and investment scams and a whole lot more the we will be cover in this chapter.

# THE IRS SCAM

Usually, seniors will get a call from someone impersonating an IRS agent. They may be requesting or demanding one's personal information or stating that one has unpaid back taxes. Sometimes the scammers may attempt to order one to pay a fine or they may even attempt to threaten a person with lawsuits, or that one will be arrested, or indicate that they will freeze one's bank account, or even threaten to suspend one's driver's license. Be aware that these are all ploys by these scammers in order to get one's monies, and in fact, these scammers gained over 6 million dollars just from this one scam alone.

People, the IRS DOES NOT contact people by telephone or email and NEVER call back an unknown number, in fact, anyones first contact with the IRS is always by mail, and there will never be any threats by any IRS agents. However, should one be in collection or owe back taxes with the IRS, they may contact you in person by knocking on your door, but not likely. In the event that this happens be sure to ask the person for a photo ID, and then call the nearest IRS office to verify that this person is really a representative of the IRS, while they wait outside

# THE HOME REPAIR SCAM

More than likely a person will knock on one's door claiming to be a contractor indicating that they are either working on and repairing someone's roof in your neighborhood and offer to repair your roof or repair your driveway while in the area. They might indicate that you need new siding or a facelift on your garage, or your gutters, and anything else they think a homeowner would believe including pest control. Granted that one could ask to see their contractor's license, but that can easily be duplicated and falsified, so that would be a waste of time. However, never and we mean never agree to any on the spot repairs from someone you don't know. Likewise, have them give you specifics concerning the name of the person in your neighborhood who is having work done by this person and then go check it out for yourself; and don't forget to ask the name of the neighbor who is having the work done and their recommendation. There are many cons that can be used to attempt to get someone's monies in these scams.

# THE INVESTMENT SCAMS

There are a multitude of investment scams that can involve fake financial advisors, pyramid scams, Ponzi scams, Church scams, fraudulent complex scams, and others that are all designed to get one's monies. Some of these scams are so elaborate that they will even go to the lengths of offering FREE lunches for attending such elaborate scams. Nevertheless, because several legitimate real estate and financial investment services market their opportunities and promotions using this same approach, one must be extremely diligent in discerning when attending these events; so be sure to ask a lot of questions and then check them out at various government facilities to validate their legitimacy.

One may be offered an affinity fraud where one is offered an opportunity or a free trip that allows one to invest in an elaborate scheme scam. One might be asked to take advantage of a cheap stock, or one may be offered a once-in-a-lifetime deal to invest in some deep sea exploration that will rake in billions in a year or two. Churches are also a great target for scammers, especially, where they have a lot of seniors attending because these are fairly wealthy churches. The goal here, is to gain the respect and trust of the congregation and indicating that a considerable percentage of the congregation's investments will be guaranteed to go back to their church if they invest into this secured investment.

These people are usually given several reasons and reasonings to base their decisions on such as they could lose their social security benefit which could be cut off, or that the return on this investment could give them more than enough money that they could out live their retirement funds, or that they would now be able to afford their health care costs, etc. In this kind of fraud situation Pastors, Ministers, and Elders of the church may become involved or be part of this scan in exchange for monies now and in the future by way of future offerings and future promises of further monetary rewards. It should be noted that several churches have been convicted across the US for being implicated and promoting such scheming scams on their unsuspecting congregations.

# THE GRANDPARENT SCAM

This is a very popular scam and probably the most widely used senior scam used by scammers today. A scammer will place a call to an older person pretending to be a grand child or great grand child in dire need of money. It goes something like this, Hi Grandpa or Grandma, do you know who this is? When the unsuspecting grandparent attempts to guess the name of the grandchild, right then and there they are had because the caller has now established a fake identity without having to do any background checking. Once the relationship is established the imposter will generally ask for money stating that they are in some kind of trouble and need money for bail, rent, or for some other reason and ask that the money be sent by Western Union. A new version of this scam is that the scammers will say they have been kidnapped and tell the grandparent that they need money to pay the kidnappers. These scam artists are a little more sophisticated in that they usually obtained more information about the grandchild either by calling them, knowing them, or through some media source like Facebook where they gained more information about them. The scammers may also be able to have someone impersonate their grandchild's voice giving the call more authenticity. If these scammers are really smart they will have called the real grandchild and tell them that they have to turn off their phone for a certain time period because they are from the cell phone company and they need to perform some maintenance task. Once the phone is off the scammers place the call to their grandparents thereby insuring that the grandparents cannot make any contact with their grandchild to verify the story.

The main thing to remember is to never send any money to anyone or anywhere until one can verify the whereabouts of their grandchild either through their parents, relatives, or friends. Seniors need to be careful because some of the smarter scam artists will have gathered information about you, your relatives, and friends from social media sources, so don't be surprised if scammers know several details about your lives. The first thing to do is to tell them you will have to call them back and then hang up. If that doesn't work, be sure to have a password established with your grandchild or ask for something only your grandchild would know about you. Never, ever, give in to any caller you can't verify before sending any money to anyone in these situations. Your goal is to get the facts about the situation and verify as much as one can before being taken in by these scammers in these situations, better to just hang-up.

# FINANCIAL SCAMS

This area covers several classifications of financial scams including Financial Advisors or Planners as some of them refer to themselves, Fake Check scams, Grant scams, House and Vacation Rental Property scams, Payday Loan scams, Timeshare scams, Affinity and Securities scams just to name a few. So let's get started going over these financial scams.

# FINANCIAL ADVISORS OR PLANNERS SCAMS

Starting with the financial advisor or planner scammers, seniors need to be aware that these people do not need to be licensed or even maintain any kind of a college degree in order to advertise as being a financial advisor or planner to be able to open their doors for business. These people can have all sorts of fake degrees hanging on their office walls attempting to give the impression that they are legitimate and qualified to offer all kinds of advice in order to get one's business. Nevertheless, one needs to be cautious when interviewing these people and be sure to have a list of questions to ask them concerning your particular situation. As an example, when we decided to start investing years ago we wanted advice on how to go about investing the way we wanted in order to satisfy our wants and desires for our retirement. With that being said, we made a list of all the financial advisors and planners in our area and made appointments to interview and talk with them.

During our interviews with these people we discovered that very few of them really knew anything about what we wanted to achieve, but all of them put on a good show trying to convince us that they were the only one's qualified to handle our finances. Needless to say, we never hired any of these people and ended up going with a stock broker that was with a small firm while living in California. Today, some 40 years later we are still with this stock broker even though he is now with a major national firm and has been promoted to vice president at his location. The beauty part of this relationship is that we get all the information we need, anytime we need it, and he has never misled us thus far.

Even though everything has been fine with our broker, seniors have to be careful, even with trusted professionals. We have heard and read of several incidents where all people, especially, seniors have been taken advantage of and ended up losing large sums of money because they did not keep up on their investments. One case in particular that stood out for us was an incident that took place by a financial advisor who had known the client's father for over 25 years. As the father aged and the children got involved, the kids started reviewing the father's statements and wondered why a certain amount of money was being used each month, but was not matching up with the investments figures. So the kids decided to call the financial institution and ask them what they were doing with the $60,000 their parents were sending them each month.

To make a long story short, the kids were told that the institution was only receiving $30,000 per month and that the distributions were regular and sufficient. As it turned out, their financial advisor had been taking the other $30,000 out of the distribution for herself. Come to find out that this had been going on for several years. After the financial advisor was convicted of fraud and embezzlement and the financial institution had to reimbursed the clients account, the institution was able to recover over 50% of the funds that were misappropriated by this now convicted financial advisor.

All people, especially, seniors need to pay close attention to the monies coming and going out of their accounts regardless of what type of accounts one may have. Just because financial advisors or planners maintain excellent credentials, experience, and give one the impression that they will be acting in one's best interest, may not always turn out to be who they say they are. One should also ask for references, client references, and anything else one deems necessary to verify that these financial advisors or planners are who they say they are. Should one not be diligent in verifying the legitimacy of these people, all and anyone can be taken advantage of, and even lose their investments in the event that these financial advisors or planners decide to close up shop and leave for another unsuspecting area in or out of one's state.

# CHECK SCAMS

Check scams are some of the more popular scams that the con artist are using, They use these fraudulent checks to convince people to exchange their checks for cash. Most of these scammers will use emails, but seniors can also be conned on a personal basis. The goal of these scammers is to convince people that they are having a hard time cashing their checks for some reason or another, and would someone or anyone be kind enough to accept their check in exchange for cash? These scammers also are likely to offer someone an added bonus for their trouble in helping them out of a jam. People, don't fall for this because the check will bounce and one will be left with no ability to reclaim their cash monies. Remember, there has to be a legitimate reason for one not to be able to cash a check at any bank, financial institution, or checking facility as long as one has legitimate personal identification. If one is approached by one of these scammers don't hesitate to deny exchanging money for checks from someone you don't know.

# THIRTEEN
# SECTION II
# GRANT SCAMS

These scammers will present themselves as government officials after they have obtained legitimate information from the various corporations in our country. These businesses are usually told that they will have an opportunity to offer financial assistance to their customers that maintain serious debt issues. These scammers then offer the opportunity to gain "GRANT" money for a processing fee. The goal of this scam is to get people to give up their savings for a chance of gaining a new lease on life. However, once the scam has been completed, all of one's personal information will be sold to the highest bidder in the black market. Since people having serious debt problems will try anything to get back in good standing, especially, seniors that are going broke as they make the best targets.

# HOUSE AND RENTAL
# PROPERTY SCAMS

Because of our housing market, future property owners may choose renting a home or other properties and the scam artists are always looking for these people. This is a relatively new trend that targets Millennials, Generation X, and the Generation Z prospects along with the retired Baby Boomers. These scam artists will advertise nonsense and fantasy properties along with appealing pictures including all the details of said properties. Naturally, the rental fees will be considerably below the current market in order to attract the most renters. However, the phone number will be local, but transferred a foreign country and after one has made an agreement, the first rent money will be made through a money transfer process normally through Western Union. Don't fall for these fake scams.

# PAYDAY LOAN SCAMS

This scam usually affects the lower class of people and those that are in dire financial straights, or maintain a lot of debt, making them extremely vulnerable to these types of scams. Payday loan scams are extremely high risk identity theft loan scams, not to mention very high interest rate loans. Normally people will see ads in throwaways papers, tabloids, from several phony websites that are designed to grab one's attention by stating that anyone can get out of debt by applying for a loan. Once these people are approved for a low-interest loan they are told, in order for them to immediately access the monies they have to pay a security fee. When the person ask what the security fee is for, they are told the fee is for checking and verifying that the person has the necessary income to repay the loan.

This is where the identity theft risk comes into play because they may also ask for the indicated bank account information in order for them to setup a means for a direct deposit to be made into one's account. People need to be alert and very cautious if they find themselves in these situations because their personal information can be compromised and either used or sold on the black market for other scammers to use at a later date. Should anyone find themselves in this situation we highly recommend that they obtain identity theft protection and if they don't have the money to pay for something like Life-lock, one can receive a free 30 day coverage by calling Experian, or visit them on the internet.

# TIMESHARE INVESTMENTS AND RESALE SCAMS

Timeshares have been one of the biggest rip offs for years not to mention being taken advantage of 3 or 4 more times by crooks stating that they can assist one in selling their timeshare properties. We have been telling people for over five decades that timeshares are one of the biggest ripoffs in the real estate market. Think about it for a minute, why would anyone want to share an ideal vacation resort property that they can use for only two weeks out of the year? It makes absolutely no sense to waste one's monies on such a scam. Then when one tries to resell their timeshare property the nightmare begins all over again because the scammers come out in force as they smell the money to be made. These crooks will attempt to sell an owner their timeshare for huge profits, but first the owners have to pay up front fees. These fees can include but not limited to new appraisal fees, advertising fees, title search fees, closing fees, broker fees and other administration fees.

In addition, people maybe told that they will get all their money back when their timeshare sells, but don't believe anything one hears unless they are willing to put it in writing, signed, and dated. In order for one to protect themselves, be sure to read any contracts before one signs because once they sign, the contract becomes binding. We recommend that one takes a copy of the contract to their attorney to review before signing, as a little bit of money can save one thousands of dollars in the long run. One last note, if anyone tells you that you will make far more than what you paid for your timeshare, they will be lying through their teeth. If one makes a few pennies on the dollars they spent, consider yourself lucky. It is also worthy to note that all real estate agents only get paid upon the closing of any sale and not before.

# AFFINITY AND SECURITIES FRAUD SCAMS

Affinity fraud scams mostly target ethnic groups all across the United States. They can also include various fraternal organizations where the con artist gains access to an event or organization by means of a close friend, in order to sell or promote fraudulent investment products. Whereas Securities fraud scams can be perpetrated on anyone by offering someone promissory notes or other security devices in exchange for money that is to be invested in an investment that will supposedly present returns of anywhere from 9% to 15% at some specified time in the future. The problem with this scam is that it will be very hard to discern its validity because the offer usually comes from a friend, or someone a person trust, or told that the offer is coming from an attorney, banker, or another trusted source that may or may not exist. With that said, one's only recourse is to maintain the sagacity to be able to differentiate if the offer is too good to be true. If it is, then one can walk away from the deal. The problem with this scam is due to the fact that most of these seniors will be extremely older, usually in their late 80's or 90's making them too old to be able to make a rational decision and they will be taken advantage of by these scammers. This is a good example why family members should stay in touch with their senior parents, never in a nagging fashion, but in an inquisitive manner to make sure one's older parent or parents are still sound of mind, especially, the older they become in their retirement years once they approach their late 80's or 90's and even once they are in their 100's or older if that is the case.

# MEDICARE AND HEALTH CARE SCAMS

As more and more people are getting ready to retire or entering retirement as well as those that have already been retired, these scams are becoming more and more prevalent and will continue to be so in the future. Usually, these scams are being perpetrated by scammers using the telephone where they indicate that they are health care or medicare representatives and are attempting to get access to one's personal information.

This can include anything from talking about the Affordable Care Act (ACA) and requesting money to assist one by guiding them through all the different areas of the ACA that they are entitled to, offering medicare refund checks, or that one needs a new Medicare card in an attempt to get one's social security number, or they may tell seniors that they will call them back at later date. They may even offer to assist seniors with getting discount medical insurance. When the scammers call back they will state that they have spoken with one of your family members, ie, Son, Daughter, or some other relative and tell you that it is okay to give them one's security numbers, driver's license numbers and any other personal information that these scammers can get and use. They may even go door-to-door to solicit the information they are seeking. Some of these scams are directed at Medicare instead of the seniors, but they can include conning the seniors into becoming unknowing accomplices.

Currently, and as mentioned before, the biggest scam now seems to be when these scam artists are promoting the Medicare refund check scam that is supposed to cover the gap in one's covered prescription drug program. Seniors are told that they will receive a check for $200 or $250 dollars, all designed to get one's details to be used for identity theft purposes. People, under no circumstances should anyone ever provide their confidential information over the telephone. In addition, one should ask for a call back number and then call Medicare and ask them if they are offering a check to reimburse one for any gaps in their prescription drug plan. If in fact that Medicare has sent out a reimbursement check, there will be no information required nor any telephone calls made to verify this transaction by Medicare. If people are ever in doubt, one should shut the door or hang up the phone on anyone attempting to extort money from them.

People may also see an advertisement in the papers or mostly on the internet or by phone by these scammers stating that seniors are entitled to all the credit and deductions they deserve including receiving very large refunds if they start filing now for free. This scam is designed to gain as much personal information as these con artist can get and then use one's scammed information to bill Medicare and keep the money according to the National Council on Aging. Furthermore, there are also health care scams that seniors need to be made aware of that may offer "Free Medical Supplies or Equipment" that will have hidden charges hidden in small print one has to sign. There may also be free medical test being offered that usually are not required or necessary.

# PRESCRIPTION AND ANTI-AGING DRUG SCAMS

Unfortunately, America uses more drugs than any other country in the world. In fact, the US only accounts for 5% of the world's population and yet its people consume 90% of the world's drugs. Our question is why? Simple, because the pharmaceutical companies offer to pay the medical doctors, and approximately 80% of the medical doctors are on the pharmaceutical companies payroll in exchange for them to get their clients on their drugs. Kind of a unique system we have here in the US today and their target, you guessed it, the seniors. It has been reported that the majority of seniors over 60 are on 10 to 18 or more drugs daily, weekly, or monthly that they have been prescribed by none other then their doctors. The sad part about this scenario is that these people think that these doctors are their friends. As long as doctors continue to make money from these people they will continue to prescribe drugs as long as they get compensated by the pharmaceutical companies. We have a simple solution that is known as "Stop Drugging America."

That being said, the majority of seniors have been put into a situation where they have to decide whether to buy their drugs or stop eating or vice versa because of the outrageous charges that the pharmaceutical companies are charging for their drugs now that they have been hooked. In turn, the seniors have been looking for cheaper drugs because they are on a fixed income. Because of this problem scammers are taking advantage of these defenseless seniors by targeting them by offering lower prices on these drugs. The scammers take their money and then never deliver, thereby jeopardizing these seniors lives.

Many seniors will also seek out online pharmacies that maintain a location outside the U. S. who then import these drugs from various countries in which the majority of these imported drugs that are nothing but phony imitations, which have little effect or more likely no effect at all, and again jeopardizing the lives of the seniors. Furthermore, the New York Times reported in one of their articles that 12% of all drugs imported from India are fake worthless drugs, and that around 45% of all U. S. pharmaceuticals are manufactured in India. This can also be true concerning drugs from China, South Korea, and Russia, although we don't have any percentage figures as of the time of this writing.

However, it would be wise for seniors not to buy their drugs from any overseas countries because other countries do not have the restrictions that America has concerning pharmaceutical companies and drug makers. Nevertheless, the FDA is placing several new regulations on foreign pharmacies that supply drugs to the U. S. and making them conform to the same standards of the America pharmaceutical makers. Nevertheless, Seniors need to be extremely careful and cautious when attempting to purchase prescription drugs from overseas pharmacies sources because one is playing Russian Roulette with their lives. If any of these drugs do not maintain certified certification or safety validations, these drugs could be inactive or outright dangerous because one never knows what they are really receiving from overseas companies and what the ingredients are that make up these drugs.

Another area in the health care is the Anti-Aging drug and products scams. As the population of seniors age, there is always a need for some to feel that they want or think they must look younger for one reason or other. And, if you are like most seniors who stay up late at night and watch a lot of TV they are inundated with a multitude of commercials advertising these fake products claiming to be the perfect products to rejuvenate one's aging or signs of aging. These commercials may also promote drug products that are supposed to aid in unwanted physical changes or problems. People need to learn to question these companies about their validity and call them first before sending them any money. Don't hesitate to ask for at least 3 references in one's area that have used their products. However, beware that these may be setup calls to people they have hired to mislead people in reference to their products. Seniors are always looking for new treatments, medications, AKA drugs, and other remedies that make them susceptible to these scammers.

These scams can function in different ways, including offering expensive treatments that can turn out to be homeopathic treatments that can be harmful to one's physical makeup or to their overall health and they do nothing more than take one's money. Scammers use the words like "Anti-Aging" as their marketing tool to attract attention to their products that can be completely phony in order to gain access to one's money. Whether it is like the fake Botox that was sold all over the U. S. that netted these scammers over 1.5 million in less than a year, or fake treatments and medication products that do absolutely nothing, there is big money to be made by scammers in the "Anti-Aging" business. People, and especially, seniors need to be aware that advertising for these products are designed to play on one's emotions, fears, and aspirations.

Nevertheless, one has to be very careful not to be maneuvered or influenced by these advertisement claims. To give people an example, we recently emailed a company that was advertising a rather expensive "Luxury Beauty Serum" by a company called Saint Jane out of California. After reading everything on their web site about this product, it sounded too good to be true. Nevertheless, a woman at this company apparently did not understand what I was asking for to be verified the first time I contacted her by email. Again, I sent a more direct email indicating what I wanted to know and this time I requested a direct and terse answers because I wanted to test their product out because it sounded like it would be great for my aging wife, who is now in her late seventies for her coming birthday. First, I asked this company several questions and after receiving their replies, I then asked for samples of their product. When their samples arrived, I had my wife try their samples and after a week or two my wife stated that the product seemed to be working as advertised and it did not bother her delicate facial skin as a redheaded woman, so we ordered this product and she loves it and her face is starting to glow and her facial wrinkles are starting to disappear making her look younger and younger. Naturally, I told my wife that for the price of this product it better do what it is supposed to do and so far it does. Therefore, we both now recommend this product because it definitely works should older women want to look younger.

People, the point of this conversation is to make sure of what one may be inclined to order, and as seniors ourselves we have the time to investigate any and all company claims before we order anything that is to good to be true. In this case we got lucky and therefore we are happy to spend the necessary extra money for a quality product that works. My wife looks better and better each and every day she uses this Saint Jane product and we will continue to order this "Luxury Beauty Serum" product as long as my wife wants to maintain her glowing facial radiance and beauty for years to come.

# COMPUTER SCAMS ALSO KNOWN AS TECH SUPPORT SCAMS

Since the majority of people today have a computer they will more than likely see pop-ups on their computer screens stating that your computer may be infected or is infected with a computer virus. Also, some people may be contacted by phone by someone claiming to be a representative of a high-tech computer company like Microsoft or Apple in an attempt to add credibility to themselves. Regardless of who these people may be, one will be told that their computer has been infected or could be under the threat of being infected by a malware virus that will or could cause severe damage to one's operating system. Most of these so called companies will have blocked phone numbers or they are from overseas scammers.

The next step of these scammers can be to offer people to download a program that will correct the problem, or one may be offered a free security check over the phone granting them access to one's computer for a fake free diagnosis analysis. Next, one will naturally be told that they found the problem and that they can clean and fix the problem for a payment of hundreds of dollars that one can pay with their credit card or by making an online payment. Those people who allow these scammers to gain access to their computer will use the time to infect one's computer with a malware virus that will damage one's operating system thereby forcing the owner to go to a third party website to confirm the damage. Once confirmed, the goal of this scam is to force the computer owner to pay for unnecessary repair work over the phone by credit card.

Once these scammers have gained remote access to one's computer they can download software to one's computers that will allow them to steal money from any accounts that one has placed on their computer. According to Microsoft, eight out of 10 people who allowed remote access to their computers had their money stolen. One in five became identity theft victims and over half of these people had their computers infected with viruses that messed-up their computers. Moreover, the cost to repair their computers, more often than not, was far greater then the money that was stolen from their computers. Also, be careful in the event one decides not to pay these scammers as they may become angry and threaten to destroy one's computer, which they cannot.

Our recommendations are to never grant anyone remote access to one's computer. If a person thinks they have a computer problem, take their computer to a local repair service center whenever possible. Don't visit any websites or install any software being unsolicited or being recommended by any callers. Unfortunately, anyone can fall victim to this type of scam and all too often many have fallen for this scam and have reported that their personal identity has been stolen a week or so after a phone call from these scammers. Never give one your last name nor one's first name if one does not know who these callers are. Unfortunately, for some reason or another these scams are subject to being very high identity theft risks, so be very careful.

One final note from the author, unless it is absolutely necessary, never put one's financial information or bank account information on one's computer. Granted it may be a pain to keep tract of one's finances every month on paper, but it is better to be safe then sorry in the long run. Remember, scammers are always on the hunt for victims, especially seniors because they are the most vulnerable.

# THIRTEEN

# SECTION III

# REVERSE MORTGAGE SCAMS

There are all sorts of scams on the market today that everyone needs to beware of and not just the seniors. We will list a few more in this section that may not be used as much as the previously aforementioned scams, but nevertheless everyone should be made aware of what these scammers are up to all around the world today and into the future.

In the reverse mortgage scams the scammers first find the public information on one's home or homes. Once they obtain this information they then send an official looking letter to the homeowner or owners offering to assess the value of their property for a fee. Again, this tactic is designed to get free money and then these scammers will offer a free home somewhere else or money in exchange for one's title to their property. Even though the popularity of the reverse mortgages have peaked in recent years these scammers are taking advantage of seniors with false offers, especially, if these properties are unsecured reverse mortgages. Seniors should never take out a reverse mortgage without calling or talking to a trusted financial professional or a Federal Housing Authority representative first.

A more recent new scam has surfaced in the market place called the Reconveyance scam, where one's property deed, which is publicly available document that is drawn when one pays their mortgage off. Since scammers can access these documents online, they write the victims offering to supply the owner or owners with these documents and will indicate threats of legal problems in the event the owner or owners refuse to get a copy and pay a fee of anywhere from $175.00 to $225.00. Every homeowner should know that they can get a copy for themselves for free or a small fee at their county records office.

# FUNERAL, CEMETERY, AND CREMATION SCAMS

All of these scams have been around for years and even involve dishonest funeral homes that prey on the grieving families. Most people are unfamiliar with the price of funeral services where these unethical funeral homes will attempt to capitalize on these people in order to get more money from them. These funeral homes have been caught selling seniors expensive caskets even if they perform a cremation. People will usually be told that they need an expensive casket or coffin in order to remember their loved one or loved one's in this manner or setting.

According to the FBI there are scam artist criminals who will read the obituaries and call or attend the funeral services of someone they don't even know, in order to take advantage of someone who is grieving at the service. The scammers will then indicate that the deceased had an outstanding debt with them in an attempt to get the relatives to settle this false debt. Our suggestion is not to answer any questions they may have and that you will call the local authorities to investigate their claims. Trust us, they will disappear from the funeral services.

We recommend that people do their research on the net before agreeing to anything being suggested by any funeral home. Also, write down any questions one may have and take them with you when visiting any funeral homes. Likewise, should one have elderly loved one's or other members that may soon pass away, be sure to check up on them and watch their finances to make sure they don't fall victims to these scams. The final scam that is another tactic of these unethical funeral homes is to take advantage of family members lack of familiarity with the cost of funeral services and they will add unnecessary charges to one's bill, including overcharging for cemetery plots. There are caskets, coffins, cremations, natural and garden burials available, so take your time, do your research, and check costs. Concerning the natural and garden burials, there are restrictions involved, so be sure to check this out before making a decision. In a natural burial, one cannot have the deceased body embalmed and there are restrictions regarding a garden burial plots also, so be sure to check. Not all cemeteries in the aUnited States will allow natural or garden burials, but one can check with different funeral homes or check on the internet.

# THE OBITUARY SCAM

As stated before, scammers will read the obituaries in the local papers and get the names of the deceased person. Once they have researched the names of the deceased relatives, they will call them and like always they will demand money for some outstanding debt that the deceased failed to pay. Be sure to question the caller and ask for a receipt and do not take anyone's word on anything they may say to one over the phone. Stand one's ground and demand valid proof that can be verified before giving anyone any money.

Another tactic of this scam is for the scammers to target widows because they are easier prey. Once the widow is targeted (known as the Mark) the scam artist shows up at their door claiming that the deceased, whom they identify, ordered something and then demands immediate payment. Once the delivery person takes the money and delivers the package, the delivery person immediately leaves the area before the victim widow realizes that the package contains nothing but old newspapers or magazines that are worthless. This has been a very lucrative scam for these scammers year after year and will continue as long as people continue to pass away, which is inevitable. Seniors need to understand that they have the right to refuse any packages that may be delivered to their door where the delivery person is demanding payments for something one has no knowledge of. Always request to see the original order form and never give anyone money at your door.

# SWEEPSTAKES AND LOTTERY SCAMS

Granted that these scams have been around for a while and one would think that they would avoid these sort of scams, but scammers are still making money from these scams. The majority of these scams are being used on the internet where people are told that they have won a sweepstakes or lottery, but they need to pay money or disclose personal and financial information before the money can be released. The goal of these scams is to collect as much money as possible from these victims before they realize that they have been taken advantage of. These scams work like this, often seniors and other people are sent a check that appears to be of considerable value and then the scam artist will collect fees or taxes on these supposed monies before their check bounces. Once the check bounces and the fees or taxes have been paid to the scammers the victims have no way of ever collecting or getting their monies back.

In lottery scams, a person's savings are not eliminated all at once, but once they send in some money their names are put on a contact list. In other words, these people are singled out to have their information sold to other scammers or they have been marked to receive future calls about other declared lottery winnings. This is known as "reload scams," that can also be used in other areas besides fake lottery scams. One way to determine the email is fake is to check the "to" address. If it's not to yours, then this is a generalized email scam that has been sent out to thousands of people. The latest version of this scam has been coming from foreign countries indicating that one has won a little over a million dollars that has been placed on a credit card or that will be sent to one by certified check providing one fills out all the requested information they have sent on their email that will request all of your personal information including one's financial bank account information so that they can make a direst deposit into one's bank account. All people need to ignore these temptations and spam, trash, or hang up and block all and any of these phone or email solicitations.

# COLLECTION AGENCY SCAMS

These types of scams can be very viscous scams not to mention extremely emotional and psychologically depressing because collection scams can be on going for long periods of time. Since collection agencies have the right to contact people who are delinquent in their monthly bill payments, these scammers will usually represent themselves as representatives of a phony collection agency. These scammers will make their claims based on real information about a person's credit history that they have researched and will threaten lawsuits if one does not comply. As a rule, these harassment phone calls will usually continue until the victim breaks down and makes a payment over the phone or they make a police report against these scammers. However, the problem with making a payment over the phone simply means that one will start receiving collection calls a few months later thereby starting the same vicious cycle all over again in yet another attempt to extort even more money from the victim or victims.

The bad part about this situation is that people who have been contacted by these collection scammers may have had their personal information violated and their identities stolen. If one does not have or maintain identity theft protection they should get some if possible. Nevertheless, it is our recommendation that one tells these collections agencies that your case has been turned over to an attorney, and don't hesitate to give these agencies the phone number of one's Attorney General's Office in their state for them to call and verify. Chances are, this tactic will put an end to any further harassment calls by any collection agency whether they are scammers or not. Furthermore, it has been our experience that these collection agencies, whether they are legitimate or not will not place a call to any Attorney's General's Office in any state whatsoever. One can also indicate that their debt claims are in the hands of one's attorney and give them the phone number of any attorneys listed in the yellow pages. Under no circumstances should one ever answer any personal or financial questions from any of these callers whether they are scammers or not.

# PHONY COUNTERFEIT SCAMS

This scam is also a very high risk identity theft scam and a very popular scam because these scammers are compelling unsuspecting people to accept fraudulent checks in exchange for cash. Since the advent of the internet many, many stores are online that will often gratify anyones particular needs. The only problem is that it is very difficult to figure out which sites are legitimate from the one's that are out to steal one's personal information. How they work is rather simple as they send out very detailed emails stating how they are having trouble cashing a check, and then asking if anyone would be kind enough to help them by giving them cash for the amount of their check.

Normally, these scammers will offer some kind of an additional incentive or other compensation for their help. The only problem is that their endorsed check bounces and the good samaritan is left without any of the money they paid these scammers for the amount of their check. Furthermore, anyone who has responded to these scammers may have had their personal and financial information breached and their identities stolen. Our recommendation is to never respond to these kind of solicitations on the internet ever, just put them into spam or trash them.

# THE PAYPAL SCAM

People may receive an email from someone claiming to represent PayPal stating that one's PayPal account has been breached and that one needs to sign in to change one's account settings. People, beware that this is a scammer who is attempting to gain access to your PayPal account information. The first thing to do is to verify the sender's email address for legitimacy and then call PayPal. Our recommendation is to always get the first and last name of the caller if possible and write it down along with any other information you may need to verify any caller one does not know. Remember, all scammers maintain all sorts of different ways at their disposal to con people out of their monies, so everyone should be on alert anytime someone they don't know calls them.

# HIGH YIELD PRIME BANK ACCOUNT SCAMS

There are only two problems with this scam, one being that there is no such thing as a high yield prime bank accounts that exist. And two, there are no such things as "secretive bank accounts," but for some reason some people believe in such things for some unknown reason. However, these scams are usually conducted by very seasoned scam artist because they target the very wealthy net worth family seniors with these so called high yield prime bank investments that are connected to secretive accounts that is supposedly only made available for theses wealthy people.

These professional scam artists will even go to the extent of fabricating complicated fake bank documents to entice these wealthy seniors in order to get them to invest as much of their monies as they can. In order to tantalize these people even further these scammers will offer French, British, Swiss or other overseas banks that these people will be doing business with. They also will tell these wealthy seniors that not only will they be able to invest with these overseas banks, but they are guaranteed to enjoy their risk free and loss free returns the same as the other millionaires. It should be pointed out that this is a very high risk scam targeting the very wealthy seniors in our society who need to be protected just like everyone else from these unscrupulous professional scammers. The best way to protect these seniors is to stay in touch with them and communicating with them on a regular bases if possible. If one is not capable to constantly checking up on these older seniors then one should jokingly ask them simple questions like; Has anyone asked them for money lately, or has anyone asked them to invest their monies with their overseas banking institutions, or has anyone offered them financial advice if they place their monies in their operations whatever they may be. Questions like these will keep you alert to what is going on with aging seniors, so ask in a humorous manner and more than likely one will learn the truth of the matter and then one can offer advice and/or look into the matter in more detail.

# THIRTEEN

# SECTION IV

# JURY DUTY SCAMS

Normally, these scam artists will impersonate local government officials. They usually call and tell the people that they have missed their jury duty and then threaten one that they will be placed under arrest immediately. Once these scammers have scared these people out of their minds, they will then ask for one to provide them with their personal information like social security numbers to prove one's identity. This scam is also a very high risk identity theft scam and it is wise to inform the caller that you need their first and last names and ask them what specific government office do they represent. At this time these scammers may realize that you are on to them and they will hang up. People need to know and realize that a local government department would never ask anyone for their social security numbers or make any threats on an unsolicited call. So be sure to question these people and never give out any of one's personal or financial information, and never ever give out one's social security numbers over the phone unless one has called the Society Security Office for information.

# CHARITY SCAMS

These types of scams don't happen very often unless there is a major disaster that has occurred in one's state, community, or in their local area. However, they can also be major disasters that have occurred in other states or even other countries like the pandemic in 2020 where these scammers will come out and start scamming people. Most people will be contacted by phone, but these scammers also will send out emails to others soliciting monies. Even though this charity scam can be disgusting to many, scammers don't really care because they are out to make free money. Scammers will claim to be representatives of a charity seeking money to assist and pay for disaster recovery services or to assist the victims of a given disaster. Naturally, any money one sends will end up in these con artist bank accounts and the good samaritan then becomes the victim. Our recommendation is that, if people want to donate monies to any charities whether disaster or otherwise, check out these charities first by calling them yourself, and never make a donation to any organization that calls one on the phone.

# FAKE MARRIAGE SCAMS

These scams are usually targeted at the retired military veterans who have no remaining families and who are living in a nursing home and are extremely susceptible to these marriage scams. In fact, a veteran nursing home administrator indicated that she has seen the nursing home nurses marry these veterans just to gain access to their service pay and their military benefits. Once these younger women nurses become their wife's, they have been observed living in the veterans homes, eating their food and driving their vehicles because they can now live off their military husband's pensions. The major problem with this scam is that there is nothing anyone can do about this situation.

# SENIOR DATING SCAMS

This is a very popular and growing scam against seniors that has cost unsuspecting American seniors over 210 million dollars and growing, known as the internet sweetheart scam. The problem starts with building a profile, looking over their selected matches and then start communicating with one's selections in an attempt to fine a potential compatible date. The problem starts with one's profile in that the majority of them are phony and can be set up by overseas people as well as local American people to attract one's attention. Unfortunately, a lot of these online relationship scams can be established based on false intentions, only to find out that they only wanted one's money or they may be looking for a free caretaker.

One may even develop emotional feelings for them, and when it comes time to meet them, something comes up like the inability for them to buy an airline ticket, or there has been a death in their family, or some other emergency, but of course, if you are kind enough to pay for their plane ticket, or fund their emergency, or whatever, they will be happy to meet you. Granted that it is not unusual for older men and women to be on the lookout for younger companions that are healthier and in better physical shape then they are, but it may indicate that they are deceiving one because they are really looking for a caretaker or a sugar daddy. The majority of seniors cannot afford to experience these situations regardless of how lonely or isolated they are in their lives.

All seniors that use the internet for dating purposes need to be on the lookout for some of these dating scams. If one will not agree to a video chat or speak to one face to face, chances are they are not who they say they are. If a person's profile maintains nothing but professional photos or the person is quite a bit younger than you are, chances are they are hiding something. Should one be told that there has suddenly been a death in the family, or they have been laid off from their job, do not and we mean do not offer to send these people any money. Our suggestion is to agree and sympathize with them and tell them that you hope things will get better for them and leave it at that. If these internet contacts indicate that they have developed feelings for one or indicate they have fallen in love with you within a few days or weeks, just agree with them indicating that you will get back to them and then spam or trash them because one is asking for trouble. Then again, they may speak broken English or are poor writers, chances are this is a con artist from outside the U. S. and it is better to delete these people. Unless of course, they indicate that English is not their native tongue in their country even though that is a great excuse because everyone speaks English.

All seniors need to be aware of some online dating strategies for their protection. Seniors can become online internet detectives if they have a dating profile or a social media profile. One can do a search with just the username or one has a phone number and when they learn their dates entire name it will be kinda like a got ya. One can also join a better dating website that provides more security as well as profile verifications. Never give out one's personal information and never fall for any financial deceptions. Don't offer money, bank information, or make out gift cards and we suggest one buy a book on scams to protect themselves.

# REAL ESTATE SCAMS

People can lose a lot of money to these scams, especially, seniors because they understand the value that land investments can have over time. These scammers will come out in force in the event of any disasters that may be natural or otherwise. They will attempt to sell land acreage, lots, or buildings at rock bottom prices and indicate that these properties can be redeveloped or rebuilt if one is willing to get in on this deal before every piece of property is sold. These properties are selling from anywhere from $5,000, $10,000, or $15,000 dollars, providing one acts now. Most scammers will indicate that these properties had a value of anywhere from $75,000 to $250,000 or more before the tragedy struck this area. However, if one takes advantage of this opportunity now, these people/investors will reap huge rewards in a short period of time.

The only problem with this scam is that the people may not realize that the land or mortgage titles don't exist or that 40 or 50 other people are on the mortgage, thereby making the transaction worthless. Meanwhile, these victims may have lost their entire retirement savings and have no recourse against these scammers because they are long gone with their monies. Unfortunately, we almost got caught up in one of these real estate scams years ago in the mountains of Julian in California, where the entire area was burned out by a massive fire burning out thousands of homes and land in 2003. Fortunately, we had already owned 5 acres in the mountains that was also burned out, but since it was vacant land it didn't really matter much to us at the time.

Nevertheless, the scammers came out in force tempting people to purchase some of these properties at major discount prices, but the only problem was that these scammers jacked up these burned out properties

2 to 3 time of what the real value was at the time. We don't know how many people got taken by these scammers, but there were many and we almost became one of them until we found out that we could not get any real answers to any of the questions we had been asking. No mortgage or title information was available at the time as we were told because of the amount of chaos that the fire had caused. Since we had been in the real estate business we knew this was an outright lie because the county recorder's office hadn't burnt down in San Diego. Had we not known some of these facts we could have been taken for thousand of dollars, but because of our educational backgrounds and real estate backgrounds we were spared the embarrassment of becoming victims. People need to be on their toes all the time when dealing with scammers and even more so if one happens to be a senior.

# WORKING FROM HOME SCAMS

Almost everyone thinks at one time or another about how great it would be to work at home. The majority of these scams are perpetrated by these scammers on the internet and we are sure a multitude of people have viewed these advertisements if they have spent any time on the web. The people who fall for these scams may go through an interview process via email or by other means. Naturally, when one is supposedly hired by these fake companies, they usually send packages to these new employee's along with detailed instructions on how to inspect the product before shipping the product to another location.

Eventually, the companies will stop communicating with their employee and send them a phony check in an amount that is far greater than the time they have worked. Naturally, the employee being honest, contact the employer stating this overpayment fact and once the company confirms this error of overpayment they simply tell the employee to send the difference back to them before they deposit the check. However, when the employee deposits their check, they find out that their check has bounced and they eventually learn that they have no chance of recovering their monies because this so called employer has disappeared.

It should also be noted that these people's identities may have been stolen as this is a very high identity thief risk due to the fact that these trusting people probably gave these scammers all of their personal information during the initial interviews. Granted one may apply for identity theft protection, but our recommendation is to never give one's personal information out over the internet whether it is by email or otherwise. Another scam is to offer other employment opportunities in order to get information and then hijack one's computer and tell the person to pay them large amounts of money or these scammers will delete all of their computer information. In this situation one either pays and gets their computer information back or loses everything that was on their computer because of lack of payment. Therefore, it is wise to always back up one's information when they are finished for the day.

# PET-FOR-SALE SCAM

Yes, there is even a pet-for-sale scam that seniors need to be aware of, especially, those seniors who enjoy having pets around in their retirement years, but then again this scam can apply to just about anyone who enjoys having pets. Like the previous scam, this scam utilizes the internet to set up phony websites that offers pet adoption services or they offer people the opportunity to donate to a worthy cause to a fake animal facility. These scammers will manage to showcase a variety of different animals that can be adopted at tremendous discounts then one could purchase on the open market. The key to this scam is to request that people are asked to pay for the shipping cost to have their pet sent to their new owner's location, Likewise, the only method of payment that will be accepted has to be by Western Union, a non-refundable money transfer, or by a money-gram payable to an overseas bank.

People need to learn not to be so gullible and to learn to research these companies before sending any money to an overseas bank for any reason. For those people that would like to verify the legitimacy of these pet-for-sale scams, they can check with ScanGuard to verify as they have the ability to secure information regarding reliable information on animal breeders that are located in one's area. It should be noted that one should never send any money to an overseas account they have never done any business with as they are asking for trouble. Overseas accounts are also one of the biggest scams going and have been for years and why people fall for these scams is beyond our comprehension at this time.

# PHONE AND EMAIL SCAMS

Phone and Email scams are the most widely used scams being used by every country around the world we live in today, and who knows what the future will bring in the way of new scamming techniques? Phone scams are mostly designed to be used on the seniors in our society, but everyone is subject to becoming prey to these phone scams too. It would be wise for people not to think they would be impervious to any phone scams, as the more sophisticated these scam criminals become anyone can become a target and a victim if they are not always alert when answering their phones.

This also applies to Email scams as well because all sorts of diabolical scams are being perpetrated and widely spread by the internet. The majority of email scams revolve around lottery and other financial scams or they may be from criminals that claim that they can make one rich providing a person can assist them or offer them assistance in some phony financial endeavor. There are a variety of countries from Africa, India, the United Kingdom, Russia, China, and several other countries that are now jumping on the scam bandwagon targeting the United States of America because of the individual wealth of our citizens. The citizens are being told that they will be given a fortune provided they fill out the information being requested only to be taken for thousands of dollars in the end.

Email is a very effective source for the scammer criminals because they can send out millions of emails and it only takes one or more victims to fall for the scam in order for these scammers to be able to recover their cost and a lot more. Other scammers will use "Phishing" scams where they make their emails look like they are official emails from some known legitimate organization or institution. A person then may be directed to another website that will also be phony, but will look like the website it is representing. These scamming sites can be anything relating to financial scams like banks, brokerages, real estate entities or anything else related to the financial industry. Nevertheless, the goal of these email scams is to obtain as much personal and financial information, bank account numbers, and even passwords, if possible, in order to steal as much money or one's personal identity as these criminals possibly can by convincing one that they are legitimate.

As an example, we recently received an email stating that someone had attempted to get into our bank account and would we be kind enough to do a security check with our bank? They even had the name of our bank and all we have to do was click the security check button on the email and we would be directed to a secure site to validate our information including our bank account information. However, we first placed a call to or bank's headquarters, explained the information in the email and was told that this was a new scam that was making these scammers a lot of money stealing funds from these unsuspecting banking clients. Headquarters thanked us for informing them and stated that they wish more people would be suspicious enough about emails such as this as it would save people and banks a lot of money. Basically, no one can be over cautious when it comes to these type of scams.

When it comes to scam phone calls, never call an unknown number back and remember that government offices will never contact people by phone or by email, only by the U. S. mail. When it comes to emails, especially, unsolicited emails, never trust these emails and never give out one's personal information online to any organization that one is not sure if they are legitimate. Should anyone ever have any doubts as to the questioning they are receiving, we recommend that one hangs up and then call the organization back directly and verify who they are, and be sure to verify the first and last name of the caller, their department, and their ID employment number.

# THE MEDICAL SCAMS

The only reason that we are going to mention this scam is because America and the rest of the world are being mislead by the media all around the world and by the organizations that are supposed to protect the people. We are talking about the World Health Organization (WHO), the U S. Department of Health and Human Services, Center for Disease Control and Prevention (CDC), Health Resources and Services (HRSA), Occupational Safety and Health Administration (OSHA), US. Environmental Protection Agency EPA, The Institute of Medicine (IOM) just to name a few as there are many more.

At the time of this writing, China has managed to release what was and is known as the Coronavirus that had been spreading all around the world at a fairly good pace infecting many people. Even though this virus was not very deadly because the majority of people have recovered that had been infected, there are still a multitude of those that have died because of their compromised immune systems and their underlying health problems. Unfortunately, the majority of these people have been the senior citizens. However, the injustice has come from all of these agencies as well as the world media by communicating to the people that this virus has caused a pandemic.

Let's set the record straight, the WHO leaders stated that this virus was being declared as a pandemic, when in fact, it was not, but according the definition of a pandemic, which "states that a pandemic spreads over a wide geographical area affecting an exceptionally high proportion of the population" was true. However, even though this virus falls into this definition the health organizations and the media immediately blew it all out of proportion to the people, causing mass hysteria among the masses that was not warranted. Instead of remaining calm and dealing with this virus for what it was, the majority of all the world leaders took it upon themselves to continue to scare all of their people by agreeing with the WHO that was out of line using the word pandemic just so they could be recognized around the world as being important?

In our opinion, this was completely uncalled for and these organizations were never held responsible for the mass chaos they caused by using the word pandemic. It is true that the people bought into the use of this propaganda word because they did not know better and to make matters worse, the world media started promoting the word pandemic that caused more people to panic all around the world. Fortunately for America they had a level headed President at the time who played down the virus situation that helped calm the people down in the US; although several less educated were eager to cast their aspersions at the President at that time because of their hatred towards the President.

To show people how irresponsible these organizations were, especially, the CDC and the various medical organizations along with the media outlets in America, they were telling the people that they needed to stock up on various items that in turn caused a rush on all stores where people bought out certain items because they panicked. By doing so, they placed the less fortunate into a bad situation because they were unable to purchase the same products that others were able to purchase.

Nevertheless, in any situation where there is a disaster, be it medical, financial, a fire, a flood, or anything else where there can possibly be an opportunity to gain free money, the scammer criminals are in the background just waiting to take people's money. Furthermore, this pandemic was no different as it has presented several areas that all scammers around the world could venture into in order to scam people out of their monies. Naturally, their main targets are the seniors as they are the most vulnerable when it comes to running scams on, but everyone else are also targets, especially, when it comes to a situation like this one. Anytime there is a world event taking place like a pandemic, this is the perfect situation for scammers to run their scams on everyone.

The main ingredient for an effective scam is misinformation, and the coronavirus pandemic is the perfect world wide playground for these criminal scammers. Be aware that major media outlets such as Facebook, Twitter, and others will usually see an increase in tech companies working overtime trying to stop the increase in activity of these con artists. The process of misinformation can be used by foreigners and various unethical groups in order to cause further public panic, or creating separation among the people, or create uncertainties about our government, people, and agencies concerning certain political parties, or even the current President and the leaders of other countries.

Another thing that all people should be aware of is that in these situations our government will be concerned about any foreign countries becoming involved that can and will manipulate public distress in order to cause voter suppression during primary elections or any upcoming elections. It is our understanding that the State Department has identified and detected over two million conspiracy theories that indicated coordinated and inauthentic activities that suggest foreign governments involvement. Any of the overseas countries could become involved with pushing false, misleading, and disinformation concerning the coronavirus or any virus or disease for that matter. As this virus continues to spread, all people may become exposed to several scams. Nonetheless, never should one provide personal information in unsolicited phone calls, emails, or by text messages. Never click on a download from anyone that one doesn't recognize and be careful from buying from sites one does not know or recognize.

Another thing to watch is phony or fake websites that maybe offering face masks, vaccines that don't exist, pharmaceutical and natural healing remedies, testing kits or anything else that maybe in short supply and at an extremely low pricing. The goal of these scammers is to try to take your monies or credit information if they can, and they can also infect one's computer if one gives them information they request or need. Likewise, people need to beware of scammers that use Amazon, Walmart and other retail selling outlets to sell a wide variety of products that have become in demand because of this virus. The problem being that these products may be unsafe products, used, damaged, out dated, or contaminated. However, in order to get people to buy these items they will usually offer an incentive in the form of rebates, bonuses, or some other incentives that they have no intentions of honoring and the person is left holding the bag so to speak. People may also find these scammers on the social media sites attempting to sell their wares. Due to the demands the coronavirus has caused people to likely buy these products without thinking twice about what they are doing in order to protect themselves and end up never receiving their products in the first place.

# WATCHING OUT FOR SOCIAL MEDIA SCAMS

The most common type of scam is the phony investment scams that can cost investors millions because the scam artists target the desire for people to invest in a phony company directly thereby bypassing the Security and Exchange Commission (SEC). The scam is all based on investing in fake coronavirus vaccine companies promising huge returns based on one's investment in any one of these companies. Even though this sounds appealing, the scammers will build up these companies making them sound irresistible because the investors will be on the ground floor when this is the first company that hits the market with the coronavirus vaccine. However, this virus has already mutated 243 times already, as of this writing and therefore, no vaccine will be capable of stopping this virus that continues to mutate. Nevertheless, these criminals will usually promote micro-cap stock and claim that this company is ready to hit the market before anyone else. People, don't fall for this particular phony scam because it is not possible. When anyone produces a vaccine for anything there is a lengthy time period that a company has to go through in order to be tested and receive approval by the Federal Drug Administration before their new vaccine is allowed to be used on people in the market place.

Another popular scam is the fundraising scam that can be used for the victims of the coronavirus or by phony charity groups in order to serve these victims' families. These scam criminals will not only use outfits like GoFundMe in order to accept donations, but they may also use testimonies with real images of people who have died of this virus and are extremely convincing in their presentations. People need to be diligent and watch for any red flags such as high pressured sales tactics attempting to gain larger donations. It is also important for people to remember that criminal scammers will always come into the market in the event of any crises that may occur around the world that will afford them the opportunity to make money.

When it comes to scams no one is safe and just about anyone can be scammed so don't think that you can't be taken in by a criminal professional scammer. The really good scammers are highly educated and well versed in manipulation tactics and they make a lot of money because of their skills. If one should run across a professional scammer we can pretty much guarantee people that they will end up losing money along with their identities if that is what they are after, so be diligent at all times when faced with a country or world crisis. People need to realize that scammers will use any tactics available to them in order to gain access to one's monies at all cost because that is how most of the criminals make money, so stay alert because the United States is a major target for all countries and the scammers around the world.

# MONEY MULE SCAMS

Even though these scams have been around for a while they usually proliferate in crises like the coronavirus situation. Basically, criminals will look for people they can prey on by playing to their natural desires to help someone that they think needs help, and the coronavirus is a perfect example. How these scams work is simple, as they may claim to be people working in the medical equipment industry and ask you to send or receive money on their behalf. Scammers can claim to be US service members stationed overseas and ask you to send or receive money on behalf of themselves or a loved one fighting the coronavirus. Scammers can claim to be with charitable organizations or affiliated with them and ask you to send or receive money on their behalf. These scammers may claim to be US citizens that have been quarantined overseas and ask you to send or receive money on behalf of themselves or a loved one fighting the coronavirus. These scammers may also claim to be US citizens working overseas that ask you to send or receive money on behalf of themselves or a loved one fighting the coronavirus.

That is why it is important for the people to recognize these warning signs, especially, as the unemployment figures continue to climb. With over 30 or 40 million Americans filing first-time unemployment claims, the work-from-home scams continue to rise. These scammers may even ask you to open a bank account or suggest you use your own bank account to transfer funds in return for some of the money. The problem with this scam is that everyday law abiding people are being tricked into doing something illegal. People need to understand that they can be prosecuted and put behind bars for aiding and abetting these scam criminals when one assist them in these Money Mule Scams.

Likewise, the FBI is warning the people to stay away from any request from strangers who may ask you to become a money mule. The FBI also suggests that one gets in touch with your local FBI office and report any incident where one may be asked to be a money mule. All people need to understand that there are no limits to what scam criminals will come up with in the future, but it is certain that scammers will continue to take advantage of the naivety of anyone who falls for these scams. Furthermore, in all the other scams, people will just lose money and suffer a little embarrassment, but with this type of scam people can be locked up for participating in these illegal scams when they are caught. People, scammers may contact you by phone, text, or email, so be alert.

# THE BOTTOM LINE

All people, need to be vigilant when it comes to unknown phone callers and unknown telephone numbers and the same applies to unknown emailers because chances are they are criminal scammers no matter how legitimate they sound. Remember this, "If it sounds too good to be true it probably is" and "as long as there is money to be had, their will always be criminals around." Should one think they have been targeted or singled out by any criminal scammer, report them to the local law enforcement office near you. Because there are endless scams out in the market place, even though we have named some of the most prevailing ones being used today in these chapters, seniors and anyone else who would like to stay abreast of the latest scams can sign up for Scam Alerts at the National Consumer Protection Bureau.

Allow us to give people an example of what we do to handle these scammer situations. First of all, if we do not recognize a telephone number we simply do not answer the phone and then block the telephone numbers. When it comes to email scams, first we read the emails and if they have anything to do with supposedly being sent any money from overseas, regardless of what country they are from, they go directly into our Spam file and then they end up in our Trash. However, because I have a wife, she sometimes forgets not to answer the phone because as every guy knows, women like to talk.

Nevertheless, she has received several calls that have been from scammers, with the most recent scammer stating that our social security cards have been cancelled and that we had to apply for replacement cards. When we managed to stop laughing at the caller, apparently he decided to hang up on us while we had been laughing. Another time she again answered the phone only to be told that she had won the lottery even though she never bought a lottery ticket, and even if she had, how would anyone know who won the lottery? Yes, one can get some very incompetent callers at times. Unfortunately, she answered the phone again and this time it was supposedly a roofing contractor stating that we needed our roof replaced as it had some damage.

Nevertheless, I told my wife to invite this contractor out to our home so we could view the damage of our roof section. When the contractor showed up he attempted to make a bunch of may be's and might be's that could happen to our home if we did not allow him to make the repairs. Then came the fun part, when he asked me what I used to do for a living, and I told him that I had been a Fraud Investigator for several attorneys in the state and that we were able to convict several fraudsters and send them to prison.

Needless to say, we never saw or heard from this so called contractor ever again as I figured that we could play the same scam con game on him. The bottom line people, is to use your heads when dealing with scam criminals because they are just as vulnerable, and even more so than you are, so have some fun. Scaring the hell out of these criminal con artist scammers is very enjoyable and rewarding for us. Needless to say, we very seldom ever get anymore scam callers, nor do we get these scammers knocking on our door anymore and we just wonder why?

The reason we wrote on this subject is because seniors along with everyone else are being taken advantage of by these criminal scammers everyday of the year and in every year to the tune of hundreds of millions of dollars. Yet no one tells anyone about these scammers and for some reason they just suffer for no reason. By exposing these unbelievable scams, people can, eventually, over come these criminal scammers, expose them and have them locked up for a long time for committing these scamming crimes. In other words, get them before they get you. Be smart, be alert, and don't become a scam victim just because you didn't know better because that is not a valid excuse in a court of law in todays world.

# FOURTEEN
# THE MEDICAL INDUSTRY
# THE GOOD AND THE BAD

We have been studying the medical industry for over 43 years now at the time of this writing due to the negligence of the surgeon that had managed to create a brain damaged handicapped child for us, only to find out the surgeon did not have the slightest idea of what the next step was after delivering our child and just before he cut the umbilical cord. Because the child was a meconium aspiration, meaning that the child had released its first bowel movement in the womb before birth, and was engrossed in its own feces just because the surgeon neglected to check below the child's vocal cords before severing the umbilical cord, this simple error caused the child to ingest this waste material when he took its first breath and out he went for 8 minutes without any oxygen. Because of the incompetence of this surgeon he literally created a brain-damaged handicapped child by handing the child to a nurse who also did not know what to do until she was told to take the child to the emergency nursery where someone finally put a rebreather bag on the child's face. Finally, our child was forced to breath and he managed to survive the next three weeks having been transported to Children's hospital downtown Los Angeles in California.

It wasn't until 9 months later that we had learned of what actually took place when the case went to court and after hearing the reason our son was now a brain damaged handicap child, which was based on doctor incompetency, that is when we decided to start investigating the medical industry. We also learned that this doctor/surgeon had 2 pending wrongful death suits against him and 3 pending medical malpractice cases against him at the time. Why this doctor was still allowed to practice and still had his license was beyond our comprehension. At the time this doctor was the replacement doctor because her primary doctor was on vacation. Nevertheless, in the last 43 plus years we have learned some very interesting things about the medical industry and their atrocities that we will be relating to the readers. In addition, we will be relating some new facts of some new discoveries that were discovered over 30 years ago that all people should be made aware of concerning the medical industry and its people and what they don't want people to know. There may be some good aspects concerning the medical industry, but we have not discovered very many in our research over the last 43 plus years, so let's get started by relating what we have learned over the years so far, as we are still studying the medical industry.

In the late forties, and through the nineties seldom did any of us ever go to see any doctors unless it was for getting stitched up or resetting broken bones. Other than the State mandated inoculations the medical industry was just another industry that everyone we knew of was staying away from them, including us. However, doctors back then were real doctors out to help the people and they would spend whatever time was necessary to assist their patients. However, in today's world one is lucky to get or receive more than 10 or 20 minutes with any so-called doctor and most of the time it is a nurse who has a higher degree on paper, but may not maintain the necessary experience to diagnose or treat anyone. In essence, people are dealing with someone who may not even be qualified to be dealing with their problems. In our opinion, the medical industry has taken a turn for the worst when it comes to doctor-patient relationships. In our opinion the medical industry needs to stop referring to people as patients and refer to people as clients because the word patient is subservient terminology and clients pay their bills.

Nevertheless, sometime in 2000 things started to radically change and the medical industry started on a massive propaganda indoctrination program to brainwash the American people. How many of you have ever seen or heard the phrase "Consult with a licensed physician or a pharmacist" or words to that effect, before consuming this or that? This propaganda has gotten so far out of hand that even people with flatulence are afraid to release gas unless they call a doctor first to make sure it is okay. If one has been studious, they will also be able to make the connection associated with the tremendous rise in medical fees and pharmaceutical fees all based on this brainwashing propaganda being directed at the American people. This has also accounted for the tremendous increases in doctors compensation since they think that if it's okay for the goose than it is okay for the ganders and everyone gets ripped off. The only problem with this sort of propaganda is that Medical Standard of Care has also become less and less over the years.

Someone needs to put a stop to this insanity because it has gotten way out of hand. The main problem is that once the medical and pharmaceutical industry started this brainwashing propaganda they managed to convince all the people to conform to their ways. Then once they had everything in place and the people brainwashed, the medical and pharmaceutical industries started increasing their prices, all at the expense of the American people. In fact, it has gotten so out of hand and outrageous monetarily that the medical industry recently stated that they expect to make over 4 trillion dollars in the year 2020 alone. Just how much more outrageous can this become at the expense of the American people?

Before going any further on this subject we would like to relate two of our favorite quotes that all people should be aware of, which are; 1) "Doctors are people who prescribe medicines of which they know little, to cure diseases of which they know less, in human beings whom they know nothing." By: Voltaire 1692-1788, and so true to this day. 2) People are warned of the medicalization by dehumanizing and the damaging effects of the so called professional intervention: "The medical establishment has become a major threat to health." By: Ivan Illich. We don't know about other people, but these two quotes come to mind anytime we are dealing with anyone in the medical industry in order to protect ourselves from any and all unnecessary medical intervention that has anything to do with our bodies. Furthermore, we make it mandatory to inform any and all medical personnel, whether doctors or otherwise that they can suggest, advise, and offer alternatives, but that we will make the decision to agree or not agree thereby stopping them from proceeding any further in any given situation.

People need to understand that just because a doctor said something, he/ she may or may not know what they are doing. In medical schools these people are taught about the human functions of the male and female bodies and they learn by working on cadavers instead of live people, thankfully. Therefore, even though they spend some time in hospital emergency rooms (ER) seldom are they exposed to all the different problems that people can encounter not realizing that it takes years to learn all the in's and out's of the human body, and even then no one can learn all there is to know. That is why doctors specialize in their given areas because it would be impossible to learn everything that could go wrong with the human body. In our opinion the General Practice doctors are the least qualified medical people around because they know very little about what they are doing in their practice. Another thing that is drilled into student doctors heads are the words "Standard of Care" that all doctors are to provide to their patients regardless of who they are, but these words have very little meaning to doctors today in the world of medicine as mentioned earlier.

Take for instance the coronavirus that encompassed the world in a short period of time in the year 2020. No one in the medical or scientific world had any idea of what this virus was even though they knew that it started in a place called Wuhan in China, but they never did figure out what caused this virus. Nevertheless, that did not stop the assumptions and speculations that erupted among all of these supposedly educated people that did nothing more than play the guessing game. Even the World Health Organization (WHO) turned out to be the worst because they went ahead and announced that they were declaring this virus to be a pandemic when it was not even though it did invade several countries, but the point being made is that this virus was not killing a lot of people at the time. Nonetheless, even with all the people that were recovering from this virus, the WHO managed to create a massive panic around the world that was not called for because it was not entirely true. Why they did what they did will probably never be known.

The question was and is; how come none of these so-called brainy-act doctors and scientist were unable to figure this situation out? Sure there was a lot of guessing going on, but not one of these doctors, specialists, scientists, nor anyone else could solve this simple question as to what caused this virus. So now, the question became why? If these doctors and others couldn't figure this virus out, what makes one think that doctors know all the things that can go wrong with the human body? They don't, unless they have experienced the same situation over and over again where they are capable of determining what is wrong in their clients. In the event doctors can't make that determination they simply subject their clients to outside tests that will cost more and in turn make them more money because of the followups once they learn the problem or problems, if they ever do.

In this situation doctors don't look for the cause anymore, but they treat the symptoms that causes more problems and that makes no sense to us because they haven't determined the cause. If one knows the cause, they can treat the problem themselves and save a lot of money, but unfortunately, that is not the way the medical field works. This is what Ivan Illich meant when he stated: "The medical establishment has become a major threat to health." Not only is the medical establishment dehumanizing the people seeking assistance, but because of the doctors medical intervention, they have also created a major threat to health care in general.

Another thing that was irritating was the fact that not one of these doctors ever thought about testing the people who were not being infected by this virus. Why would one not want to know what was preventing these people from getting infected and rejecting this virus? It would seem logical that at least one of these doctors or scientists would have figured this out so they could determine how to stop the spread of this virus. And people wonder why doctors, scientists, specialists, and others prefer to play the guessing game as opposed to knowing how to solve a world pandemic problem as indicated by the WHO that started all of this chaos. Instead, these medical people have just assumed that all people were infected one way or another without having any evidence to back up their assumptions. They all just assumed that everyone was asymptomatic, which is a bogus term meaning one may or one may not be infected with this virus. Kinda of boggles the brain doesn't it? Doctors are no longer in the business of helping people get healthy, but to insist on prescribing prescription medications, AKA drugs. Since over 80 percent of all doctors are on the pharmaceutical payrolls, it is no wonder why doctors are no longer interested in finding and treating the causes of any disorders or diseases. Find the cause and eliminate the problem, but finding a doctor to do that is slim to none in today's medical field.

# FOURTEEN

# SECTION II

# THINGS THAT WE HAVE LEARNED

Do people know that one's blood rebuilds every 120 days? Do people know that the two worst indicators of a person's health is Blood Pressure (BP) and Cholesterol readings? Do people know that BP testing was established over 120 years ago? A little outdated don't you think? Did people know that one's BP should be based on one's age plus 100? Do people know that one's BP will eventually be checked by Pulse Pressure (PP)? At 40 and below one is healthy and 41 and higher in PP something may be wrong with one's body? Did one know that the death rate is 4 times higher in people with 120 and less in systolic pressure and that BP of 161 in older people live longer according to the American Medical Association Journal stated on Nov. 8, 2006: 296 (18) 2217-2226? Do you know that all humans including animal bodies are self healing, self regulating, and self controlling? Did people know that the leading cause of death in the US is medical care according to the American Medical Association right behind heart disease and cancer?

Do people know that they are being lied to by all of the medical health organizations in the medical industry? Do people know that high BP does not cause heart attacks or strokes and there is no valid medical or scientific evidence to validate this fact. Look it up on the internet where they do nothing but lie to the people by pointing out other problems that clog the arteries that has nothing to do with BP. Do people know that if one has high BP for over 10 years without having any health problems they are considered to be normal? Did people know that heavy weight lifters, body builders, and extreme sports athletes are usually in the high BP ranges and have had BP readings as high as 400/200 and are perfectly okay? Unfortunately, doctors do not keep up to date on BP situations and they do not ask questions of these people and yet they attempt to lower or increase people's BP if these people do not fall into their ideal BP readings. Did people know that there is no cut-and dried definition of high blood pressure? The point being made is that doctors still don't realize that there are always exceptions to the guidelines and attempting to control one's BP with drugs goes against all biological laws.

Did people know that every few years the Joint National Committee (JNC) establishes new BP guidelines by basically, rolling the dice? Where did the guideline of 120/80 come from? The JNC: JNC 6 stated BP should be 140/90, JNC 7 stated BP should be 120/80, JNC 8 stated BP should be 150/90 and now 150/95 for people over 60 years of age. And along comes JNC 9 that states BP should be 130/80 and yet the American Medical Association indicates that people over 60 years of age should have BP reading of 161 or higher over 90, 95 or higher and indicated that these people live longer and have healthier lives. People, the JNC is comprised of some doctors, some pharmaceutical personnel and others that are people that know little or nothing about BP and yet they attempt to establish guidelines for everyone based on and still practicing 120 year old testing procedures and data. Do people know that back in the 60's and 70's BP was 170/100? Likewise, every time the JNC changed the BP standards since then, the pharmaceutical companies increased their incomes by 5 billion dollars. Now maybe people can understand why these JNC people insist on making and setting new BP standards. No one can expect a 60, 70, or older person to have the same BP as an 18 or 20 year old person as that is not even logical to expect. Did you know that BP meds increase one's chances of having a stroke by 1/3 for each med taken. Talking while taking BP reading can go up by 50% and Diuretics (most common) have the highest mortality rates. People with low BP readings have an increase chance of developing cancer and dementia, which leads to Alzheimer's disease and all of the aforementioned has been documented.

# BLOOD FUNCTIONS

Probably one of the more important functions of the body, but yet we have asked several doctors and nurses to explain how the blood functions and what it does in and for the body. Never have we ever gotten the correct answers concerning such a vital function of the human body, so here we go. Blood supplies Oxygen to the tissues. Blood supplies Nutrients throughout the body. Blood assists in removing Waste materials from the body. Blood aids the Immunological functions of the body. Blood controls Coagulation and is the self repair mechanism of the body. Blood transports Hormones throughout the body. Blood signals tissue damage when one is cut and bleeding. Blood also regulates and controls the body's PH and finally, Blood regulates and controls one's body core temperature. It would seem to us that all doctor's and nurses would at least know what blood does in the human body and yet none of them know anything about what blood does. Nevertheless, these people continue to take one's BP incorrectly having no idea of what blood does in the human body and these people are supposedly taking care of people—why?

It has also been proven that the higher the BP the lower the death rates which is contrary to what the ignorant doctors and the medical industry are telling everyone. Nor do doctors or anyone else have any proof or evidence that supports the fact that high BP causes heart attacks or strokes. In the meantime, people need to know that BP can change with the time of the day, a rise in the temperature, talking, having a full bladder, eating, drinking, or smoking within the last hour, standing, sitting, or lying down and all of these mentioned can have an influence on a person's BP measurements throughout any given day. It has become quite apparent that there is very little common sense today in the medical industry and these people are not being taught anything about critical thinking when it comes to treating their clients. For example, do people know that diabetes is not a disease, but a process that can easily be reversed in 30 days just by changing one's diet and by juicing? For those of you who are interested they can go to **drjohnbergman.com** and discover just how simple it is to eliminate diabetes by watching his U-Tube videos.

# A NEW DRUG THAT SENIORS NEED TO KNOW ABOUT THAT REPLACES OPOIDS AND THEIR DERIVATIVES FOR PAIN

The company is called AcelRx Pharmaceuticals, Inc. and has developed a product designated as DSUVIA that does the same thing that opioids and their derivatives do without the side effects that opioids can cause. This product has been approved for the treatment of acute pain for the U. S. Military. DSUIVA is now in all US Army sets, kits, and outfits instead of opioids. This product has also been tested by 2 hospitals that has resulted in a substantial decrease in the time one is required to be in the post-anesthesia care unit (PACU); and the second result has dramatically decreased the IV opioid requirements in the PACU. In another situation there were 4 people undergoing abdominal surgery. These cases usually take about an hour or so depending on the complexity. However, the nurses in the PACU as well as the anesthesiologist were hesitant to believe that a single dose of DSUVIA would be all a patient would need for opioid analgesia. To say the results were quite unbelievable is not an overstatement. The results were minimum compared to other IV opioids that were required during the operation process without the after effects of using IV opioids.

So how does this effect the seniors? For years the elderly with multiple comorbidities (the presents of two chronic diseases or conditions) that decline very rapidly after an acute traumatic event. These people are initially admitted to an emergency facility after they have slip on a sidewalk or some other slippery surface and incur a myriad of hip fractures, hip femur, other fractures and other types of injuries. In some cases , these patients are never discharged back home and are sent to a skilled nursing facility never to return to their homes again.

Treatment of severe pain can require repeated does of opioids which can activate metabolites (a substance formed or necessary for metabolism) that can build up over time, especially when renal function is diminished, which is common in the elderly. This process can result in confusion, delirium, mental clouding and can impair mobility, leading to extended rehabilitation stays. This company felt that if they could use their DSUVIA in the treatment of these patients, they could avoid the downward physical regression. Therefore, they went to a hospital emergency department to test their theory. First was a 93 year old gentleman who had broken his hip and was dosed with DSUVIA. When they went back to check on him after surgery, he was comfortable, awake, reading the newspaper and doing the crossword puzzle. That was not something one would normally see every day.

The second patient was an elderly woman, she also had fallen and broke her hip, and she was initially dosed with IV Dilaudid, that is a common treatment. However, the patient was very confused after the dosing and disoriented and her family was very concerned. The Dilaudid was let to wear off for a few hours, and then she was re-dosed with DSUVIA. It was unbelievable in that her pain was controlled, and she was lucid and her family was very relieved. These were just two examples of what has been observed over time again and again with these elderly trauma patient using DSUVIA. Eventually, DSUVIA will be used in every hospital and emergency facilities in the U.S and around the world without the additional side effects of using opioids. Now seniors can ask for this DSU-VIA drug to stop any severe pain that they may encounter by falling and breaking hips, arms, legs or any other bones or severe injuries, and if the hospital or emergency department hasn't approved the use of the DSU-VIA, request to be transferred or have one's family members move you to another hospital facility that has approved the use of this new drug. It would also be advisable to call any and all hospitals ahead of time and ask them if they have been authorized to use DSUVIA. Seems to us that this would be far better then for seniors spending the rest of one's life in some nursing facility all drugged up when it is not necessary.

# PHYSICAL, CHEMICAL, AND EMOTIONAL STRESS

So what is causing heart attacks and strokes? Glad you asked that question because even though the medical personnel want to pretend that they know what they are talking about, they in fact don't. What if Physical, Chemical, and Emotional Stress is responsible for just about all medical problems and diseases that people have today and will have in the future? What if these problems are being caused by medical intervention, which is causing the harm? Physical stress is pretty much self explanatory, but do people think that too much stress could cause a heart attack? Sure it can, especially, as one ages. Could physical stress cause a stroke? That is also very possible depending on the situation in which a stroke occurs. Let's look at some other things that can cause heart attacks as they are a major killer of people all around the world. Do people know that NASID'S cause over 20% of all heart attacks and taking Aspirin (baby or regular), Motrin, Alive, Ibuprofen, Naproxen and other NASID'S increase congestive heart failure by 60% not to mention that these NASID'S destroy the cartilage in the human body.

Furthermore, NASID"S can cause a 25% increase in hearing loss, have an 80% risk of miscarriage, responsible for over 7000 hospitalizations every year for GI complications, and between 10% and 20% increase risks of allergic reactions. Concerning Aspirin, it is the fourth leading over-the-counter drug in America that is the leading cause of liver disease. Oh, the medical industry forgot to tell people that little tidbit?

In addition, NASID'S will decrease cartilage production, causes accelerated bone destruction, and inhibits proteoglycan production, which are the building blocks of cartilage in the human body. What people need to understand is that doctors have little or no training or knowledge of nutrition and that is why they are so ignorant about people using nutrition to aid themselves in getting better. In essence, one is taking money out of the pockets of the doctors and that is why the majority of them are against nutrition.

As an example, a few years ago my wife had a female problem and went to see a doctor, but before he saw her she had already gotten a urine test because she knew that the doctor would request one. Nevertheless, upon seeing the doctor and after answering all of his questions the doctor asked her if she was taking vitamins because she was so healthy at her age and she said yes. However, my wife knew to never tell any doctor what she is taking and to ask the doctor why he inquired. Next, the doctor told her she needed to get a urine test, that she had already done and she was treated and on her way home in no time. The point being made is that doctors know little or nothing about nutrition and they will do whatever they think is necessary to discourage people from taking vitamins or anything else that will heal them without the intervention of any medical personnel just because they are in business of making money from their practice and the selling of pharmaceutical drugs.

Another example occurred during the coronavirus pandemic. During that time we had the family using a nebulizer with colloidal silver and we were always going out to all kinds of places because very few people were out and about. Colloidal silver is an excellent product that actually kills viruses and pneumonia, among other aliments that one can look up on the internet. Naturally, there are a lot of negative articles, mostly by the medical community that they don't want people to know about and colloidal silver is one of them. Having said that, the medical and dental industries have kept this product a secret as they have been using colloidal silver for healing purposes for a very long time, but they don't want the people to know because it works, exceptionally well, for all sorts of things affecting the human body. Having used colloidal silver for several years now we knew that we would never get any kind of virus no matter what we did or where we went because colloidal silver had never let us down regardless of how we have aged.

The major factor of colloidal silver is that there are no chemicals in the product that can cause the harm that vaccines can cause, especially, the new coronavirus vaccines that everyone has been trying to develop. Granted that the vaccine may or may not work, but we knew that almost every vaccine contains chemicals that can cause everyone harm now or in the future in the human body and brain and that is why we use colloidal sliver. We also use apricot seeds and iodine, both of which kill viruses. Not only does apricot seeds eliminate every known kind of cancer, but one of its side effects is that is kills viruses. The medical industry is well aware of the fact that iodine kills all known viruses because they use iodine all the time for themselves and on their clients. We take 6 drops of J. Crow's Lugol's 2% Iodine diluted in water every morning and at night before going to bed and we are never concerned about catching or contracting any viruses from anywhere or anyone.

# CHEMICAL STRESSORS

Let's look at some chemical stressors that can have major effects on the human body starting with Vaccinations, Medications (Drugs), Environmental Toxins, Non Organic and GMO Foods, Nutritional Deforestries, and Chemical Food Additives. However, one of the biggest chemical food stressors that is causing the most damage to people was given the approval by the Food and Drug Administration (FDA) to be used on our food crops. Do people know that originally, the FDA was a chemical organization that monitored chemicals before they developed into the FDA everyone knows today?

Nevertheless, the FDA approved the use of a chemical called GLYPHO-SITE that is being sprayed on all of our food products as a weed killer. However, what they don't tell the people is that glyphosite causes the following: Depression, Brain defects, Autism, Skeletal and Brain Mal-formations, Parkinson's disease, DNA Damage, Neurotoxicity, Multiple Sclerosis, Alzheimer's disease, Cancer, Reproductive Toxicity, Gastro-intestinal disease, Endocrine Disruption, Obesity, Infertility, Cardiovascular diseases, and Allergies just to name a few things that glyphosite can do to the human body. However, glyphosite does clear the weeds so that farmers can plant more food that is then sprayed with this chemical. It kind of makes us wonder if the FDA approves these chemical products to perpetuate and continue to proliferate the medical and pharmaceutical industries?

# LET'S TALK ABOUT THE CHEMICAL ALUMINUM

Aluminum is and has been used in most all vaccines and is known to do the following to the human body: Aluminum interferes with Gene expression, it damages Cell membranes, it disrupts energy metabolism, it alters DNA and the normal regulation of Gene function, it coagulates Protein, increases Vascular endothelial adhesiveness thereby increasing cardiovascular disease, and enhances Excitotoxicity in the brain and increases brain inflammation.

This is all brought to people by the FDA otherwise known as the Fraud Deception Administration of America. Using aluminum in vaccines is the major cause of Alzheimer's disease in the United States today. So if the vaccines don't kill people, they will have problems down the road because aluminum enters the brain and eventually destroys it. All people need to learn to read the warning sheets that come with all vaccines to be able to determine if they want to be injected with these deadly foreign chemicals that will destroy the human body and brain. This will include the new pandemic coronavirus vaccines because no one knows what deadly chemicals these vaccines will have in them, but read the warning sheets that must be provided with any vaccines before deciding to accept or reject being vaccinated.

All doctors and medical personnel need to learn that the human body is intelligent and knows how to react to any given situation and stop being arrogant to think they know more about the human body, which they know nothing, and respect every person's body because the body knows more than they do. All doctors learn and know that the body is self healing, self regulation, and self controlling, but for some unknown reason they refuse to respect the intelligence of the human body. The body has an adaptive physical response system built into it called the Autonomic Nervous System (PNS) that is designed to Resist-Digest and performs Repairs. The body also has a Simpathic Nervous System (SNS) that is designed to initiate the Fight or Flight system in any given situation one encounters. However, both the PNS and SNS systems can only occur one at a time and don't ask us why the acronym for the Autonomic Nervous System is PSN because we did not make it up in the first place.

# EMOTIONAL STRESS

As people already know emotional stress can also be anything and based on almost anything and it all depends on the individual. Because every person is different, everyone will not be affected with the same things that can cause them emotional stress. Since we are not psychologist or psychiatrist we are not able to give people advice, however, we will give the reader a small list of things that can cause one to experience stress due to some of the following circumstances: Depression, Irritability, Temper problems, Anxiety, Sleeping problems, Lashing out at people for no reason, Unexplained physical problems, Dramatic weight fluctuation problems, Trouble remembering things, Experiencing a low sex drive, Having low energy problems throughout the day, Concentration problems, Fatigue, Compulsive behavior problems, Avoidance coping, and many, many more situations that people can experience.

As time goes on stress can and will have the ability to exacerbate a person's misery and make everything seem worse than it is. Likewise, emotional stress has been proven to weaken the human body, accounting for all of the aforementioned above. A lot of emotional stress problems can be caused by sudden changes in the body, or by low blood sugar, dehydration, exhaustion and overheating. Also different medications (Drugs), heat, insect bites and even foods and chemicals can cause emotional stress. Some people will need to seek help to overcome some or most of these stress problems, but it has also been shown that most stress problems will disappear on their own over time. If people would like more information on stress issues they can go to **drjohnbergman.com** site and type in "Emotional Freedom Zone" and get all the information they want or may need to cope with any problems that may have been caused by emotional stress factors.

# FOURTEEN

# SECTION III

# WHAT DOES CHOLESTEROL DO?

Cholesterol is the body repair substance. It is a powerful antioxidant and cholesterol along with BP are poor health indicators. Did you know that there is no good or bad cholesterol? Did you know that any unused cholesterol returns to the liver? Did you know that the body needs cholesterol to build healthy cells? Did you know that LDL cholesterol is needed to carry cholesterol to an injured area of the body? Did you know that no cell can form without cholesterol? Did you know that low cholesterol causes cancer, depression, and increases in strokes? Did you know that lowering cholesterol using statins can cause headache, joint pain, muscle pain, constipation, stomach pain, indigestion, nausea, skin rashes, sleep problems, cold symptoms, unexplained muscle pain, tenderness, or weakness, dark urine, pain and burning when urinating, and depletes CO-Q10 in the body. Did you know that when medical scientist took the CO-Q10 out of the statins that heart failure rate doubled?

Did you know that the body needs cholesterol to produce progesterone, estrogen, testosterone, and cortisol to protect against cancer. Taking statins has been shown to increase breast cancer by 1500 percent, lower cholesterol levels decreases the survival rates from strokes.

Did you know that cholesterol is vital for proper neurological function and plays a key role in the formation of memory and the uptake of hormones in the brain, including serotonin. Cholesterol is vital for the body's repair process, cholesterol is the precursor for vitamin D, cholesterol is needed for bile salts for the digestion of fats, cholesterol is a vital antioxidant protecting the body from cancer and aging, cholesterol is the main molecule in the brain, cholesterol is the precursor to all hormones and promotes healing and sex hormones. Did you know that cholesterol lowering diets and drugs cause blood sugar problems, allergies, edema, asthma, mineral deficiencies, chronic inflammation, reduces libido, infertility, causes reproduction problems and difficulties in healing. Needless to say, cholesterol is a vital substance for the function of the human body and attempting to alter human physiology with any chemicals is insanity.

# THINGS SENIORS SHOULD KNOW ABOUT DRUGS THAT CAUSE DEMENTIA

ANTIDEPRESSANTS DRUGS
ANTIHISTAMINES
ANTI-PARKINSON DRUGS
ANTI-ANXIERTY MEDICATIONS
NARCOTICS

CARDIOVASCULAR
CORTICOSTERIOS
ANTICONVULSANTS
SEDATIVES
AND OTHERS

# DRUGS THAT CAUSE EPIGENETIC CHANGES IN THE HUMAN BODY

To keep this simple, Epigenetic's, basically, changes and alters the physical structure of DNA. Epigenetic's refers to the external modification to DNA that turns genes "on" or "off." However, these modifications do not change the DNA sequence, but instead, they effect how cells read genes.

| | |
|---|---|
| Anti-Inflammatories drugs | Statin cholesterol lowering |
| Beta Blockers | Anesthetics |
| Diuretics | Antibiotics |
| Tamoxifen | Methotrexate |

# VIOLATING BIOLOGICAL LAW

Giving or taking a chemical to alter physiology violates biological law and that includes trying to control everyones' BP and Cholesterol with drugs, ie: chemicals. Example: The flu shot increases one's chances of developing diabetes, and taking 5 consecutive annual flu shots has been proven to increase a person's chances of developing Alzheimer's by 75% because of the aluminum in the vaccine. There are 9 other chemicals in the flu shot that are known to be deadly to the human body.

People, the major problem is that all of you are being experimented on by the medical industry, pharmaceutical industry, and our government. This may be hard to accept, but all diseases are being caused by the Medical, Pharmaceutical, Chemical, and Food industries that leads to Physical, Chemical, and Emotional Stressors. In other words, all diseases are nothing more than an adaptive physical response to the chemicals being put into your bodies. These can be in the form of drugs, AKA medications, vaccines that contain dangerous chemicals that will destroy one's body and brain, unhealthy foods like processed and GMO foods, chemicals from all sort of industries including the medical and pharmaceutical industries. Therefore, it is recommended that everyone read the literature that comes with all vaccines including the flu vaccine that list the chemicals (required by Law) that one is agreeing to allow to enter one's body. People need to understand that they are being killed off slowly every year because they are allowing all of this activity to take place without questioning anything. Should these industries try to make anything mandatory, take them to court and make them justify anything that they try to mandate.

# THE MAJORITY OF DISEASES ARE MAN MADE

Unless one is born with a disease, diseases are created by the medical, chemical, and food industry and the chemicals they use or put into people's bodies supplied and concocted by the pharmaceutical companies and others. The chemicals that are being developed by the pharmaceutical companies are being made without scientific studies or testing, otherwise they could not get their manufactured drugs patented. Moreover, there are no adequate time testing requirements of these man made drugs by the FDA before they grant patents to the pharmaceutical companies based strictly on the propaganda supplied to the FDA by these companies and that is pure insanity. The real testing grounds for these made-up chemicals are the American people and primarily the babies, kids, and seniors and if they die, these companies don't care because it is all about profits. These pharmaceutical companies will just make another chemical and again test it on the American babies, kids, seniors and people have been told that there is currently no legal recourse against these vaccines and pharmaceutical companies, including the CDC, who's job it is to promote and sell these vaccines. Nevertheless, we have discovered that people do have recourse against the medical industry if the products they use cause severe or deadly results on one's loved ones, but that is not much of a gratification for losing a loved one.

Take for example the bio-toxic flu shot as it is very deadly in its makeup. For example, the flu shot contains *Egg proteins: including avian contaminant viruses. *Gelatin: can cause allergic reactions and anaphylaxis are usually associated with sensitivity to eggs or gelatin. *Polysorbate 80 (Tween80 ™) can cause severe allergic reactions including anaphylaxis. Also associated with infertility in female mice. *Formaldehyde: known carcinogen. *Triton X 100: a strong detergent. *Sucrose: table sugar. *Resin: known to cause allergic reactions. *Gentamicin: an antibiotic and *Thimerosal: mercury is still in multiple flu shot vials. *As stated before most vaccines contain Aluminum that causes Alzheimers and Dementia because it affects the brain. We listed 10 foreign chemicals that are used in vaccines that are known to be extremely hazardous to human life. So, is the bio-toxic flu shot effective? Not in babies: a study of more then 294,000 children found that there was no evidence that injecting at 6-24 months of age with a flu shot was no more effective than a placebo. In children over 2 yrs of age, the flu shot was only effective 33% of the time in preventing the flu. Reference: Vaccines for preventing influenza in healthy children. The Cochrane Database of Systematic Reviews 2 (2008). Not in children with asthma and a study failed to provide evidence that the flu vaccine prevents pediatric asthma exacerbation. Not in adults: In a review of 48 reports with more than 66,000 adults, "Vaccinations of healthy adults only reduced the risk of influenza by 6% and reduced the number of missed work days by less than one day (0. 16) days. It did not reduce the number of people needing to go to the hospital or take time off work. Reference: vaccines for healthy adults. Same review company, Review 1 (2006). Not in the elderly: In 64 studies in 98 flu seasons. For the elderly living in nursing homes, the flu shots were non-significant for preventing the flu. For the elderly living in the community, flu vaccines were not significantly effective against influenza, ILI or pneumonia. Reference: "Vaccines for preventing influenza in the elderly. Same review company, Review 3 (2006).

What about the Swine Flu shot? Some of the H1N1 swine flu vaccines that was made by Novartis made with Per. C6 cells (human retina cells) contained MF59, a potentially debilitating adjuvant. MF-59 is an oil based adjuvant primarily composed of squalene. All rats injected with squalene adjuvants developed a disease that left them crippled, causing them to drag their paralyzed hindquarters across their cages. Injected squalene can cause sever arthritis and severe immune responses, such as autoimmune arthritis and lupus. Rated 3 on a scale of 4. The only bad part about all of these vaccines is that all pharmaceuticals companies are now protected from accountability, unless criminal intent to do harm can be proven by the injured party. They are protected from liability even if they know the vaccine or drug will be harmful. This needs to be overturned in the courts because the people are at the mercy of these unethical pharmaceutical companies. Everyone needs to speak up in order to maintain their freedom. What can the people do? Spread the word by *Giving this information to everyone you know.

*Contact first responders (EMT's, Paramedics, Fireman, etc.). Let them know that they will be the first to get the flu shots. *Talk to local police and discuss concern about mandatory vaccinations. *Talk to as many people as you can at church, in the grocery store, with kids' parents that play with your kids, so forth and so on. *Contact local council members about your liberties. People will need their support to maintain one's rights to refuse any vaccinations. Write short articles for local, community papers and others. Connect with local activist groups that support the second amendment issues, the environmental and animal rights and help spread the word. *As stated by Margaret Mead, "Never doubt that a small group of people can change the world, indeed it is the only thing that ever has. Everyone needs to beware of the pandemic vaccines and know what chemicals are in them because your life may depend on it. It should also be noted that these vaccine companies will not allow their families to take the vaccines they develop because they are aware of the hazards and consequences involved with these vaccines, but it is okay to test them on you and your families.

# ALTERED GENES ASSOCIATED WITH GMO

| | |
|---|---|
| Insulin Regulation | Cholesterol Synthesis |
| Cell Signaling | Protein Formation |

It should be noted that several countries around the world will not allow GMO crops from the US into their countries because of the known health risks and the unknown consequences of human consumption. Although, in the U.S.A. GMO is approved and being used in just about everything along with Herbicides, Pesticides, Sterile pollen, Altered oils, Protein composition, etc. In other words "If man makes it, don't eat it." Remember our discussion on the chemical glyphosate? Always be prepared to protect yourself and your loved one's.

# WHAT SENIORS NEED TO KNOW ABOUT SALT

For every study that suggests that salt is unhealthy, there are just as many that state salt is healthy. In fact, low salt diets may have side effects when salt intake is cut, the body responds by releasing renin and aldosterone, an enzyme and a hormone, respectively, that increases BP. Furthermore, unless we have clear data, the Medical Industry and other anti-salt campaigns are not just based on shaky science, they are ultimately unfair. As stated by Hillel Cohen, an epidemiologist at the Albert Einstein College of Medicine, "A great number of promises are being made to the public with regard to this enormous benefit that saves lives." "But it is all based on wild extrapolations."

Now that scientific devices have become more precise, the correlation between salt intake and poor health has remained unsubstantiated. A large study by Inter-Salt published in 1988, compared sodium intake with BP in people from 52 International Research Centers and found no relationship between sodium intake and the prevalence of hypertension. In fact, the population that ate the most salt, about 14,000 milligrams a day had a lower median BP than the population that ate the least, about 7,000 milligrams a day.

The US Department of Health and Human Services, published a review of 11 reduction salt trials and stated: that over the long term, low salt diets, compared to normal diets, decreased Systolic BP in healthy people by 1.1 millimeters of mercury and Diastolic BP by 0.6 mmhm. That is like going from 120/80 to 119/79. The review concluded that, "Intensive intervention, unsuited to primary medical care or population prevention programs, provide only minimal reduction in BP during long-term trials." As an example, we take a teaspoon of potassium with a 1/2 teaspoon of Himalayan salt every morning and evening in a half glass of water for years now and have never ever had any problems whatsoever and feel great. That is about a 8 to 1 mixture, but the body needs salt.

# ONE OF THE MOST DEADLY SWEETENER'S SUCARLOSE

Sucralose has been shown to be a migraine trigger, induce skin rashes, dizziness, diarrhea, muscle aches, headaches, stomach pain, cramping, agitation, numbness, and bladder problems in people. In addition, it is shown to lead to weight gain, and blood sugar issues like type 2 diabetes. Decreases red blood cells, enlarges and calcifies your kidneys, interferes with sperm production and increases infertility in men, and resulted in spontaneous abortions in almost 50% of rabbits fed sucralose in one study. The rabbit study also resulted in an elevated death rate among those that consumed sucralose as opposed to those that did not. Sucralose is a substance chemically similar to and used in the pesticide DDT. Sucralose causes heart diseases, metabolic syndrome, obesity, alters insulin response, alters genes, causes inflammatory bowel diseases, and can destroy up to 50% of healthy intestinal bacteria just to name a few of the problems by ingesting sucralose. Sucralose is one of the most insidious substance known to mankind that is now being used in just about everything and anything people can ingest. The bad part about sucralose is that it binds to various molecules in the body and hides there for decades while you consume more and more sucralose that eventually breaks loose and your body is flooded with diseases causing irreparable damage that can't be cured including cancers, Alzheimer's and Dementia, in addition to any and all of the above aforementioned diseases and problems. The use and approval of sucralose is not only unethical and unmoral, it is outright criminal. Note: this is only one product out of the thousand of others the Fraud Deceptive Administration known as the FDA has approved with inadequate testing. It should also be known that the FDA was originally the Chemistry Board before becoming the FDA. Now we know why we have so many approved chemical companies being allowed to poison the American food crops. However, don't take our word with regard to sucralose, but look it up yourself as your life could depend on it.

# FOURTEEN
# SECTION IV
# WHAT IS THE ENDOCANNABINOLD SYSTEM IN THE HUMAN BODY?

We are going to expose to the people a system in the human body that very few people know about, including doctors and the majority of the medical industry, but many people behind the scenes who know of this system have been very secretive for over thirty years since it was discovered and the question is why? Why are they hiding this system, how it works, and how anyone can make it function better for the benefit of the human body and the human race? We will try to keep this as simple as we can so that all readers will get a better understanding of their endocannabinold systems within their bodies.

The endocannabinold system is responsible for maintaining the homeostasis in the body. The definition of which is, "Any self regulating process by which the biological systems tends to maintain its stability while adjusting to conditions that are optimal for survival. If homeostasis is successful, life continues, if unsuccessful , disaster or death ensues." Endo relates to endogenous, meaning that it originates within the body. Cannabinoids refer to a group of compounds that activate this system as there are endocannabinold receptors located all throughout the body and found on the surface of the cells in the brain, organs, tissues, glands, skin, bone, immune cells, liver, fat tissue, heart, blood vessels, skeletal muscles, kidneys and the gastrointestinal tract. These compounds interact with these cannabinol receptors to regulate basic functions such as pain, sleep, mood, memory, appetite, apnea, fibromyalgia, post traumatic stress disorder, social anxiety, traumatic brain injury, Tourette's syndrome, immune function, metabolism, reproductive functions, seizures and many more problems that the body can encounter that scientists currently know of at this time with many more discoveries to come.

The cannabinol system is made up of cannabinoid receptors, endocannabinoids, and metabolic enzymes. The body produces natural occurring endocannabinoids and the cannabis plant produces phytocannabinoids. The last system is the metabolic enzymes system that destroys the endocannabinoids when they are used up and no longer required by the body. The endocannabinold system also affects all the neurotransmitter levels and is important in emotions, pain, or whether a person is going to have a seizure or not, as well as any functions one can name, and not just the brain.

# THE TWO MAIN RECEPTORS

So just exactly what are receptors? They are known as CB1 and CB2 receptors and each one responds to different cannabinoids even though some cannabinoids can interact with both. CB1 is mostly found in the brain and spinal cord and CB2 is mostly in other parts of the body and are responsible for a wide range of biological immune functions. There is also what is known as Exogenous cannabinoids meaning that they originate outside of the body. For example, cannabinoids found in the marijuana plant maintains tetrahydrocannabinol (THC) and cannabidiol (CBD), which are considered to be exogenous. Likewise, when these products are combined and consumed they interact with the cannabinol receptors that then produce physical and psychological effects in the body.

It is important to know that the CB2 receptors, when activated, will reduce inflammation, which is an immune response that plays a major role in several diseases and conditions that can affect one's body. However, only the THC has the ability to bind to both CB1 and CB2 receptors thereby activating both the brains neurological system and the bodies immune system. On the other hand CBD without THC will not bind directly to the cannabinoid receptors. Instead, CBD works by inhibiting an enzyme called FAAH (fatty acid amide hydrolase), that is responsible for the breakdown of anandamide, which is the most important endocannabinoid in the body. Scientists now know of two major cannabinoids that are produced naturally by the body known as 2-AG and anandamide. Anandamide was the first to be discovered and comes from the Sanskrit word ananda meaning bliss referring to its unique effects on the mind and body. The 2-AG (2-arachidonoyl glycerol) is found at higher concentrations in the brain, whereas anandamide is found at higher concentrations in the immune system throughout the body, and both can bind to CB1 and CB2 receptors. Endocannabinoids are neurotransmitters meaning that they are only produced when the body needs them and they only last for a short time.

THC on the other hand is the psychoactive product of marijuana that causes the "high" feelings of elations, which can cause an increase in appetite, increase in socialization, relaxation, and other effects. However, THC can also cause physical, memory, and motor impairments such as dizziness, increased heart rates, dry mouth and other impairments when used in abundance. THC has been shown to reduce seizures in both children and adults. CBD on the other hand has been shown to reduce the psychoactive effects that can be caused by THC thereby benefiting a large range of psychological disorders, such as depression, schizophrenia, anxieties and other psychological problems. CBD also has neuroprotective effects where the CBD protects the brain from damage after an injury. Let's now take a look at some important aspects that everyone should know about the various CBD products that are currently being sold to the public and what to look for that would be suited for them.

# CBD OR CBD WITH THC ?

This is a question that people are always asking and the decision is left up to the people to decide. When we first started using CBD products we started with a product containing both CBD and THC with the THC that was less than 3 percent or an infinitesimal amount that did not seem to bother any one of us. Nevertheless, as time went on we searched for some stronger CBD, only this time we decided to try the CBD without the THC in it because the product not only contained the CBD, but also CBC, CBG, CBN, CBDV, and natural TERPENES. Thus far they both seem to work just fine. So, it comes down to a personal decision as to which one a person elects to use, or like us, we now use the CBD without the THC.

All of these cannabinoids serve a different purpose in the body, but yet they are all compatible and all are derived from the marijuana plant. All of these cannabinoids have been found to have several therapeutic effects for the brain and nervous system as well as the immune system throughout the human body. People can buy all kinds of different CBD products as they have been legalized by the US government and they come in a variety of strengths from 300 milligrams up to 5000 milligram bottles. However, what people need to pay attention to is the number of milligrams of actual CBD that is used in each because the actual CBD contents vary considerably from product to product.

The amount of CBD will determine just how effective the CBD product will be for the users. The actual CBD content can range from 10 milligrams to as much as 120 milligrams or more depending on the vendor, but we prefer the CBD that contains 1000 milligrams, but has 40 milligrams of actual CBD that works the best for us and 33 milligrams of the CBC, CBG, CBN, CBDV for a total of 73 milligrams of actual CBD products. Therefore, it is important to question the sellers of any CBD products as to the actual content of CBD that they put into their products. For example, a product may indicate 1000 milligrams strength of CBD and yet the actual CBD content may be only 20 or 30 percent. On the other hand, another CBD product may contain 600 milligrams, but contains 40 percent of actual CBD. Therefore, it will depend on the individual as to how much actual CBD content they want in their product and in this situation the better buy would be the 600 milligram bottle as opposed to the 1000 milligram bottle because the 600 milligram solution contains more actual CBD in its content. People can now see why it is important to question all vendors as to the actual content of the CBD in their CBD products because that is what is most important.

# FOURTEEN

# SECTION V

# SENIORS NEED TO KNOW HOW THE ENDOCANNABINOID SYSTEM RELATES TO THEIR HEALTH

The endocannabinoid system was discovered over 30 years ago and yet the scientists are still playing around with mice and rats knowing that this system will have a major impact on the people in our society. They also know that people will not have to rely on doctors or the medical and pharmaceutical industries as much as they currently are and therefore delaying their research that people need to know about now and not later. Furthermore, not only is this system overlooked by the medical industry it is not even taught in any of our medical schools and definitely not in any of our veterinary schools. And the question is

WHY? The endocannabinoid system is a major part of the human and animal bodies and yet the medical doctors and veterinarians are being misled about a major piece of science that has been hidden from their consciousness thereby delaying the research on a subject matter that is extremely important to human physiology, and especially for seniors.

We now know that the endocannabinoid system regulates several basic functions of the human body as previously mentioned, but it also includes Digestion, Movement, Cardiovascular functions, Temperature, Neuroprotection, and Neural development. The endocannabinoid system also reacts and responds to all kinds of illness. In fact, tumor cells have shown more cannabinoid receptors than healthy cells. Likewise, it has been shown that endocannabinoid levels increase with various diseases like Alzheimer's and Parkinson's in an attempt to eliminate and correct these problems within the body. In addition, homeostasis is the key element in the biology of all living things and has the ability to stabilize internal conditions that are necessary for survival. In other words, failure of the body to achieve homeostasis results in the development of diseases. Nevertheless, the role of the endocannabinoid system in maintaining homeostasis is a very unique system that should have an army of medical scientists working on this subject for the betterment of all humanity. The body's ability to adjust to changes and maintain homeostasis directly reflects the health of that organism and any interruptions to the physiological balance will cause health problems.

It is also known the cannabinoids attach to cannabinoid receptors unlocking the receptors causing changes in how cells function that causes different effects in the body. We also know that there are as many as 113 or more different cannabinoids that are produced by the marijuana plant and scientists and the medical world have no idea of what these cannabinoids will do to assist the human body by eliminating all sorts of diseases. Nevertheless, we currently know that the endocannabinoid system plays a major role in the pathology of a multitude of disorders and that they serve as a protective role in these medical conditions. We now know that conditions like pain, inflammation, vomiting, and diseases like Alzheimer's, Huntington's, and Parkinson's and Tourette's Syndrome, along with Obesity, Cardiovascular problems, Metabolic Syndrome, Schizophrenia, Multiple Sclerosis,

Glaucoma, Anorexia, Epilepsy, Cancer, and other Seizure Disorders can be eliminated by modifying and controlling the endocannabinoid system in the human body.

It has taken over 30 years since the discovery of the endocannabinoid system in the human body for medical scientists to discover just a small portion of the endocannabinoid system and what it will cure, and yet they are not teaching this information to our medical students. However, it has recently been noted that the American Medical Association and the American College of Physicians are just now requesting more research be done into cannabis and its impact on the human body. Nevertheless, we guess it is better late than never, but the medical industry needs to understand how CBD with THC and how just CBD by itself effects the endocannabinoid system in exogenous when it is introduced into the body. Even though we currently have very little knowledge of what CBD with THC or just CBD will do to enhance the brain and nervous system and the entire human immune system we can only wonder what will be discovered in the future.

It is our belief that we are just now getting started into a new era of medical discoveries that will completely alter the current methods that are being used in today's medical practices. How long it will take will depend on the people who will demand further exploration into this amazing endocannabinoid human and animal body systems. Even though it has taken us 30 years to find out about this amazing system the people can now push and demand further research be done at a faster pace because the people everywhere have the right to know how they can better take care of their bodies without the interference and intrusion of the medical industry.

In closing, all seniors should understand the implications and the importance of their endocannabinoid systems and how they can adjust or manipulate this system to stave off health problems and possible diseases as they age. The older one becomes the more susceptible one is to all sorts of medical problems, but if one has the ability to manipulate their cannabinoid system, be it the brain or nervous system or their immune system, they would be able to live a longer life knowing that they can take care of themselves until the end. We are in our seventies and with the use of the CBD products we buy, we function as if we are in our forties or early fifties. We don't worry about diseases or any other medical problems and we have never used medications (drugs) for anything and nor will we. And now, with the understanding of the endocannabinoid system and how to activate it and enhance its function neither of us for see any medical problems occurring as we continue to age. Granted the medical system will not like this, but we honestly do not care what they like or don't like because it is our responsibility to take care of ourselves, each and every-one of us. Just think, no more medical intervention or very little of it and the elimination of medications AKA drugs. Living a healthier and better retirement life without all the worries everyone should not have to deal with in their retirement years.

Understanding how people can turn their mitochondria body system back several years will enhance their brain thinking ability, decision making, memory and remembrance ability that will be better then the younger generations. In addition, seniors will be able to turn back their aging time anywhere from 20 to 30 years or more once they understand the correlation between their endocannabinold system and their mitochondria system. As an example, everyone we met or see thinks we are in our 40's or 50's and they have no idea that both of us are in our 70's with one of us just a few years away from being 80. We tell people that we are just senior kids out having fun.

BEING ABLE TO RETIRE

KNOWING THAT ONE CAN TAKE CARE

OF THEMSELVES AND

BECOMING

DEBT-FREE AND WELL-OFF

LIVING WITHIN YOUR MEANS

IS OUR WISH

FOR ALL OF YOU!


GOOD LUCK AND BEST WISHES


MARK KOVACH

AUTHOR

# BONUS SECTION
# NEGOTIATING BONUS

THE FOLLOWING NEGOTIATING INFORMATION

WILL NOT ONLY BE WORTH THE ENTIRE COST OF

THIS BOOK, BUT IT WILL ALSO BE SOMETHING

THAT YOU CAN USE FOR THE REST OF YOUR LIFE

TO SAVE AND SAVE YOU THOUSANDS OF DOLLARS

WHEN YOU ARE BUYING OR SELLING ANYTHING!

THIS INFORMATION IS COMPLIMENTS OF

MARK KOVACH

# How to Negotiate on Anything

As we sit here pondering the above statement, we are trying to think of something that is not negotiable in this world and beyond. As far as the world as we know it is concerned, we really can't think of anything that can't be negotiated. However, if there is a heavenly world out there beyond our world, then we can think of several things that would not be negotiable. For example, we know that God's work—the Holy Bible, heaven, natural occurrences, etc.—are not negotiable. We know that the Scriptures in the Holy Bible are not negotiable (this was contributed by my wife). We know that one's infilling by the Holy Spirit cannot be negotiated. We know that the universe, with its stars and planets, is not negotiable. We know that natural disasters and occurrences like tornadoes, earthquakes, rain, wind, snow, day, and night are not negotiable. However, other than the above mentioned things, everything is negotiable in our world of retail sales. Therefore, the two rules we are going to give you can be used in nearly every aspect of your life.

## RULE # 1

## EVERYTHING IS NEGOTIABLE!

## RULE # 2

## REFER TO RULE # 1

# Negotiating Guidelines

Basically, as with everything else in this world, there are guidelines that you need to understand before you start a negotiation.

You must learn to enter all negotiations with a win-win-win thought process in mind.

You must know and identify what you want.

You should have a good idea of what the fair market value is concerning anything that you want to negotiate on.

You must be willing to give and take.

You must have financial capability.

You must accumulate as much factual information concerning what you want to negotiate on ahead of time.

You must be willing to ask for what you want or you will not even get started in the negotiation process.

You must be willing to walk away from any transaction.

You must be objective.

You must have patience.

You must learn to relax and appear as though your ability to negotiate is nothing more than an everyday routine.

You must learn to analyze people and situations as quickly as possible.

You must never appear to be doubtful or hesitant.

You must learn to trade off.

You must learn to become an expert at developing alternatives.

# The Win-Win-Win Situation

Keep in mind that when you start a negotiation, you want a win-win-win situation. In other words, this means that you will win, the other person will win, and the company, store, manufacturer, vendor, or any other entity will also win. Now, you may be wondering, *if this is the case, how can anyone win and yet still have a win-win-win situation?* Simple!

Allow me to explain some basic facts to keep in mind when it comes to negotiating. We will start with a monetary item. For every product that you would like to acquire, the seller must have a certain built-in profit structure. The only question a seller has in that situation is, how much of a profit? All products or commodities must have a sufficient profit structure surrounding them to ensure that everyone will benefit if the buyer makes the purchase. This includes the seller's place of business, as well as the employees. This is otherwise referred to as overhead or the cost of doing business.

As an example, let's consider the purchase of a car. First of all, you have a seller (private or commercial) who has an asking price. However, what you may not know is that the seller has two more prices in mind, the sellers wanting price and the seller's accepting price. Likewise, buyers have three prices in mind. This may sound a little strange, but some buyers actually have the asking price in mind as their offering price, and in fact, these buyers will usually end up paying the asking price. However, most buyers will have an offering price, a wanting price, and a paying price.

Now, let's view a win-win-win situation. The seller starts off with his best asking price and the buyer starts off with his best offering price. Whether or not the buyer is aware of it, he has just started negotiating. In turn, the seller becomes realistic, understanding that he will not receive his best wanting price because the buyer's best wanting price is still below the seller's best wanting price. The seller then informs the buyer of the price that he is willing to sell the car for, or the seller's accepting price.

Let's look at your first lesson in the art of negotiating. The seller has just indicated to the buyer what his accepting price will be, but don't believe him! As with every negotiation transaction that we have been involved with, the seller always has a rock-bottom or final accepting price. The buyer now indicates his paying price, or the price that he is willing and able to pay for the car. At this point, one of two things will occur: (1) the buyer will make the deal and everyone will be happy, or (2) neither party will conclude the transaction. Why might the latter occur? Because, it is not a win-win-win situation.

If you are dealing with a commercial car dealership, there may not be a sufficient profit in the transaction or a sufficient incentive from the car manufacturer for the seller to cover his overhead expenses. Likewise, there may not be a sufficient profit for the private-party seller in the event that he has to pay off an existing loan balance or have sufficient money left over to make a down payment on another vehicle. However—and this is a very important point to remember—the buyer needs to realize that this is the point in his negotiation at which he can make a final offer in order to consummate the transaction! Unfortunately, it is at this point in the negotiation that most people would walk away because they have become upset or frustrated, feeling that they have not been treated fairly by the seller or that the seller does not want to do business with them. This is not true!

At this point in the negotiation, the seller is trying to tell the buyer what his rock-bottom or final accepting price will be for the transaction to be consummated. As the buyer, you must be in a position to either accept the seller's rock-bottom price, realizing that the deal will not go any further, or be willing to ask for additional concessions, such as an additional 25 percent discount on accessories, for which most dealerships will offer 10 percent. Both of you might settle for 15 percent if that is what it takes to close the transaction. Otherwise, you must be willing to walk away from the transaction!

# Know and Identify
# What You Want

Learning the negotiating technique is not difficult. So why don't we negotiate? Simple: because we don't know what we want, and when we finally realize what we want, we usually end up paying the full price. Notice we said *usually*. This is because we personally never pay the full price for anything because we know what we want before we decide to make a purchase or a commitment. More importantly, we know what we are willing to pay to get what we want, and if our offer is not enough, we simply walk away and go elsewhere.

In the event that you gain nothing more out of this information, remember this: any product is only worth what someone is willing to pay for it! Allow us to rephrase this for clarification. Any product is only of value to the person who makes the purchase, and the price paid is the value to that person and that person only!

Knowing and identifying exactly what you want before you attempt to negotiate will afford you the opportunity to search the marketplace to learn what different prices are being quoted for the same product. The more knowledge that you can accumulate concerning the product that you would like to purchase, the better your negotiating position will be when you are ready to negotiate. In order to become a good negotiator, you must understand that there is more to closing a transaction than just being right. You have to learn to develop the insight to look beyond what most people are concerned about and to eliminate any possibility of tunnel vision, which the majority of people have been taught since birth. In other words, know what you want, and try to think outside of the box!

# Know or Learn About the Market Value

Regardless of what you want to purchase, know or learn what the current market value is for that particular product. This means that whether you are considering buying a bicycle for yourself or the kids, carpet for your home, fixtures, clothing, diamonds, jewelry, home additions, a home loan—you name it—knowing what the current market value is will place you way ahead of the other person in the negotiating process.

What does it take to learn about the market value of any given product? No less than three inquiries. Depending on the price of the product, as many as five to ten or more inquiries may be needed. As a rule, we will only start to negotiate on a product priced from $1,000 to $5,000 after having made a minimum of three inquiries in the marketplace. For products priced from $5,000 up to $25,000, we will make anywhere from five to ten inquiries before deciding to negotiate. For any product priced above $25,000, we will make a minimum of ten inquiries, and then we will incorporate time (as in hours, days, weeks, or months) before making a decision to negotiate. Why? Because we want to know what the market value is as well as what the price fluctuations are in the current marketplace.

Once we have obtained this information, we will then decide the price we would like to purchase the product for as well as what we would be willing to pay. Unless we were willing to make those inquiries, we would never have any idea what the product would be worth on the open market. Not knowing better, we (like everyone else) would end up paying the full market price when we could have saved a considerable amount of hard-earned money had we simply taken the time to research the market.

By learning the art of negotiating, the average person can save hundreds and thousands of dollars throughout his or her lifetime, and can become a successful negotiator. Nevertheless, with knowledge and skillful negotiations, anyone can learn to gain the leading edge in the negotiating process. As a negotiator, you will need the ability to develop and use every bit of knowledge, experience, and information you have gained thus far in your lifetime, which will place you above the rest of the crowd. Moreover, each time you make a choice to buy something, you will be doing so, because you have negotiated the value and benefits that you want to receive.

# Give and Take

Once you have decided that what you want is really what you want and you have researched the marketplace, you should have a better-than-average idea of the true value of the product that you would like to purchase. Now you should be ready to negotiate. Negotiating is fun, but being effective at it is an art. The negotiating techniques mentioned in the beginning of this section will not only help you appear more confident and perform accordingly, but practicing these techniques will also allow you to improve your concentration and alertness during the negotiating process. Remember: never lose sight of your objective. As a negotiator, you should remain calm and appear as though using your ability to negotiate is an everyday event. As you continue to practice, using your negotiating skills will then become as normal as saying your name when you introduce yourself.

In order for negotiations to be effective, you must understand the concept of give and take. Effective negotiations will convert your knowledge, experience, and information into dollar savings. Your ability to become an effective negotiator will depend on your ability to give and take in the negotiating process. The word *give* in this sense does not mean that you are to give away your rights, freedom, enjoyment, or money. On the contrary, in the art of negotiating, the word *give* means knowing what is right, fair, and equitable and placing yourself in your opponent's position.

The word *take* in this sense does not mean that you are to rip your opponent apart, show no mercy, or show no consideration or empathy. In the art of negotiating, the word *take* means knowing when to seek an alternative, concede to a valid point, restructure the offer, or be prepared to walk away until you have had the time to reconsider your position as well as that of your opponents. Once you have learned and understood the concept of give and take, you will be on your way to becoming an extremely effective negotiator. As you build confidence, your negotiating abilities will continue to improve and advance.

In the above two scenarios, you have and maintain the same common denominator, that is nothing more than a tool, which is money. If you think, and use money as a tool, you will be able to manipulate just about everything and anything you want or desire in your lifetime.

# Financial Capability and Asking for What You Want

Never enter a negotiating process without having the financial capability to follow through with the transaction. A good negotiator may spend hours, days, weeks, months, or years negotiating for some particular item, but if he or she does not have the financial capability to follow through with the transaction, it would be a complete waste of time, money and energy. If you negotiate and you get what you want, you must be prepared and have the financial capability to close the transaction. The only time the above statement does not apply is in the event that you are out practicing your negotiating techniques. Incidentally, when you think you are ready to go out and practice negotiating, the best places to practice happen to be the hardest places to deal with, such as car dealerships, carpet and flooring dealers, large retail outlets, furniture companies, and building and plumbing supply companies. Even though you may not get what you want, the negotiating experience you gain will be invaluable, and the continued practice will only help sharpen your negotiating skills. Caution: Even though you may make some ridiculous request while you are practicing negotiating, be careful not to get so caught up in the process that your opponent goes along with your request, and you end up in a situation in which you have to perform or you can never show your face in the area again.

When you are out practicing your negotiating techniques, be sure to negotiate on an item that you know you will never be able to get your price on so as not to place yourself in an embarrassing and awkward position.

On the other hand, when you are serious about acquiring an item, be sure to ask for what you want and be specific; otherwise you will never get what you really want. For example, let's say you want to buy a car. Be sure to ask for everything you want on that particular car and then ask for additional items that you don't want or even need on the car before you begin to negotiate on the final price. Why? Simple: making concessions by giving up certain items you asked for, but really don't want or need, will make the car salesperson feel guilty, which in turn will give you a much better shot at getting the price you want to pay for the car. Remember the give-and-take scenario? Well, in this situation asking for more than you want or need allows you the ability to take what you do want and give back what you really didn't want in the first place—but your opponent doesn't know what you are doing or thinking, as he or she just wants to make the deal if at all possible.

One thing about cars that everyone should remember is that buying any car is always a losing proposition because of depreciation. Car dealerships and manufacturers have been ripping off the general public for generations. As an example, let's look at a typical car transaction. Let's say the manufacturer is offering a family-and-friends discount of $2,000 in addition to the dealership's $1,500 discount if you purchase in a particular month. The average car on the market today runs around $30,000 out the door (OTD), so if we were to subtract the total incentives of $3,500 off the sticker price of $30,000, we could see that you would be able to purchase this car for only $26,500. Not bad? This is a total rip off! Even with the added manufacturer's discounts, people are only getting approximately a 12 percent discount, and if you were to drive off the dealer's car lot and immediately drive back on and request your money back, the dealer would only give you approximately $20,100 for the brand-new, discounted car.

When any car clears the dealer's car lot, the price drops by one-third, or 33 percent. This immediate depreciation rate is a figure all dealers use to calculate a repurchase, assuming the car is immediately returned to the dealer's car lot.

Therefore, when you are out negotiating for a new car, you should always start at the 30 percent mark in an attempt to get a 25 percent discount, and you should never go below a 20 percent discount if at all possible. Only once in our lifetime have we been able to get a full 30 percent discount on a new car. However, we have been able to get 25 percent most of the time, and we have never bought a car at less than a 20 percent discount. In other words, we would normally buy the above $30,000 car for between $22,500 (a 25 percent discount) and $24,000 (a 20 percent discount). If the car dealer insists that he or she will not be able to make any money by selling the car at a 20 percent or 25 percent discount, don't believe a word of it, even if he or she is willing to show you the purchase invoice. Ask the dealer to show you the manufacturer's invoice and not the dealership's made-up invoice, where they add on to the manufacturer's invoice.

Most car salespersons will normally avoid showing you the manufacturer's invoice if they can get away with it, or they will avoid the question by misdirecting the conversation in an attempt to get you to buy at the dealership invoice price. Don't buy it and insist on seeing the manufacturer's invoice and/or inform the dealership that X amount of dollars is all that you are willing to pay for the car, and then shut up! Why? For he or she who speaks first will lose in the negotiating process. We have even gone outside and waited for the dealer to make the first response, because it put us back in the driver's seat, so to speak. Likewise, when the dealer comes back with a response, don't give him a response right away, but rather take your time and tell him that you will have to think over the offer. Now, after you have taken some time to think it over, and if you believe that the offer does not meet with your expectations, tell the dealer that you will get back to him after you have had time to check with other dealers, and then slowly walk away from the offer. Why? Simple: because should your offer for the car be within reason, the salesperson will inform the sales manager that you are going to another dealer. We can guarantee you that at that time someone from the dealership will catch you before you can get to your car and drive off.

This is the time in the negotiation process where you must maintain your composure and stand firm with your offer. Let the dealer squirm for a while, while you just listen to what he has to say and never agree with him or even nod your head on anything he is asking or saying—these questions and statements are known as little closes, a technique used to get you to the final closing. After all is said and done and you believe that you have negotiated your best deal, close the transaction. On the other hand, if you still believe that the dealership has not done what they can to meet your offer price, walk away and go to another dealership and start negotiating again—only this time you will be armed with the information from the previous dealership that will give you the edge when you start negotiating for the same car. The trick here is to take the best price the previous dealer gave you, knock off another $2,000 or $3,000, and inform the new dealer that this is the best price that the previous dealer was able to offer you. But tell the new dealer that if a better deal could be struck, you would be happy to do business with their dealership. Again, shut up at this point, for he or she who speaks first loses.

Provided that you have the time, patience, and stamina, you will find out what you can really purchase the car for, as the new dealership will bend over backward trying to meet or beat the previous dealership's offer. Caution: a typical dealership response will be to ask you to get the offer in writing from the previous dealership. Don't fall for this tactic; instead, start laughing and say, "Sure, like the previous dealership would be willing to put their best offer in writing so we could go elsewhere and shop for a better deal? Would your dealership do the same? We seriously doubt it! So, either we can do business with your dealership, or we can go back and do business with the previous dealership. It doesn't make much difference to us because we only want to buy the car from the dealership offering the best pricing." Again, shut up at this point! This is when you can just kick back and relax and let the dealer come up with his best deal.

When the dealer comes back and gives you his so-called best offer, you can accept the offer, reject the offer, or take his best offer and go to another dealership and start negotiating all over again. Depending on the amount of time you are willing to invest, along with the amount of money you want to save, you can negotiate as many times as you want to.

As an example, we once went to a total of five different dealerships over five consecutive weekends before we finally made a deal to buy a particular SUV that we wanted, and we ended up getting a 22 percent discount off the sticker price, excluding the dealership's add-on pricing. This process of negotiating can be used on anything that you might be inclined to purchase. Going from one dealer to another with the same merchandise will always give you better insight as to what you will eventually be able to purchase the item for in the open marketplace.

# Thinking on Your Feet

In order to become a great negotiator, you must have the ability to think on your feet. Over the years we have negotiated with many different kinds of people on all sorts of things—cars, boats, homes, land, printing materials, clothing, etc.—and the one thing that seems to stop most people from negotiating is that they don't enjoy conflict or are afraid they may get caught up in a rapid-fire question-and-answer situation that they wouldn't know how to handle, which includes my wife! Then again, there are those people who just don't have any idea that one can negotiate on anything in this world and are willing to pay the asking price, just like my wife before she met me. However, contrary to popular belief, negotiating can and will save you hundreds of thousands of dollars over your lifetime if you learn how to do it correctly.

In the beginning of any negotiation process, each person is sizing up his or her opponent, and the process will usually proceed slowly until one or the other opponent finds a weakness in the other, at which time that person will concentrate on that weakness. The primary weakness that we have observed over our years of negotiating with people is their inability to think on their feet in a rapid-fire question-and-answer situation. This is how it works: First come the introductions; next the feeling-out process; next the process of finding out if the people negotiating know what they really want, determining if they can afford whatever it is they are negotiating for, and determining whether they are willing to trade or willing to give and take.

Once the above information has been assessed, and just when the buyers involved believe that they are going to be able to negotiate their deal, this is the time the salesperson start rapidly firing questions at their opponents. The goal in this situation is to continue to ask questions as fast as possible, avoiding the answers and attempting to place the buyers in an uncomfortable situation by making them feel guilty or as though they would be taking the food off the dealer's table and the clothes off the dealer's children's backs. Now, if you are a beginner at negotiating, you need to avoid a rapid-fire question-and-answer situation, and the best way to do this is to simply ask your opponent to restate the first question, even if he is already on the third or fourth question. This technique is used by attorneys in a court of law all the time, and your attorney should teach you how to handle this situation, which is the same way I had to learn the hard way. You must slow your opponent down and take them off track as fast as you can. As time goes on and your negotiating knowledge and abilities continue to increase, handling a rapid-fire question-and-answer situation will become second nature because you will have learned how to think on your feet in order to handle it.

# Trading Off or Developing Alternatives

One of the great advantages of negotiating is having the ability to trade off or develop alternatives during the negotiating process. If you remember the section entitled *"Financial Capability and Asking for What You Want,"* you will recall that we showed you how to ask for more than you want or need when negotiating the purchase of a car. Using this same scenario, let's say you asked for a six-CD changer, an MP3 player, upgraded wheels, a special roof rack, and a towing package including all the special wiring. You really don't want or need these things, but if the deal is negotiated properly, you would be willing to take these items. Your salesperson goes out of the room to see the sales manager in an attempt to get you the best price for your new car. This process can take anywhere from fifteen minutes to forty-five minutes or more, depending on how long they want you to squirm around in their little office before they think you are ready to leave the dealership. Suddenly your salesperson shows up with a big smile on his face and says, "Congratulations! The price of your new car will be [X], and the monthly payments will only be [Y], and the car has everything you wanted." However, instead of offering you your negotiated price for the car, the salesperson gives you a price that is way out of line.

When you hear this news, you will normally think that you have been hit upside your head with a sledgehammer and that everything you have been negotiating on went in one of the salesperson's ears and out the other. This is the point when most people will walk away from the dealership or pay the quoted price. But this is not so for the professional negotiator, as this is the time when all your abilities, knowledge, and skills come into play. The real negotiation is about to begin. At this time you should inform your opponent that there seems to be a considerable difference between what you are willing to buy the car for and what the dealership wants you to pay for the car. Just ignore the surprised look that comes over the face of your salesperson, and begin to give back or trade off and develop alternatives in exchange for a better price for the car.

Inform the salesperson that as much as you would like to have the six-CD changer, you will have to settle for a regular CD player if he is willing to lower the price and downgrade the radio system. Likewise, as much as you really want the MP3 player, ask how much they will knock off the price if you give it up. The upgraded wheels are great, but ask how much can be saved if standard wheels are substituted. Tell the dealer that though you really need the roof rack, you will have to forego buying it because you can't afford it, then ask how much will be saved without the roof rack. Besides trading off, do you see what we are doing to the salesperson? We are taking our time and making

240

not only the immediate salesperson feel guilty, but we are also making the invisible opponent (the sales manager) feel guilty. Each time you trade off something, make sure the salesperson goes back to the sales manager for confirmation. The more your opponent has to go back and forth, the better your chances are of getting exactly what you wanted in the first place as far as the price of the car is concerned.

Likewise, having the ability to develop alternatives is just as important as trading off when negotiating. Using the same scenario as above, when the negotiating situation seems to come to a point where no one is willing to continue to give and take, developing alternatives comes into play.

For example, let's say you are getting very close to getting the car you want at the price you want by trading off, but there still remains a difference of, say, $2,000 or $3,000. What do you do? Come up with alternatives, such as stating to your salesperson, "I might be willing to accept the car at the price you have quoted us, provided we can get a 25 percent discount on accessories or a 25 percent discount on parts or free car washes any time we bring the car in for service as long as we own the car." Ask for the same regarding any other services that the dealership may provide in offers to continue to get your business after the sale. Now, you might get a 10 percent discount on parts and a 15 to 20 percent discount on any additional accessories you may want sometime in the future, but remember, every time you buy parts or accessories at a negotiated discount, you will be closing the gap on the sales price of the car over any given period during which you own the car and do business with the same dealership.

One final thought in dealing with car dealerships: don't think for one minute that you are taking the food and clothing away from your opponent, and don't believe any dealer who tells you that they paid the manufacturer's suggested retail price (MSRP) for the vehicle, as this is outright ludicrous. Think about this for a minute: when times get hard and retail sales drop off and a recession might be on the way, it is not unusual for car dealerships to start cutting their prices in order to attract business.

When things get really tough and a recession has taken hold of our society, you see car dealerships advertising and selling vehicles at half of the MSRP sticker price and not at the dealership's total add-on prices. We are currently living in Texas, and as we are writing this book, day after day we see and hear the car dealerships advertising to sell their vehicles for half off the MSRP. Therefore, if it is possible for a car dealership to sell a vehicle for half the price indicated on the MSRP and still be able to make money, you as a potential buyer should not be too concerned with the idea that you may be taking advantage of any dealership, as they have been gouging the general public for years.

All of the above negotiating information has been used and tested again and again by us, and it never ceases to amaze us that people do not negotiate when they know that they have absolutely nothing to lose and everything to gain in the form of dollar savings.

# NEGOTIATION EXAMPLE

To give the readers an example of what they can accomplish and save and make by negotiating we will use two of our most expensive purchases and a sale that we completed. The first was the purchase of a mobile home in a trailer park about a half mile from the beach in California some years ago. We had been living in a condo in Laguna Niguel and it was costing us $2,200.00 dollars a month just to make ends meet on the unit and did not include our living expenses at the time. After talking it over my wife and me decided to look for a mobile home to rent or buy in order to cut our expenses. While driving around different trailer parks my wife saw a for RENT sign on a unit and when she told me later that day we both went to look at the unit and decided to call the owners who naturally were not in. Nevertheless the owners had returned our call and we made arrangements to meet. Upon meeting we indicated that we would agree to the rent and they agreed and we all left.

Having dealt with a lot of people over the years we had developed the sagacity to read people in a matter of seconds and after thinking about our meeting we decided to see if these owners were willing to sell the unit because they were in a hurry to rent the property. Therefore, we called the owners again and asked them if they were interested in selling their mobile home? They responded with yes and we made arrangements to meet again. Since the mobile home was in bad shape the owner stated that they would take $2,500 hundred for the property if we were willing to take over their payments, which confirmed my suspicions that these owners wanted to get ride of this mobile home. Granted this was not much of a negotiation process , but it does get better. As another week went by the owners called us again and we made arrangements to meet again to finalize everything.

Upon meeting again, the owners had someone with them and after introductions this new person interjected and stated that he thought it was not fair to accept the $2,500 hundred dollars for the mobile home. At this point we asked this person if they had a vested interest in the property? When he said no, we turned to the owner and asked them what they thought would be a fair selling price and they responded with $5,000 dollars. Now this opened up a great negotiating platform for us as we could ask for trade offs if we needed or wanted them. We then asked the owners why when they had already told us and we agreed to the $2,500 price? The owners responded stating that they had some other property in San Diego that they had to pay off in the amount of, you guessed, it $2,500 dollars.

Nevertheless, we agreed and said that we would give them a check for $5,000 dollars and that we would make the monthly mobile home pay-ments each month as we paid them to put toward their remaining pay-ments as they requested. Next we stated that we would need the tax write offs and again they agreed to let us pay their taxes on the unit and lastly we would draw up all the real estate contracts that would protect both parties and again they agreed. So we made another appointment to meet with the owners again to sign all the documents the following weekend. Now my wife and I were both real estate agents in addition to one of us being a loan officer so we wrote up a sales contract and a lease to own contract so as not to activate the alienation cause, also known as an acceleration clause used by banks that would make their loan all due and payable in full on their bank should they sell their mobile home.

Basically, what we were doing is what is known as an "All Inclusive Trust Deed" known as an "AITD" in the real estate business. In other words we were agreeing to take over their remaining payments of $30,000 dollars payable at $500 dollars a month until the unit was paid in full. Now since this trailer park was where everyone owned the land our land fee was an additional $75.00 per month, which was unheard of at that time. So we ended up buying the unit for $5000.00 dollars having a payment of $500.00 dollars plus a $75.00 dollar space lease, which was also a write-off because it was classified as a land payment. We then gave them a copy of the sales agreement contract and a copy of the lease agreement that we then had recorded in the event that their bank wanted to view the lease contract.

We then took the next year to gut and refurbished the unit and then sold my wife's condo and moved in to our newly remodeled mobile home. At the time I told my wife that as long as we live within our means it would not take long to get back up on our feet to be able to do whatever we wanted to. We were now saving over $2,200.00 dollars a month. In the meantime I set my wife up with a processing company for a year or so and then we opened our own Processing company, opened a Real Estate Company in addition to a Loan Company in Irvine, California. For the next seven years we lived this way and having made enough money to retire on we decided to sell the mobile home.

We figured that we could get at least $159,000 for the mobile home, but we listed it for $300,000.00 because after all this was California. The first offer came in at $260,000 dollars and we accepted, but eventually the person who assured us that they would never walkaway from a deal, walked away and we were back at square one again. Nonetheless, we fixed what needed to be fixed and re-listed again, only this time we listed for $395,000 dollars even though nothing had ever sold anywhere near this price including a 5 bedroom mobile home in our trailer park. About a week later we got an offer of $315,000 dollars and I turned it down and thought my wife was going to have a fit as she was in total disbelief. However, we had two more buyers that had come by, both of which were really interested in buying. So I informed the first buyers real estate agent that we would give their client the first right of refusal if we received a better offer. Three days later the same buyer came back with an offer of $330,000 dollar cash offer and this time we accepted because we had only expected to get $150,000 for the Mobile home originally. Even though the unit was now in excellent shape and completely redone with all new three-quarter inch plaster board throughout, including the entire ceilings in addition to putting in fixtures that are only found in million dollar homes, our unit was definitely a one of a kind mobile home. No one in the park had even come close to the price we received for the unit We paid off the remaining balance from the previous owners and still had over $300,000 dollars left over. The readers can now understand what they can save and make by learning to negotiate using the right techniques.

The next example deals with a brand new home we decided to buy and the builders were asking $320,000 dollars for their newly built home. We offered $250,000 for the home and they came back with $310,000, we came back with $275,000 and the builder came back with $300,000 and stated that was as far as he would go so we agreed depending on an appraisal and an inspection and they agreed. The appraisal came in right on target, but the inspection revealed some major problems. We then told the builder that they had to rebuild the chimney and reinforce it and repair the roof damage. The builder refused and we walked away from the deal.

We spent the next 30 days looking at 10 houses a day when we finally came across the one we wanted to buy. What we didn't know was that the house was almost finished and that the for sale sign had just been placed on the property 30 minutes before we got there. Later we found out that the house has been sold to a couple in Florida, but that they forgot to tell the builder that it would be a contingency sale. This meant that the buyers would have to sell their home out of Florida first before buying this home and the deal fell through because the builder had to go to court to get a release or discharge before they could resell the property again. This process cost the builder a lot of time and money because they could not sell the home until granted a release from the court.

When we asked the price of the home we were told $320,000 the same as the other home, but now knowing the builder was hurting because they could not sell the home without the release we offered $200,000 for the home. Naturally, the builder came back with 310,000 and we came back with 210, 000. This went on and on until we reached $250,000 and the builder came back with $255,000 and we agreed. The only problem was that we forgot to make the offer pending an appraisal which came at $245,000 because the real estate market had started taking a turn for the worst as we were entering the beginning of the financial crises. Knowing that the builder had lost money we decided to forget the $10,000 dollar difference and bought the house pending its completion.

We went back to California to pack up and made our arrangements to move into our new home in Texas to retire. In addition, we want to point out to the readers that we had made a little over $300,000 by negotiating on one deal and saved another $65,000 on another deal not to mention saving a total of $196,000 dollars negotiating on all new furnishing for both the mobile home and the new house thereby saving a little over $561,000 dollars just by negotiating. Likewise, these figures do not include yard equipment such as a tractor, O-turn lawnmowers, shrubbery trimming equipment, tree trimming equipment along with furnishing our 3 car garage and nor does it include the additional cement for extending both of our driveways and adding a circular drive in front of our home. Nevertheless, this negotiating information can be used for just about anything a person may desire, keeping in mind that the end result can add up to be major savings over one's lifetime.

WIN-WIN-WIN

NEGOTIATING TECHNIQUE

REMEMBER,

SUCCESS IS NOT AN ACCIDENT

AND WHEN ALL ELSE FAILS,

NEGOTIATE!

Wishing all of you good fortune in all of
your negotiation endeavors,

Sincerely,
Mark Kovach
Author

# Other Books By Mark Kovach

## Making Parenting Simple Handbook
## By Mark Kovach

The basic concept of Making Parenting Simple Handbook is to train your child while they are developing in the womb or as soon after birth up until the age of 5 or 6 that are the most critical years of a child's life. The book includes chapters on how to protect your child, especially, girls under the age of 21 and a whole lot more of relevant parental information concerning older children.

## Home Buying and Financing 101
## By Mark Kovach

This book Home Buying & Financing 101 Second Edition is a **MUST READ** for anyone who may be considering Buying a Home and Understanding the Financial details and implications of financing their new home which was originally written and designed for the Loan Officers and Real Estate Agents and now for the general public which includes new updates and subjects such as the Reverse Mortgage and how to never lose your home plus other information that was designed for the benefit of the general home-buying public.

# How To Establish Your Credit
# By Mark Kovach

This "How to Establish Your Credit" book will offer people some helpful suggestions and scenarios that we talk about in the banking industry, along with my real estate banking experience with inputs that will assist the reader to become familiar and to get a better understanding of how to establish or expand their banking credit. Over the years we have noticed that most bank customers do not know the proper people in the banks or how to use the banks to their advantage. Our hope is that this book will assist people in establishing and expanding their credit needs with a better understanding of what bankers are looking for in establishing your personal basic and advanced credit needs. We also cover and discuss the requirements needed for business credit and credit expansion.

Made in the USA
Columbia, SC
31 July 2021